Industrial Evolution

Through the Eighties with

Cabaret Voltaire

Mick Fish

First published in 2002
by SAF Publishing under the Poptomes imprint

SAF Publishing Ltd.
Unit 7, Shaftesbury Centre
85 Barlby Road
London. W10 6BN
ENGLAND

email: info@safpublishing.com

www.safpublishing.com

ISBN 0 946719 46 2

Printed in England by the Cromwell Press, Trowbridge, Wiltshire.

foreword and acknowledgements

When the second edition of a book I compiled about the group Cabaret Voltaire went out of print in the early nineties, to my surprise certain individuals started inquiring as to when a third edition might appear. Apparently there was still some interest in the group, even though they had all but ceased operations. My initial reaction was a curt but polite, "No way". Being many years since I had originally put the book together, I thought it was time to lay the whole business to rest.

Nevertheless, as I thought about the suggestion, so a subplot to the original book surfaced and an altogether different idea began to form in my mind. I started to think more about the time when the book was originally written – specifically a period of turmoil, particularly for those who felt shipwrecked by the changing tide of the eighties. As I began to piece the first tentative bits of the jigsaw together, a parallel path started to emerge, whether as the member of a Sheffield industrial band, or like myself as a local government worker at the Council refuse depot.

Ultimately, this book is about the eighties. It is neither a full biography of Cabaret Voltaire nor an autobiography. For those that are wondering, yes I did do other things than just work at the Council by day, and write about Cabaret Voltaire by night. Also, to add some form of continuity from the two previous editions of *Cabaret Voltaire: The Art of the Sixth Sense*, all the transcripts to the interviews that appeared in that book are reproduced here as appendices.

Due to the skewed mists of time, not to mention chemical and alcohol imbalances, certain stories and anecdotes have had to be coaxed from the dusty corners of an oft-addled brain. In this I am eternally grateful to Dave Hallbery, Paul Widger and Roger Quail for helpful guidance in filling in gaps where holes in my memory appeared. Thanks to Bruce Morrison for additional guidance, and introducing me to places in the world that I would surely never have gone to. Thanks also to Iain Forsyth, for comments and suggestions, Karen O'Brien and Noreen Hallbery for a female perspective, and to Paul Smith for background information over the years. Thanks also to those others that were there: Alan Fish (no relation), Ron Wright, Charlie Collins, Pete Hope, Pete Care, Karen Howard, Viv Spencer-Grey and John Clayton amongst others.

A very personal thanks goes to Teresa for listening, and to Ben for teaching me more than he could ever imagine.

The biggest thanks must ultimately go to Richard H. Kirk, Stephen Mallinder and Chris Watson from Cabaret Voltaire for their wit, wisdom and being the initial inspiration for my first book. For without them, or that book, this one would surely never have existed.

Special thanks must also go to Richard Kirk and Lynne Clarke for hospitality beyond the call of duty (especially clearing up the trail of spent beer tinnies I often left in my wake).

I also extend my thanks to all the other people, too numerous to mention, who have provided me with help and encouragement. I trust you know who you are, chances are I may not.

Certain names in the sections referring to the Council Depot have been changed to protect both the innocent and the guilty.

"Every search begins with beginner's luck. And every search ends with the victor's being severely tested."

Paulo Coelho, The Alchemist

INTRODUCTION

one night in Heaven

We were in Heaven. Not literally of course. There was a distinct lack of fluffy white angels floating around. This particular paradise was Europe's largest gay disco. But on the night in question there was a distinct lack of muscle-bound moustachioed patrons dancing around to Hi-nrg. Instead it was a grey and dismal Monday night in April, and an amphetamine-fuelled crowd of London's night creatures had donned long raincoats and turned out to see The Fall. As a light rain pattered the empty streets outside and the final few commuters rushed for their last trains home, for some of us there was not much else to do but cling to the underbelly of late night drinking and hanging out.

For my part, come the morning I knew that I wasn't going to be allowed the luxury of a lay-in to nurse away the hangover, or to blunt the sharp nerve endings and aching arms once the speed had wended its merry way from my bloodstream. By 9am I would be back at my desk, staring blearily at piles of paperwork. It felt like the dual life led by an adulterer as I attempted to keep separate the two very distinct sides of my life. Working for the Council by day I tried to hide the after affects of the previous night's indulgences, hanging around at gigs by night I tried to make out that I wasn't stuck in a dead end job. Like all deceptions, it was a tiring business.

It was Spring 1983 and we were all supposedly fishes being happily swept along by a boom-time current created by the Tories and Mrs Thatcher. Not that the nocturnal reptiles that crept around Heaven's corridors showed much interest in either boom or bust. They were too busy being seen at the right places, maintaining a presence amongst London's rock hierarchy. In the damp moon-glow which hung under the night sky, the rest of the population was tucking themselves into bed, apparently happy in the knowl-edge that they had never had it so good. In the suburbs that radi-ated outwards from the Embankment, dreams were filled with ideas like buying houses and selling them a few months later for a huge profit.

As a kid who had been brought up in the sixties, I was far from feeling buoyant in this accelerating tide. In fact, I was slowly watching all the foundations of my life crumbling about me. Thatcherism was rampaging seemingly unstoppably over what I saw as the mainstays of my outlook on life. The Tories' general manifesto was, "We don't like it, so we'll scrap it." The Unions, the GLC, even the local Council I worked for were all under threat of execution. It felt like I was walking around with an evic-tion notice around my neck which read "me next".

As The Fall hit the stage, I was hitting full tilt on my own little game of amphetamine pinball. Nerves jangling, teeth on edge, I stood and watched a few numbers and was less than impressed. Mark Smith was marshalling his troops into what was then known as Northern psychobilly, but it sounded more like a bad tempered rumble to me – the band's sound being bounced around by unforgiving walls more used to soaking up pounding mechanoid dance beats. By the time the group's racket had swirled around the rafters and back to my ears it was like listening through a blanket of cotton wool. I wandered around the cavern-ous interior. The bar beckoned.

As ever, the speed was easing my foot harder onto the drinking accelerator pedal – was this the fourth or fifth pint? Who was counting. The bar was crowded and the odd celebrity could always be spotted downing a beer. At a back table was Marc Almond, sitting there like a regular down his local pub. The video jukebox churned out "Boys Keep Swinging" by David Bowie. The sight of Bowie in drag was very in keeping with the surroundings, whilst the lyrics of "they'll never clone ya, when you're a boy" seemed a little odd when the place would be packed to the gills with just that for the rest of the week.

I did my best at mingling until I bumped into Mal from Cabaret Voltaire and we joked about something or another. He had this feline ability to glide effortlessly from one conversation to the next. In attitude Mal always acted like a man who courted fame. By then, Mal appeared content to swan about in the glow of semi-stardom, but with a front consisting of cheap sulphate and not-so cheap Stella Artois I was quite comfortable with gently taking the piss out of him – semi-pop star or not.

The Cabs, as they were affectionately known, had indeed never had it so good. At the time it was hard to tell whether or not they were poised for greater things. They were two months away from releasing their album *The Crackdown* and their relationship with new manager Stevo was reaping rewards in terms of coverage in the press and on TV.

Mal was never backward in talking up his career. Names were dropped, cool bands saluted. The usual flow of record company-speak abounded. However, this outer sheen hid an inner frailty, a slowly emerging reality that he was fronting a band that was facing a dilemma. They were four years down the rock 'n' roll road. From sitting proudly amongst the cream at the top of the indie milk, they were about to find out that the mainstream pop world was an altogether more turbulent liquid. Oh, and one other small point – as the band's singer, Mal couldn't really sing. But heck, who gave a shit about that. Mark Smith hardly sang, and in those days Marc Almond didn't sing in tune half the time.

All three – Mark, Mal and Marc – were typical of those who had cut their teeth on the entrepreneurial and artistic explosion that followed punk. Inevitably, they now found themselves hovering around the fringes of respectability. For Mal's part he was a member of a band that had helped create a strand of music that was being broadly termed Industrial. It was something I kidded myself I knew a bit about. For a few weekends a year I even hung out in Sheffield, where Cabaret Voltaire committed their dark noises to tape and were doing quite nicely thank you as a result. For the rest of the year, my job at the local Depot was all about the real noises of industry; refuse compactors, sledgehammers, rivet guns and welding machines.

At the bar, Stevo darted a look our way that seemed to say, "Why the fuck is Mal bothering to talk to that schmuck?" Well, fuck him, I thought. Rumour had it that he couldn't even read, but that itself was probably just part of the hype surrounding the Some Bizarre empire. Mal offered to buy me a drink – he was always generous and seemed to have money. Turning down a drink had yet to enter my particular phrase book.

"You'll get served quicker if you get the barman with the checked shirt and the moustache." I offered as a valuable tip.

It took him a few seconds to realise they all had checked shirts and moustaches. He turned round, smiled with one corner of his mouth curling up the way it did, and mouthed the words "very funny". We joked a bit about gay clones when he came back. My pint had what looked like a pubic hair in it. I wondered if it was one of the barman's. I daren't even think about how it might have got in there. Christ, a couple of the barmen looked awfully thin. An irrational AIDS panic raced through me like a new line of speed – knowledge about its transmission was then an inexact science (AIDS I hasten to add, not speed). Fuck, what was I thinking? This was madness. I fished the hair out of my pint and took a big slurp.

As the evening wore on I withdrew into myself and let the speed do most of the talking. Conversation was easy when everyone seemed to be on something. After all, who was going to remember the bullshit the next day anyway. The poorer ones opted for cheap sulphate, the less monetarily challenged had a couple of grammes of coke secreted on their person somewhere. But everyone was too cool to brag about drugs, you were either on them or your weren't. It was a Monday night in Heaven – odds on you were on something.

For some reason the bullshit got around to books.

"Read so-and-so?"

"Yeah, of course," meaning we all knew what the cover looked like but hadn't actually read it.

"Ever read *The Sailor Who Fell from Grace with the Sea*?" I asked.

"What's it about?" Mal said.

"Urmm. A sailor who falls into the sea," I quickly ventured.

"Yeah. Right. Fuck off," Mal laughed.

For some reason the idea sprang into my mind to say to Mal that I was surprised nobody had done a book about the Cabs. A speed idea – I mean they were kind of hip at that time, but a book? By the time I had finished the sentence the whole notion seemed faintly ridiculous. "So, why don't you write one?" came the response. The speed said, "I could do that." The drink said, "Get another pint in and don't be a prat." The speed won out and ten amphetamine minutes later I was a budding author.

That I had little grasp of how to write a book was obvious, probably still is. But the one thing that hanging around with the Cabs for any length of time had taught me was that you could do whatever you liked just as long as you had the notion to do so. To some, this might seem a fact of little insight. For me, having been brought up with the belief that the proper training and education was necessary before attempting anything, it was a revelation. Here were two guys from Sheffield whose grasp of music was, to put it politely, rudimentary. If you were being rude, and there were some critics who were, they couldn't really play a note. But far from deterring them, this seemed the perfect starting point for making music. Steeped as they were in all things avant-garde, they had no problem filling their heads with notions of becoming an experimental music band.

Standing in Heaven, speeding away, half-drunk, I had convinced myself that this blurred excitement was what life was all about. In truth, I was a marooned 27-year-old. There was nothing anchoring me to the ground – the muddled sixties thinking that had preoccupied my teens had receded, leaving the music and drugs, but little else. Worse still, a new wave of eighties thinking had left me washed up on a shore where my insecurities about life were coming home to roost. Far from being at the centre of anything, I was in fact stuck on a traffic island watching life move past me like a speeding car.

At the centre of my insular little universe was a continuing fascination with the music world and all its attendant trappings. But I was now light years away from the very confused youngster who had burdened the likes of Hendrix, Morrison and Lennon with expectations they hadn't a chance of fulfilling. As the amphetamines and alcohol helped me to stumble onto a night bus at Trafalgar Square, that naive and obsessive fourteen year old seemed like a different person altogether. I could no longer imagine quite how any of those teenage thoughts could have been crammed inside my body. My dreams had somehow got lost, seeped through my sallow skin and escaped into the atmosphere. My mind now raced as if it were going nowhere, hurtling me toward an uncertain future.

I crawled into bed with the book idea still swimming around in my head before drifting off into a fitful sleep. In four hours time I would have to be at the local Depot, traipsing my way through the dustmen to get to my ramshackle office.

PART ONE

this is entertainment – "welcome to the Rat Club"

It was Xmas 1977, and my own little Industrial Revolution was about to begin. I'd already had to rethink my musical education when most of the music I had previously held dear was well and truly spat at by punk. Even though I was old enough to feel a Bob Harris-like pull of loyalty to the old wave, I was ready for the change of musical direction that punk engendered. But, as 1977 was coming to the close of a frantic musical year, not even punk could have prepared me for what was to come. My musical world was about to be thrown into an even more off-kilter orbit.

I was in my final year at University and rather than dirtying my hands with the smudgy print of the live listings section in the weekly music press, my time would have been better spent scouring the graduate appointment pages of the daily broad sheets. Many of my fellow students at the London School of Economics had forsaken fretting about what was a hot new LP in favour of turning their attentions toward the thorny issue of a career.

Not me. The Xmas holidays were following an all-too familiar pattern. I had signed on with some temp agencies in the hope of the odd day's work in local warehouses and factories. I was also already acclimatising my liver for the festive season by upping the intake of alcohol, ensuring the following few weeks would be a hazy blur. Once again, Christmas would be a never-ending round of joke-swapping and late night drinking. And of course going to see the odd gig or two.

Browsing the double-size Christmas issue of *Sounds*, my eye was drawn to a small entry about a gig to be held at a venue called the Rat Club. The evening was to be hosted by a band called Throbbing Gristle. By the name I assumed them to be a punk band of sorts.

"Come on, this is an absolute must," I chimed, as I rung round a few mates, "What sort of band calls themselves Throbbing Gristle?!"

"Hey, I just got these dead good drainpipe trousers," enthused my mate Bruce, ignoring the question. Getting off the point was Bruce's speciality. *Marquee Moon* by Television was blaring so loudly on his stereo I could hardly hear him. Whilst I had spent the last three years wandering somewhat disinterestedly through the LSE's corridors, Bruce's graduate days had been spent at the University of East Anglia's grey, fortress-like campus.

Bruce was an old school friend and was gawky, unpredictable and funny. As a sixteen-year-old public school boys we had been quick to join a group of kids that hung around at "smokers corner", smoking joints and dropping the odd Mandrax or Tyenol to reach the required level of being "spaced out". We accompanied our morning spliff with endless talk about LPs by an exotic array of West Coast bands. Somehow, names like the Grateful Dead, Jefferson Airplane, The Doors, Moby Grape, Mothers of Invention, Quicksilver Messenger Service and Spirit, conjured up a feeling of indescribable mystical excitement. At public school, English bands didn't really cut the mustard.

Bruce and I also shared a loathing for anything remotely approaching sport. My contribution to a typical afternoon's Rugby match was to be sent off for wearing a scarf and gloves. "It isn't a bloody fashion show Fish," I was told and promptly given detention. Bruce, not to be outdone, was sent off for tackling me whilst I prepared to rid myself of the wretched ball as quickly as possible. Not a crime, you'd have thought, until the master refereeing the game realised we were on the same side. As we giggled like a couple of hysterical schoolgirls, the other side scored an easy try. More detention.

Having completed his University education in an amphetamine flurry, Bruce was still worryingly thin. He had also decided that living in England wasn't going to suit his overall bohemian out-look and was talking about finding an escape route abroad. With his long legs squeezed into tight drainpipes, battered baseball boots and shoulder length locks, he looked a bit like Joey Ramone. Musically too, his penchant was for anything remotely New York-ish like Richard Hell and the New York Dolls. Anyway, eventually Bruce warmed to the idea of Throbbing Gristle.

Dave was as small as Bruce was lanky. By the beginning of the seventies, the ripples created by the Woodstock Generation had barely spread as far as leafy, suburban Kenton. As a result, the length of my hair was still likely to send curtains twitching, and as Dave was the only other long-haired 14-year-old on my block we forged an immediate friendship.

By 1977, we both met punk with open arms – well, let's say we had both visited the barbers. The previous years had been spent seeing endless groups, exchanging numerous LPs (some decidedly dodgy), buying guitars, swapping riffs, forming bands, splitting over musical differences, planning difficult second albums, writing concept albums and generally dreaming of the big time. Usual teenage stuff – and usually ending up down the pub. Had we applied the same dedication to writing music as we had to imbibing ale, no doubt our back catalogue would now be being remixed and prepared for a deluxe CD re-issue.

In stark contrast to the public school West Coast leanings of Bruce and myself, Dave's more down-to-earth comprehensive edu-cation had led him toward music with a more abrasive edge. Having started out a Cream and Black Sabbath freak, by 1977 he was more likely to sing anything from ATV's catalogue, usually "How Much Longer".

"Yeah, fuck it, I'm up for anything," he replied in his half-cockney, Steve Marriott kind of way, after finding out that the evening's entertainment was to be provided by the inimitably named Throbbing Gristle.

Then there was Paul. Ever since we had briefly played in a band together, Paul had slotted nicely into our drinking and gig-going circle, despite being a few years younger than the rest of us. He was an angular faced guy with a blond bouffant, who had sailed through his punk graduation with a degree in Wire and the Buzzcocks. His predictable reaction to a gig by Throbbing Gristle was an eager, "You can count me in."

Punk had given us all the kick up the arse (sometimes literally) we needed. But it was a brief but bright firework, and in truth we were all beginning to tire of seeing the safety-pinned, three chord thrashers that had emerged in the wake of the Sex Pistols. It had, however, left us all with a craving for exotic musical entertainment beyond the expected.

The Rat Club turned out to be the downstairs bar in the Valentino Rooms at the Bedford Corner Hotel just off the Tottenham Court Road. As we looked down the steep stairway, there was no sign of anyone to take our money, no explanation of what was going on down there. We listened to see if we could hear any music wafting up from the bowels. Nothing.

"We could always go to the pub first, and then make up our minds," someone suggested, fearing that we could be descending towards London's belated equivalent of Altamont. The brief description of the band in *Sounds* had quoted the singer, one Geneesis P-Orridge, as saying that many of the group's fans were Hell's Angels.

"Fuck it, there's four of us, and it's only a few quid to get in. If it's shit we can always go to the pub later."

We tentatively braved our way down into the hall to be met by a sparse crowd including some of London's arty punks, some pissed Australians and a handful of transvestites. Hardly a regular crowd. "If this lot are Hell's Angels, then I'm Marlon Brando," I thought.

"You're standing in the right place there, mate", Paul was informed. "The strippers are coming out of that door behind you."

So it was that we discovered that evening's bill also included Candy and her performing Gorilla. Musical variation was to be supplied by the pianist from Thunderclap Newman's group called

Thunderflag. They had either taken one look at the audience and fled in fear, or been offered something better, because they never showed. Instead the bald head of free-form saxophonist Lol Coxhill took to the stage to prove the saxophone can sound like anything from a constipated budgerigar to a grumbling fart.

Even before the main attraction took centre stage, there was a decidedly strange feeling about the whole proceedings. Throbbing Gristle turned out to be unlike any group we had ever seen – on first hearing they sounded like categorically the worst, even taking into account some of the excruciating punk copyists we had witnessed over the previous months.

It all started with a brief snippet of Bing Crosby singing "White Christmas", then the band – three guys and girl – took to the stage. The noise that followed was a continual turgid drone. It was like they had managed to condense the ear-splitting crescendo of a huge factory and squeeze it into a small room.

Suddenly I had this overwhelming feeling that I was witnessing the ultimate nadir of punk – the sort of nihilism that reduced music to a complete and utterly horrible din. After fifteen minutes, it was becoming so hurtful on the ears we were all laughing uncontrollably as a way to just relieve the tension. In the back of my mind, I had already decided this was one of my favourite bands of all time.

After half an hour of uninterrupted torture, we realised that there was to be no respite from this unrelenting aural assault. We had no difficulty in accounting for the time we had spent suspended in this noisy hell, as a LED clock ticked over behind the group. We later found out that each performance was timed to last exactly one hour. One number was indistinguishable from the next. It was a painful assault on the senses, like being forced to listen to Lou Reed's *Metal Machine Music* at excruciating volume.

Watching the band was somewhat impaired by two bright, white spotlights aimed directly at the audience. Dave was so transfixed that he spent the whole hour standing on a chair staring into one of them. The combined effect was like being forced to stand next to a giant compactor's terrifying rumble, whilst being caught in Colditz-like searchlights. After a while I felt my brain becoming so addled it was difficult to distinguish whether the sound was coming from inside or outside my head. My head was literally turning into a piece of throbbing gristle – which I guess was the general idea.

Then it was over. There followed a surreal debate, between the promoter and those brave souls remaining in the audience, as to the success of the sonic journey we had all just undertaken. "That was fucking rubbish, give us our money back," was a typical call.

"What sort of gig was this?" was all I could think. Not only were the support acts a succession of strippers, but there was an on-the-spot autopsy into the evening's goings-on.

"What happened to the guy from Thunderclap Newman?" someone shouted.

"You mean to tell me," Paul turned to me, "some cunt's just sat through that thinking they're finally going to get a rendition of 'Something in the Air'."

The rather flustered promoter being heckled with abuse was the same guy that had actually ended the evening dancing with Candy's performing Gorilla – no one else had volunteered. His other folly appeared to be a suicidal keenness to get feedback from anyone brave enough to have endured Throbbing Gristle's set.

As the closing debate quickly deteriorated into a slanging match, we were in danger of missing our last train home. With the abusive language still hanging in the air, I made my way to the toilet to be met with the sight of a guy hitching up his dress and pissing at the urinal. "Just another average night out," I joked to myself. I knew that however good my descriptive powers were, trying to paint the evening's goings-on to anyone the next day would fall short in applying the right brush strokes.

On my return, I prised Dave off the same chair he had been perched on for the last hour – from the expression on his face you'd have thought he'd just spent the last hour in an abattoir. I rescued Paul from the verge of launching into the debacle of a debate. That just left Bruce. My first guess was right. He was trying to rub his ears back to life as he nursed a last beer at the bar.

"Well, that's what I call a night out," I said, as we ducked into the underground station, rather proud of myself that I had discovered the evening. No one was arguing. In truth none of us could hear fuck all.

spread the virus – "keeping it minimal"

Back at college the next term, my fellow students were getting excited about the upcoming tour by Lynyrd Skynyrd. But I couldn't share their excitement for Southern fried guitar riffery. As I sat in the canteen watching them drink their hot Ribena, for some inexplicable reason an LSE favourite tipple, I could literally feel my life being dragged off in an altogether different direction. The beer monsters and dope fiends of the past two years were evaporating before my eyes. Every day they looked more and more like budding stockbrokers. They were sensible enough to let their musical preferences take a back seat in favour of getting "a life".

But I just couldn't let go that easily. When I wasn't going to see bands, I found myself tangled up in earnest and heated discussions down the boozer over what was supposedly new and happening. Was Elvis Costello better than Graham Parker? We all agreed Joe Jackson was shit. Who was the better singer, Tom Petty or Willy Deville? Which label had the better acts, Stiff or Chiswick? Were punk bands using the major labels, or were the major labels manipulating them? We were musically obsessed, or more correctly just plain obsessed with arguing.

Every now and then, the debate would swing toward the experimental end of the dial. It was then that someone would inevitably refer to our Rat Club experience. Suffice to say, in a few short months the evening had achieved legendary status and become the yardstick against which anything remotely outrageous was measured. Almost unintentionally we were beginning to debate TG's pros and cons. God forbid, we were entertaining the idea that they were actually rather good. Debate was replaced by excitement when, in February 1978, we discovered that their first LP, confusingly entitled *Second Annual Report*, had just been released in a limited edition of 785 copies. I thought the title to be a piece of inspired surrealism. It later transpired rather disappointingly that a "first annual report" did actually exist, albeit only in the form of a limited tape distributed amongst the group's friends.

We had to wonder which record label had been mad enough to put up the money to commit this unrelenting noise to vinyl. It was really no surprise that the mystery investors turned out to be the group themselves. The LP sported such commercial sounding ditties as "Maggot Death" and "Slug Bait", while the sleeve notes claimed that some of the music was the soundtrack to their film *After Cease To Exist*. It almost went without saying that most reasonable people, if they'd have bothered to listen to it, would have considered both sides to be totally unlistenable cack.

Slowly, it began to sink in through my skin that the whole aura around the group was essentially that old cliché, "love them or hate them, you couldn't ignore them". To some they were a nauseous joke akin to the most pernicious of farts, to others their noise was a serious artistic endeavour. Most importantly, it was really impossible to distinguish which of the two opinions was most accurate.

"If an artist can get away with presenting a totally white canvas and call it a painting," I ruminated over a pint of Stella Artois, a tipple whose potency had prompted the nickname God's sperm, "then TG can release a record of raw noise and call it music." Oh boy, was I getting to grips with this minimalism lark.

Once I had managed to rid myself of the hangover an excess intake of God's seminal fluid had left me with, I realised here was something I *could* get excited about. Meaning TG, of course, not lager. I was already totally convinced about Stella's place at the top of the lager league. Not that it hadn't been a toughly contested season, with the redoubtable Stella fighting off notable challenges from "Headache Holsten" and "Loopy Brew Lowenbrau" sometimes also referred to as "Liquid LSD".

TG had all the DIY ethics of punk, but none of that 1,2,3,4, bash, bash, boredom, anarchy stuff. No thrashing and spitting, just people hanging around waiting for the next arty happening. Having spent the previous ten years comparing guitarists and endlessly debating musical merit, it was almost a relief to finally find a group that had none whatsoever.

Dipping our toes into the world of TG was like acquiring membership to some weird little secret society. It also officially pronounced the opening of a record-buying "silly season". The hunt was on for the most outrageous, loudest, most inane 45s we could find. Anyone chancing upon something particularly funny or controversial was generally slapped on the back at weekly playback sessions. Sooner or later, everyone got awarded an extra pint of God's emission for musical services beyond the call of duty. The weekly goal was to be able to brag about being the first to have latched on to a particularly obscure bunch of weirdos.

In Virgin Records I showed Paul the cover to a record depicting a guy stabbing a duck. We both laughed. Back at home we sat in my room and tried to figure out whether my new purchase should be played at 33 or 45. The record didn't sound remotely normal at either speed. We decided The Residents were dead cool, whoever they were.

Other days we would sit around filling in order forms from Chris Cutler's Recommended Records for obscure delights like Albert Marcoeur, Etron Fou Leloublan and the Reverend Ron Pate and the Debonairs. Our appetite for musical silliness knew no bounds. I even invested in two LPs by Alvarro, "the Chilean with the singing nose", one of which delighted under the title of *Drinking My Own Sperm*. However, we declined to follow Alvarro's example and stuck to God's sperm instead.

One particularly rainy afternoon, Paul and I finally put our newly found eclecticism to some use and recorded a few avant-garde ditties together – one of which was the result of what happens if you let two nerds loose with an echo machine, a typewriter and a balloon. In a desperate attempt to find a new guitar sound, we even resorted to playing them with our feet. The resulting opus was called "Seagulls" and kept us amused until the pub opened. But anything more musically ambitious was out of the question. Even by then Paul and I had decided that our respective epitaphs should read "They didn't do an awful lot, but they had a few drinks." So drink we did.

partially submerged – "digging deeper"

It was at the end of a particularly rigorous lunchtime session that I suddenly realised that I was staggering out of the LSE's Three Tuns Bar for the last time. It was June 1978 and I was officially no longer a student. As I looked blearily into the bright sunlight casting thin shadows beneath Holborn's high buildings, I thought to myself, "So, what's next?" If I hadn't been so drunk, no doubt it would have brought on some form of panic attack.

As I toddled off down Kingsway, there had been no need for tearful good-byes. I had been so busy down my local pub, or hanging around the Marquee Club, that I had completely forgotten that one of the aims of University was to broaden ones' horizons and make new friends. In the end I even lost contact with Andy, a tall, likeable dope freak with a shock of tight curls. Andy's contribution to my well-being was convincing me to give up smoking cigarettes.

"Look," he said, "if you smoke one joint and then another, you get more stoned. If you have a drink, and then another, you get more pissed. If you smoke a cigarette, and then another, what exactly do you get more of?"

It was difficult to argue with logic like that, so from that moment on I enthusiastically replaced cigarettes with joints. It was progress of sorts, I guessed.

This progression seemed all the more sensible, as I was beginning to open my ears to the delights of booming bass heavy dub reggae. What I found more difficult to handle was my inability to drink vast quantities of beer if the day followed a hazy path set by two large joints for breakfast. My thirst for ale was unquenchable and soon the dope was losing a battle it could never win. God's Sperm 1, the devil's weed 0.

The truth of the matter was that I was more excited by the clandestine nature of the drug taking than the actual effect of the drug itself. By the time I left academia behind, I had not only tired of my compatriots giggling dope talk, but also the way many of them were pumped up with their own self-importance and the ineffectual bluster of make-believe politics.

When the rather unspectacular piece of paper with BA Geography written on it dropped quietly through my door, I jumped around joking, "What the fuck am I supposed to do with this". It was a prophetic remark. My Geography degree (a disinterested 2:2) rather than being an instant passport to a career, was something that prospective employers weren't exactly queuing up to talk to me about. As the rejection letters began piling up, it should have been time for that panic attack. Instead, I set off down the pub to celebrate the fact that I could add letters to the end of my name should I so desire.

One lunchtime I managed to pass the pub without going in, and found myself sitting in the local job centre instead.

"So what exactly do you see yourself doing?" asked the guy behind the desk.

"Oh, here we go again," I thought, looking blearily at him. "Why all these damn questions?"

Both my parents and the school careers master had posed a similar conundrum. More often than not, I retorted with a question of my own.

"What do you suggest?" was all I could ever think to reply.

Secretly, I was hoping that somebody would just hand me the address of some place where I could be paid loads of dosh for doing next-to-nothing, preferably connected with the music business.

In the end I filled in a stack of forms and wandered off to have a game of pitch-and-putt with Paul. "Perhaps I could become a professional golfer," I thought, after hitting a rather impressive 36 over the 9 par-3 holes.

Some days I went down to the local library and stared gloomily at the patchwork of job advertisements in the back pages of the newspapers. The longer I stared at the print, the more it became evident that I didn't want any of these jobs, even though I had about as much chance of getting them as becoming an astronaut. At least the weekly music press was written in phrases I could understand – although I have to say I occasionally struggled to fathom those penned by Paul Morley or Ian Penman.

Having spare time on my hands at least gave me an opportunity to do a bit of homework on TG. Being an arch self-publicist it wasn't difficult to ascertain that the main driving force behind the group was the pixie-faced P-Orridge. Slightly less well advertised was the fact that he was actually Neal Megson from Hull. He had rechristened himself Genesis P-Orridge when the Royal Mail decided to prosecute him for sending obscene postcards through the post. Hence the initials GP-O (General Post Office).

Gen, as his name was soon shortened to, was also TG's bass player and singer. I use both terms loosely, he could really do neither. His bass playing was an almost random thuddy twang, whilst his singing voice had a childlike nasally whine. But his musical talents were virtuoso-like compared to his guitarist girl-friend – the part time stripper Cosey Fanni Tutti (real name Christine Newby). Most bands, even punk bands, had male lead guitarists that liked to swagger around the stage striking Keith Richards poses. Cosey Fanni Tutti was not only a woman, but one who couldn't really play in the conventional sense – at the Rat

Club she had spent a considerable amount of time knitting. When stirred to action, much of her playing consisted of attacking the strings with a bottleneck. Unsurprisingly, Bonnie Raitt's position as queen of the slide guitar was not in danger.

As I waded ever deeper into the murky moat surrounding the TG encampment, so I found out about P-Orridge and Tutti's past actions as a performance art group known as COUM and the notorious *Prostitution* exhibition they had staged at the ICA. It turned out that P-Orridge had spent much of the early seventies utilising his connections in the contemporary art world to stage various outrageous art happenings.

The ICA's 1976 retrospective of COUM's artistic efforts had caused somewhat of a major scandal in the media, even reaching the front page of one daily newspaper where the whole enterprise was deemed to be an outrageous misuse of Arts Council money. One MP went as far as to call them "the wreckers of civilisation". Not only were many of the exhibits – including one featuring used tampons called "It's That Time of the Month Again" – considered obscene, but during a fight at the opening P-Orridge broke a finger. He was clearly utilising his true talent in life – upsetting people.

Much of the scandal revolved around a faction who argued that P-Orridge was exploiting his girlfriend Tutti. The fact that she was in on the joke and also posed regularly for nude magazines as well as being a stripper in London's East End didn't dissuade their detractors.

Despite the media splurge surrounding the exhibition, P-Orridge's thirst for notoriety remained unquenched. As a performance artist, he no doubt sussed that he was only upsetting the gallery establishment. So, having achieved his fifteen minutes of fame by shocking the art world, it was now time to turn his attentions to the music business. P-Orridge's masterstroke, if you can call it that, was to form a group that shared punk's love for shock tactics, but was musically altogether more abrasive and difficult.

For all their badmouthing of dinosaur rock bands, punk groups were still looking to gain mileage from the trusted format of singer, guitar, bass and drums. It was mostly a throwback to the old sixties garage bands. Many of the hardcore punk bands (or New Wave groups as they were increasingly being called) were merely repeating the old rock 'n' roll routine, only with safety pins stuck through their noses. They may have directed their vitriol toward the hippies, but they still sat around smoking spliff and dropping the odd tab or two of acid.

TG seemed to be saying that there was no point in trying to shock people with straight-ahead rock 'n' roll. The way forward was to use the new technology of synthesizers and noise generators to produce an unholy and confrontational cacophony. If the Rat Club was anything to go by, they had succeeded admirably.

The name Throbbing Gristle came from the Humberside slang for an erection. It was chosen specifically as the most embarrassing name they could think of for anyone having to go into a store to ask for a record. P-Orridge and Tutti had already enlisted the services of Peter "Sleazy" Christopherson, formerly a member of the design company Hipgnosis. (P-Orridge and Tutti can be seen snogging semi-naked in the bath for the cover of UFO's Hipgnosis designed *Force It* sleeve. Bath taps – faucets – get it? Well, it was the sort of visual pun Hipgnosis were keen on.) It seemed strange that the guy once responsible for the cover design to some of the most overblown progressive rock records was now part of a group that sounded like it was trying to kill off rock 'n' roll for good.

TG's fourth member was Chris Carter, the youthful looking Abba fan. With his newly acquired pudding-basin haircut he looked like a fresh-faced kid that had fallen in with the wrong crowd. "Why's a nice boy like that hanging around with those ruffians?" my mother would no doubt have commented. Well as it happened they had a reason for befriending their new innocent looking mate. Carter knew all about drum machines, sequencers and synthesizers.

So that was the four piece line-up; a female guitarist and part-time stripper, a bass player and all-round exhibitionist, a gay ex-sleeve designer, and a synthesizer player who looked like a physics student. It was hardly the recipe for the new Beatles, but strangely the whole arrangement had a certain internal symmetry.

The fact that they had decided to release records on their own label, based at P-Orridge and Fanni Tutti's Hackney home, reflected punk's DIY methodology. Apparently after their first LP sold out, a couple of offers of record deals did come in, but P-Orridge retorted that he would only be interested in signing to K-Tel!

There was a sinister edge to TG involving a gratuitous and rather sensationalist interest in anything remotely macabre. Their Industrial label's logo consisted of the Auschwitz concentration camp chimney, whilst their badge consisted of the letters T&G placed in front of a lightning flash similar to that used by Oswald Moseley in the thirties. From the outset, TG's primary interest was uncovering anything that was normally considered taboo.

For inspiration, the group lent on two previous arch-exponents of the taboo, namely William Burroughs and Aleister Crowley. True, Bowie had already flirted with the Burroughs connection, and Jimmy Page the Crowley one, but TG's manifesto (yes, they were that serious about it all) was based around a more literal translation of both men's ideas. Unlike Bowie or Zeppelin, the last thing on TG's collective mind was translating these ideas into rock's already ransacked heritage.

I had originally discovered Burroughs, Ginsberg and the Beats back at school. Having worked my way backwards from Grateful Dead records, through the Merry Pranksters to Cassady and Kerouac, and finally Burroughs. As a long-haired sixteen year old, I was happy to sit on the train home imagining that one day I too would be hitting the peyote trail in South America, or holing myself up in Tangier trying to write the ultimate Beat novel. Inevitably the whole clandestine and subversive nature of much Beat literature was part of its appeal. With wild and weird sex scenes, drug language, and science fiction sequences, surely Burroughs' books were great stuff.

I was less convinced about the beast himself, Aleister Crowley. All that black magic hocus pocus was difficult to differentiate from Dennis Wheatley or the blood and slapstick of Hammer horror movies as far as I was concerned. P-Orridge, on the other hand was running with it all like the proverbial bat out of hell. Like Crowley before him, he had already convinced himself, and his band of followers, that he was some kind of modern day shaman. His interviews were already reading more like sermons or the rantings of some crazed extremist than informed discussion. The fact that he appeared to disdain the idea of pubs was surely a nonsensical piece of snobbery. My particular altar was going to remain the public bar, no matter what anyone else preached.

So, while I waited for another opportunity to see one of TG's rare live appearances, I contented myself by relaxing at home to their newly released single "United". This wasn't as strange a paradox as one might first have imagined, as the record displayed an altogether different side to the band. Their new record was almost a pop tune, singing the praises of the sexual union. This lighter upbeat mood was immediately dispelled when flipping the record over to be confronted with "Zyklon B Zombie", a song named after the Zyklon B extermination gas used by the Nazis.

Despite the darker tones that were starting to spew out of my record player, the summer of 1978 still retained an air of innocence. I had quickly recovered from any employment panics and resolved that I would have to make do on the dole – a proper job would just have to wait until I was ready. Paul, having just left school, then suggested that I apply for a temp job at the same place where he was currently employed. An absolutely spiffing idea I thought to myself as I strolled in to start work at the mail order division of a company specializing in clothes for those too tall or wide to be catered for by high street shops.

The job was typical of temporary work, enabling us to laugh at our work mates, those stuck labouring at dead end jobs with little chance of breaking out of their little prison. Paul and I were high-minded, arrogant outsiders, student temps that were paid more than the ordinary staff.

By the second week we were completely into our stride. Paul, considered too disruptive amongst his all-female table, was moved onto the same table as me. The fact that we were mates and likely to cause more trouble together than apart seemed to elude the manager, a man who had no arse as far as we could ascertain. His legs appeared to join directly onto his back.

The first two weeks flew by as I found out what a triple G-cup bra looked like – basically two parachutes with a strap at the back. We found ourselves confronted with letters from sad individuals who were so fat they couldn't get out of their own front doors.

"Look that's me on the left in a dress I bought from you – and by the way can I have the photo back," was typical of the type of letter that would accompany an order.

Such evidence of gross obesity should have made us feel pity, but in truth we could do little else but laugh. Even the most politically correct had to chuckle at the fact that a certain Mrs Tubby had an account with the company. Everyday there was something new to amaze us. If only college had been this interesting.

We had no idea why we were doing jobs like E-stamping, which unsurprisingly consisted of stamping the letter "E" on completed orders. To ease the boredom, we took to stamping to a rhythm. Up-to-date new wave favourites like "United" and tracks from Wire's *Pink Flag* were plundered for good E-stamping beats. Sooner or later the old wave would get a look in and the drum intro to "Honky Tonk Women" would get hammered out.

a touch of evil – "the film-makers co-op"

Over a rather greasy lunch in the canteen, I was flicking through the music press, when I suddenly exclaimed, "Fuck me, the Gristle are playing again." I excitedly showed the entry to Paul, resulting in a particularly frenzied E-stamping version of "U-ni-ted" that afternoon. On returning home I rang up Dave to make sure he kept the date free.

No amount of E-stamping could have prepared us for our second immersion into the live sound of TG. Even though our new weirdo tastes had generally stretched our lugholes out of shape, we were about to push our belief in TG's musical ideas to the limit.

The gig in question was held at an odd sort of building around the back of Camden called the London Film-Makers Co-op – standard venues were too ordinary for TG. Getting in meant climbing a set of fire escape stairs, at the top of which we were each handed a TG badge. We were just in time to see some Burroughs' films, swiftly followed by the group's own infamous *After Cease To Exist*.

All I can safely recall about the film was a scene involving a guy lying prostrate on some kind of operating table. There then followed a simulated castration (was it simulated? – it looked so real!) by a woman with a pair of scissors. By the time I looked round, Paul had disappeared. He had gone outside and vomited. From this moment on I knew there was something very wrong about the whole evening. There was already a palpable violent tension in the air when the screen was lifted to reveal the group launching into a number called "Hamburger Lady". This I later discovered was not about a woman working at the local Wimpy bar but about a lady who had the misfortune of having been half burnt alive – nice one.

Behind the group were signs saying "death factory". Like at the Rat Club, the whole turgid morass of sound started to pummel the stomach and turn the head into a stodgy muddle. This time around, some of the audience wasn't prepared to just sit back and watch. All of a sudden a group of women, later reported to be members of the Raincoats and the Slits, were so incensed by the music that they had picked up some chairs and were throwing them at the stage. P-Orridge's rather ungainly response was to lift his bass guitar over his head and hit out at one of the women as if he were trying to cull a seal.

The lights went on and suddenly it was like being plugged back into the real world. "Thanks for ruining it", someone (Jon Savage, I think) shouted out. People were looking at each other with that, "What the fuck was all that about?" expression on their faces. With the evil genie having been let out of its bottle, the gig was over. It was clear that the band would not be coming back on.

The group later claimed that the problems were due to their ion-iser having broken down. This machine was supposed to negate the effects of the ultrasonic frequencies that they claimed to use during a performance. In interviews Gen and his cohorts would make a great deal of the fact that people were prone to report all sorts of sensations, including instant orgasm, at live gigs. The con-tents of Paul's stomach being splayed over a Camden pavement was patently typical of a less pleasurable reaction.

Ever keen to document their history as it happened, the tape of this performance (the group recorded every concert they played and released it on their Industrial label), featured the music fol-lowed by a discussion amongst the group about the night's pro-ceedings. Another anecdote to the whole evening was that P-Orridge started receiving death threats on the group's answering machine. One voice stated, "You haven't got long left." Another message featured a woman's voice stating, "You're going to get well and truly done over." The whole dark world in which the group had immersed themselves, begged for these extreme reactions. But never ones to waste an opportunity, these answerphone messages duly appeared on the group's next LP *DOA*.

For a while I couldn't really get my head around this new side to Throbbing Gristle. In a naive way I had enjoyed the idea of flirting with the macabre and sinister, but did I really want to know if the outcome was the evening I had just witnessed. In reality, the actual violence was less than the brawls we had increasingly witnessed at many punk gigs. Even so, there was something deeply disturbing about the whole event. For days afterwards, the film, Paul vomiting, the chairs flying around, replayed in my mind over and over again. For me TG had evolved from being a decadent type of art/punk joke into something ugly and tainted.

Paul and I met the following morning at the Tumble Inn Cafe in Alperton for our usual cup of tea with globules of grease floating on the surface. Paul had totally recovered his equilibrium and laughed about vomiting, but I had to wonder about a group that could make someone physically throw up. My misgivings were compounded in that week's *Sounds* which featured an article about TG "holidaying" in Auschwitz. All of this seemed to me to be stretching the Nazi connections close to breaking point. In response to such allegations, the group was adamant that they were apolitical. But I had to wonder at what point they would draw the line? I decided for the moment I would reserve judgement and see what the group did next.

Like all good things, the summer job wasn't built to last. Paul and I were almost tearful as we sat downing a few pints in the Pleasure Boat in Alperton on our final day. Paul had no real reason to be dismayed, he was just about to start his first year at Sheffield University. I, on the other hand, had no plans at all. As one for the road turned into six, I looked into the bottom of my glass. Once again the beer stain seemed to form a frothy message. It read, "So, what's next?" It was clearly time for another panic attack.

The end of any summer is depressing, but the shortening days of this particular one seemed to have a particular poignancy. My head was exploding with so much great music, it was almost like being sixteen all over again. We continued to down copious pints, puff away at the occasional giant-sized spliff, play pitch-and-putt, and attend so many gigs I sometimes wondered if the whole of Britain's youth had picked up a guitar, learned three chords and written a bunch of power-pop songs.

During a hot September we drove around in Dave's car with Keith Hudson's *Pick A Dub* or the Fatman Ridim Section blaring out of his speakers, a fourpack of beer on the back seat and a lump of hash nestling in the glove compartment. For all we cared we were in the heart of Kingston, Jamaica. In fact we were still in Kenton. A reality made all the more obvious when the weather took its usual turn for the worse and winter began to set in. The storm clouds were also gathering over my prospects and it was beginning to look like I was the only one with no future.

So, as Paul prepared to go off to college in Sheffield, I once again trod the familiar path to the local job centre. "See you in a couple of months", he said, throwing a few student necessities into a bag. I half envied him for making the break, but I still wondered at the wisdom of leaving the capital in favour of the provincial option.

With my meagre dole money, I had to cut down on the gigs, the drink and dope, until such time as I could see a way of financing my lifestyle again. That's how things stayed until Xmas when I landed another temporary job – this time demonstrating toys in the local Debenhams department store. I had already crossed paths with the toy industry – one of my stranger holiday jobs had been painting garden Wombles. As I sat applying splashes of paint to Wellington or Uncle Bulgaria, I had to think to myself, "What the fuck am I doing?" The self-same comment once again passed my lips as I demonstrated games to snotty, loud-mouthed kids. Behind me, the "I want to be like you-hoo-hoo" song from the *Jungle Book* blared away on permanent rotation. If that wasn't bad enough, I was exposed to germs I didn't even know existed. As a result for the whole six weeks I had a permanent cold.

It was almost exactly a year to the day when the Rat Club crew; Paul (back for Xmas from Sheffield), Dave, Bruce and myself reconvened for Public Image Ltd's first gig on Christmas Day, 1978. If we needed any persuading that punk was dead, then this was it. All the downstairs seating had been removed from The Rainbow in Finsbury Park, a foolish decision by the venue as the evening disintegrated into a series of brawls that made the disturbance at TG's Camden gig seem like a kindergarten pie fight. Intimidating skinheads shouted down the support act Linton Kwesi Johnson and then tried to knock each others brains out. In two short years, the good natured pogoing throng of 1976 had turned into a hoard of football terrace bully boys intent on exercise their fists.

It was all made a bigger shame by the fact that Public Image Ltd were actually rather good. When not imploring their audience to stop their frenzied fighting, they whipped up a fair old musical frenzy of their own. However, it is difficult to enjoy a band, however good, whilst avoiding a stray Doctor Marten being lodged into one's rump. The idea of a gig on Christmas night had greatly appealed to us – after all it was the only night of the year all the pubs were closed – but we ended up wishing we had stayed at home pulling crackers to Morecambe And Wise.

For the rest of the Xmas break I celebrated the fact that I had an income by learning to make as many of the recipes in a newly acquired book of cocktails – a particular favourite was a Vodka concoction called a Lover's Nocturne. Paul and I would stagger back to our respective homes at 5 or 6 in the morning. It was that kind of Christmas. For a whole week I never saw daylight.

PART TWO

drinking gasoline – "welcome to Central Depot"

By the beginning of 1979, those that still chose to call themselves punks were a bunch of rather sad tossers in bondage trousers and Mohican haircuts posing for tourists down the King's Road whilst exacting the mandatory ten pence from anyone stupid enough to give it to them. For my part, I could see it was time for me to abandon my own particular "no future" mentality. In truth I had lost count of which panic attack this was. Try as I might to hide from reality, I was simply going to have to apply my mind to earning a living. If I wasn't careful, the weekly trip to the local DHSS office was all that life was now offering me. Economically restrictive, I was wary of being set adrift on a money-less raft called the dole. Nevertheless, was I really going to have to enter the real world?

The Catch 22 of my quandary was that I needed an income. Drinking down the pub every night was proving to be an expensive business. But I was genuinely at a loss as to why any company would want to employ an aimless 23-year old. I continued to quote my educational qualifications, but I had to wonder if these weren't more of a hindrance than a help. I even wondered if it weren't better to put on application forms, "listening to reggae, smoking spliff and drinking beer".

Temp agencies, unsurprisingly, only provided temporary solutions. This work only lasted a few weeks and then it was back to the whole rigmarole of signing on again, endlessly filling in all the relevant forms. Working part-weeks meant more forms to fill in. It was hardly surprising people threw up their hands in horror and said, "I give up, just send us the Giro." Like it or not, there was nowhere left to run. Regular employment was beckoning me like an ugly seductress.

Then, one morning I picked up the phone to be greeted by the voice of the girl from the local job centre.

"I've got this full time clerical job at the local Council just come in and I immediately thought of you. Do you want to give it a try?" she announced in a rather patronising tone.

For a few seconds my head spun with a mixture of my usual morning hangover and the panic associated with having to make a decision at such an early hour. Do I want this? Could I forgive myself for turning down the opportunity to earn some regular money? Nobody had been able to tell me what to do with my life – now all of a sudden someone was trying to convince me that my future lay with the local Council.

What she had failed to tell me was that the job was actually down the local rubbish tip, rather than at the newly built Civic Centre. It was in one the Centre's over-heated and over-white offices that I was interviewed by a fat, red-faced Yorkshireman who tried to convince me that, with my qualifications, it was only a matter of time before I would be climbing the local government ladder. I wasn't even sure if I wanted to be on the bottom rung in the first place.

"After all Mr Fish," he assured me, "there's no reason why you shouldn't be looking on the Depot as a springboard to greater things."

As I looked out of the window, you could just about see the Depot. Bathed in a grey January mist, it looked about as hospitable as a mediaeval castle. It certainly didn't look much like a springboard to anything.

The following week, I was sitting in my favourite corner of our local pub, trying to avoid the stuffing that regularly protruded from the badly upholstered seats. As ever I was trying to make a pint look like a quart.

"Fuck it", I announced to the amazed faces of my drinking companions, "I've just accepted this job at the local Council." They may well have looked stunned, but no-one was more shocked by this news than me. Previously I had been having panic attacks at not being able to find a job, now I was having one because I had found one.

And so it was that on a bitterly cold January day I trudged through the black slushy remains of the previous week's snowfall and into Central Depot. As I stared at the muddle of prefabricated shacks and run down office buildings, I realised that the years of loafing around were now a memory. I was entering the same world as the sad fucks I had been so quick to take the piss out of as a student. Having spent the last few years floating around in the rarified air of academia and marijuana, the only whiff that met my nostrils that first morning was that of rotting refuse.

I was full of little ploys to make the finality of full-time employment seem rosier than it actually was. The reality of the situation was that this was not a holiday job where I could just jack it all in if the mood took me. Working life was now all about contracts of employment, flexi-time sheets, Unions, health and safety regulations – the whole bit. I had entered the permanent workforce. This was the beginning of a monotonous motorway that stretched out before me. The signposts read, "Destination – retirement at 65."

As I sat and wrote off a long letter to Bruce detailing my life's goings on, I couldn't help but recall the time when we had shared a joint on the way back from school, wondering where our respective lives would lead. Bruce had started to put his dreams into action and had moved to Cairo where he was teaching English at a British Council school. Hopping onto a push bike and cycling the mile or so to the Depot was hardly the stuff my dreams had been made of, but I assured Bruce in confident phrases that this was a stop-gap while I got my shit together. The difference between our two lives was made all the more apparent when I got his reply. Cairo sounded like an alien planet, and he was already making regular deposits at the bank of experience.

Typically, my arrival at Central Depot coincided with a refuse strike. The Trade Unions were still buoyed up by the fact that they had managed to reduce the country to a 3-day week under the labour government. At Central Depot I soon found out that it was the Union stewards who still called all the shots. This particular January they were demanding something or another – no doubt related to pay. So, instead of taking up my post in the Transport Office, I was marched into the Cleansing Department's portacabin. For the first three weeks I was lucky enough to have earned the opportunity to answer irate calls from local residents who had not seen so much as a hint of a dustman since they had called for their Xmas bonus.

"What's your name?" I was asked. You were obliged to tell them.

"Right then Mr Fish, I want you to know that I know the Mayor personally, and if something isn't done about the stinking heap of garbage piling up outside my house I am going to hold you personally responsible."

I soon found out that the Mayor was an extremely popular chap with a long list of close friends.

Then of course there were those who started, "I know it's not your fault but..."

"Wait, don't tell me," I felt like butting in, "You're going to give me a fucking earful anyway".

After a couple of days, the abuse was running off my back faster than water off the proverbially groomed duck. Slightly less easy to deflect were the comments of those closer to home.

"Shouldn't you be aiming a bit higher than a clerk's job down the local depot?" friends and family would inquire rather stonily of me.

I supposed they were right, but what did I care? At least I had a job. I was hardly the first University-educated, middle-class kid to end up throwing years of education down the pan.

"Is this what you studied all those years for? To end up at the local refuse tip!" my parents lost no time in reminding me.

I felt, however, that I had just about found my natural level. If education's job was to instil an individual with the get-up-and-go required for betterment, then in my case it had sadly failed. Maybe the fact that I had won a free place to public school meant I didn't feel guilty about this apparent squandering of my education. In any event, I couldn't really see the old boy's magazine, in amongst all my classmates' tales of success, running the story that I had now landed himself a job as the lowest paid clerical assistant at the local Council.

The way I looked at it, public school turned out its fair share of politicians, scientists, writers, actors and media personalities, somewhere along the line a stray misfit would surely end up at the local rubbish tip. In the odd confused moment, I even convinced myself that my new position possessed a dash of bohemian glamour that theirs surely lacked.

The refuse strike over, the work that landed on my desk in the Transport Department hardly had the complexities necessitating any kind of education, let alone a degree. For what it was worth, my task was to fill Big Viv's shoes. I soon found out that everyone acquired a nickname sooner or later. My predecessor had been so appropriately re-christened because he was called Viv and was about 6 foot 5 inches tall. It turned out that Big Viv also had big ideas and was using the Depot as a springboard just as I had been told to do. He wasn't going to let the dust settle under his feet and had applied to evening college. His promotion involved a move down the corridor and into the Highways Department.

As I slipped into Viv's vacant chair, I discerned it was my job to fill in cards that recorded the amount of Petrol, Derv and Gas that each of the Council's vehicles had consumed that particular week. That the totals on these record cards never followed any mathematical or logical pattern, and implied that dustcarts only did one mile to the gallon, seemed to concern no-one. I knew little about petrol consumption, but even I wasn't stupid enough to ignore the obvious inference that a lot of juice was finding its way into vehicles other than those owned by the Council. I was already well enough versed in the ways of Central Depot to know that the response to my mentioning this slight anomaly would have been, "Fuck me. Well done, Sherlock. Now keep your fucking mouth shut."

In the end I thought it wise to casually mention my informed analysis of the petrol cards to Big Viv as he swanned through our office showing off his new Council-issue donkey jacket.

"Of course, my sheet never adds up come the end of the week," I tossed in with a newly acquired nonchalance.

"Don't worry Micky Boy," as he had taken to calling me, "nothing much adds up around here."

He wasn't wrong about that. Big Viv already had the necessary local authority ambivalence toward discrepancy that meant he blended in admirably. I decided the smart move was to follow suit. Potentially, as an undergraduate (something I kept very quiet about), I could have stuck out like a particularly bruised digit. Very quickly I resolved to pick up enough hints of how to disappear into the background.

"Keeping your head down is the name of the game," Viv reminded me as we partook of the tarry liquid that passed for canteen tea.

In fact there were so many people trying to duck out of view, it was a bit like taking part in a limbo competition. The most successful candidates almost became ghost-like shrouds. To reach that shadowy state where no-one really knew or cared about what you were supposed to be doing was the ultimate achievement.

Council employment was a safety net for a whole fraternity of oddballs and freeloaders who couldn't get jobs elsewhere. Not forgetting those that had all but given up on life altogether – jesters who had forsaken serious employment in favour of a quiet life. I guess I had to include myself somewhere in amongst their number. Anyone with an ounce of get-up-and-go, headed straight for the private sector. Those wanting a cushy number with job security, ended up in some form of public employment. Cushy numbers were right up my alley.

Occasionally the odd career-minded individual would turn up like an unwelcome vicar at a black mass. "Oh, he'll never last," was the common assessment. "Anyway, what's the jumped-up little fucker trying to prove?"

Generally, they were right. Anyone with initiative didn't last, nor did they prove much. An alliance of the Union and Personnel departments usually made sure of that. Nobody wanted the little boat called HMS Depot rocked. Everyone was quite happy to drift unanchored in a sea of inefficiency.

news from nowhere – "a transport of delights"

It really came as no surprise that I found myself working in an office with a right strange crew. Never had I met a man so bitter at the world as Joe – a bitterness that mostly surfaced as a torrent of abuse directed at anyone remotely in a position of authority. This of course didn't include me, so we would share each other's fags – I had rejected Andy's college logic and reverted to bashing the baccy by this time.

Joe was really a disagreeable weasel of a man. Although in his forties he was still living with his mother about whom he was religiously protective – most evenings they went down their local pub together. His cloth-capped belligerence clearly delineated what he considered to be part of his job and what wasn't. Woe betide anyone who suggested he step over this barrier by asking him to undertake a duty he didn't consider to be his. Joe's deep-seated hatred of humanity was traceable back to the time when his application to emigrate to Canada had been turned down. I was sure the real reason was the Canadians were clever enough not to want a grumpy fucker like him, but the official version was that they considered him unsuitable as he only had one kidney.

For Joe, most authority figures were "those fucking bastards". The torrent of abuse aimed at anyone remotely successful in life remained largely unchecked. At times he was likely to refer to Britain in general, and more specifically the Council, as "this fucking stinking shithole." The word "fucking" accompanied most verbs and nouns, often breaking them up, so he would talk about the self-same bosses as "those bastards in admini-fucking-stration". No matter what he was doing, or who he was talking to, come tea break he would get out the paper, put his feet up on the desk and start to curse the world through a moustache that hid his rotten yellowing teeth.

Over the other side of the office was Jock. He was a bumbling Scotsman who had lost a leg in the War and chain-smoked menthol cigarettes like the trooper he once was. He would bundle together his paperwork under one arm, his crutch under the other, and with a fag drooping from his mouth march off to the photocopying room. (Back then photocopiers were so large that they needed a room to themselves.) Jock couldn't give a flying fuck what people did as long as it didn't involve him. In the evening he folded himself into his three-wheeler invalid car, back home to his German wife, believe it or not. Everyone seemed to be full of such contradictions. Having spent much of his life with one leg should have left him with more bitterness than Joe, but it hadn't.

Joe had one kidney, Jock one leg, but Alec the boss had two of everything he should have had, as far as I knew. He certainly had two tufts of white hair that sprouted from either side of his bald head. He also had a blotchy red face that looked like it was due to drink, but was just bad skin. Alec was a well meaning and jolly soul who cared little about what his staff was doing. Humility glowed from him like one of Dickens' good-hearted characters. Instead of attending to Council business, he spent his whole day organising weekend trips for the elderly on behalf of a charity whose name escapes me. A born gossiper, he laughed at everything, even when being sworn at by the refuse drivers.

"Oh well, we'll just add it onto next week's pay, if that's alright with you?" he would ask, smiling benignly at the huge hunk of a dustman looming threateningly over his desk.

"The fuck it is," was the predictable response.

He would then tease the driver to the point of threatened Union involvement only to back down on the very brink.

"Oh alright, I'll have a special packet made up for you to pick up this afternoon," he would beam. It was all exquisitely timed. Nothing phased Alec.

"Right then, I'm just off up the Ivory Tower," he would chirp, having finally seen off the queue of drivers waiting to complain about their pay packets. The Ivory Tower was his name for the Civic Centre. Most other people referred to those that worked there as "the enemy".

I could see that Alec had perfected what Big Viv had described as "the art of disappearing". His answer was to spend a lot of time lost in the corridors of power at the Civic Centre. But far from sucking up to the higher echelons, he could be tracked down gossiping with Marjorie in Accounts, Jean in Personnel, or the girls who worked in the Pay division. Generally, Alec was the type of man who preferred talking to women. He was far happier with all the "Blimey, did they?" or "Crikey, I never knew that" of Civic Centre banter, than he was with the "fuck this" and "fuck that" type of exchanges that went on down the Depot.

Like Jock, Alec had also spent time in the forces during the War. As a bomber navigator his position was to sit beneath the gunners, who often in the heat of battle pissed themselves with nerves. He would tell us that quite often he would return to base covered in their urine. Of course, to me the War was just the memory of endless childhood repeats of *All Our Yesterdays*, not the harsh reality that it represented to Jock or Alec. To their credit, both of them joked about these wartime memories, but underneath it all I knew there were scars that had never really healed. They'd seen stuff that Joe and I could only thank our lucky stars we hadn't. Only of course Joe didn't have any lucky stars because the whole world was picking on him on purpose to make his life miser-fucking-able.

The final member of the Transport Department's team was the funeral director's wife, the formidable Margie. She was a woman as wide as she was tall, waddling around with her huge pointed breasts before her. Margie always had a cold of some sort on that huge chest of hers, and subsequently croaked rather than talked. Alec and she would laugh as he tippled a little whiskey into her mid-afternoon tea – purely medicinal you understand.

Margie was painstakingly methodical about things. Whilst the rest of us would chuck papers we didn't know what to do with in our bottom drawer, she would embark with evangelical zeal on a search for the proper home for them. The fact that the whole office looked like a bomb site, irked her generally tidy nature.

"Oh sit down and drink your tea, woman," Joe would say as he watched her trying to clear the heaps of meaningless old papers into filing boxes.

The Depot was really no place for any woman who couldn't hold her own, or ignore the filthy language and work surfaces. But I had no doubt that Margie could have gone ten rounds with any of the dustmen if so roused. She could also play the coy, helpless woman when it suited her. Equally easily she could turn mid-sentence, barking out instructions like a snappy little terrier. For the first few weeks Margie generally looked at me suspiciously and whispered to Alec that she thought I wasn't up to the job. By the end of the month she was acting like an elderly protective Aunt. I didn't quite know what I'd done to elicit this change of heart, but I presumed I'd passed some kind of probationary test.

All in all, even I had to admit that we made a very odd bunch. The others no doubt thought I must be the oddest of the lot, to be happy to sit in a cold draughty office with a petrol sheet in front of me when I had a university degree collecting dust at home. Nevertheless, the office was good humoured and we were all there mainly for the pay packet at the end of the month. Job satisfaction wasn't talked about, let alone expected. There was no office politics as such – we were hardly battling egos on the look out for promotion. Nobody was getting ideas above their station. Everyone got on with what they had to do, and most importantly we all covered for anyone that wasn't in the office for whatever reason.

Accepting ones lot was the name of the game. Alec, Jock and Margie were waiting to retire, Joe had all but retired from life in general, and I was beginning to feel I wasn't far behind him.

expect nothing – "the weird bunch"

The Transport office was a little oasis compared with the overgrown and gnarled appearance of the rest of the yard – not to mention the battered and grizzly faces of many of its workforce. Nothing in my so far rather sheltered and rarified upbringing could have prepared me for the rag tag bunch of weirdos that had found a home within the Depot's windswept confines. Everyone had strange stories to tell. In fact some people seemed to do nothing but walk from department to department giving out their version of the world as they saw it. It was almost like they were on a kind of chat show conveyor belt, propelling them round and round the yard, espousing their life stories to anyone who would listen.

"Of course, when they opened the gates to Auschwitz, I was then an 18-year old army sergeant. After seeing those piles of bodies, not to mention the smell, my hair turned completely grey overnight."

This was Johnny V, as he strode around our office passing the time of day. His hair had never returned to its original colour. Unfortunately, I wasn't sure whether the rest of his grey matter had returned either. In the next sentence he was recounting stories about his prize-winning orchids. I never did find out exactly what Johnny V's job was.

Occasionally the big Admin head who had advised me about the Depot being a springboard would come by.

"Are you getting on alright, Mr Fish?" he would ask.

Or he would draw me aside conspiratorially and say, "I keep having a word with them in Planning, and I'm sure you'll get something up at Civic Centre sooner or later."

At first I stupidly thought his whispering was a demonstration of some kind of favouritism. But I soon realised that he probably didn't want anyone to overhear because he was talking fictional nonsense. He wasn't remotely interested in my career prospects. His main concern was to keep up his quota of clerical staff so he could continue to justify his senior admin position. And so it was that I began to learn some of the Council's own language. In fact, "later" really meant "never". As the crow flew, there might only have been half a mile between the Civic Centre and its Depot satellite, but in terms of moving upward between the two, I might as well have been stranded on the moon.

Many people from the Civic Centre liked to conveniently forget that the Depot existed and were even scared to walk through its gates. When they did, for the sake of safety, they would arrive en-masse. Not only was it their opinion that the Depot was a collecting point for all the domestic refuse in the borough, but it was also a suitable place for all the human flotsam and jetsam that lurked at the bottom of life's septic tank. As a result it wasn't long before I too was joining in the general conspiracy that dictated that the Depot was a no-go area where the enemy from the Civic Centre entered at their peril.

I had now sided with all the drivers, sewermen, canteen ladies, not to mention deformed and weird characters whose only job was to wander around the yard with a broom. I may well have shared the lack of ambition, but I liked to think I didn't share the general ignorance about hygiene. No part of my upbringing so far was enough to prepare me for the general level of low life behaviour and uncleanliness that proliferated in my new work place. Never before had I come across so many people who smelled that bad before. Noses were generally blown on shirt sleeves, grease and dirt covered everything, and the canteen was a health inspector's nightmare. Also, the average Neanderthal caveman would have turned his nose up at the toilets. Suffice to say I am still at a loss to understand what makes people shit on the floor rather than down the pan provided. It was as if words like hygiene, deodorant or soap were yet to enter the vocabulary.

At first I wondered if every morning I wasn't hopping off my bike and stepping into a Hieronymous Bosch painting. That being said, most of the workforce – an apt description as you literally had to force most of them to work – were well meaning enough. After getting to know my name, they always addressed me directly and good naturedly. For a start I didn't wear a shirt and tie, I dressed in jeans. Neither was I dashing around trying to make a good impression on anybody. It was almost like they could sense that I was on their side.

Very quickly I was warned about whom to avoid. Certain individuals, if not certifiable, were genuinely unhinged. For these people the Depot was the ideal compromise – a half way sanctuary between the dole office and the mental asylum. Put another way, they were too much trouble for the Job Centre to handle, but not quite nutty enough to be locked away. Most of the worst offenders were allocated a sweeper's trolley and sent out to clear up the borough's roads. It was considered an achievement if they all returned with their trolleys intact.

It was also generally wise to leave those whose breath smelt of alcohol at nine in the morning to their own devices. As I walked in the Depot gates, I pretended not to see those drivers who swigged at Vodka bottles in their cabs. Drunk driving was one of the few misdemeanours that the Union found difficult to defend and was potentially a sackable offense. The driver for Round 11 was a particular culprit. Round 11 was a "booze gang".

"No driver for Round 4 this morning, it'll have to be done on overtime," came the shout from the outer office. Round 4 was a "needle gang". The junkies, like the boozers, gravitated toward each other. Other gangs would be the complete opposite. The fit and healthy would try to finish work by 10am in the morning so they would be the first to be offered any overtime. I supposed these were the "money gangs".

As I began to re-align myself to my new environment, I comforted myself that I was really more at home in my new job than if I had to somehow conform.

"I can't be arsed with all that travelling up town." I was trying to convince friends that the idea of cycling around the corner to work had its appeal.

It was somehow comforting not to be surrounded by people who were endlessly fretting about the right career moves. Mostly at the Depot, people came to work, got pissed at the weekend, got into a fight on Saturday night and shagged the missus twice a week.

During long boring afternoons spent transferring petrol totals against different vehicle registrations, I would drift off into a trance and think about all my fellow students from college. I imagined them all with important jobs, strutting around the City in pin stripe suits. I was undeterred – jobs, suits and ties were still a "bad trip" so to speak. Clearly others were happy to abandon their teenage principles in favour of getting on with their lives and careers. Why was that? I already knew the answer to this question, it basically read, "They had grown up."

I didn't want to know anything about growing up. To me, it meant cutting down drinking, buying the odd classical record, worrying about pension plans and the like. The whole business made me shudder. Try as I might I couldn't wriggle out of my teenage hippie clothing. Not literally of course. By the late seventies the long hair, army great coat and loon pants had all been dispatched to the bin. My outlook on life, however, was less easy to change. Maybe I had simply read too many back issues of *OZ* or *IT*. Needless to say, I wasn't just running out of step with the rest of the nation, I was on a different running track altogether. The Conservative party that had just been elected to power under their new leader Margaret Thatcher was hardly drawing upon the same political dogma as me.

Underneath it all, I was rather stupidly comforted by the notion that just around the corner was some kind of job involved with music that I could slip into. This was really mythical nonsense. I was doing absolutely nothing about getting such a job. The closest I was getting to any kind of music was as a regular punter on the London gig circuit. I still vaguely had ambitions of forming a band, or making some music. Usual half-baked nonsense.

The general lethargy that prevailed at the Depot was beginning to seep into my bloodstream like a virus. After six months of listening to Joe moaning, Margie croaking, Jock cussing his crutches, and drinking the endless tea we all drank, I was slowly becoming institutionalised. Very soon I had all but stopped applying for other jobs. I was still hoping someone might appear out of the mist, take my hand and show me a way of doing something with my life. But increasingly this pallid optimism was disappearing as fast as the refuse being shovelled into the back of the refuse carts.

on every other street – "Sheffield calling"

During his first year at Sheffield University, Paul made the occasional trip back to London. In a couple of terms at college, he had acquired the confidence I had failed to achieve in three years. He wrote me letters detailing all the bands that were playing at the University, what records he was buying, and all sorts of other silliness. The three-year difference in our ages meant that he was free from the entangled web of sixties thinking that had preoccupied my teenage years.

Life for Paul was a much more straight-ahead business; birds, ciggies and beers. To him, books like *On The Road* and *Naked Lunch* were just a good read, they weren't the blueprint for a way of thinking about life. A comprehensive education meant he was grounded in a world of reality that I seemed incapable of inhabiting. Going to school in Hampstead's leafy suburbs had sheltered me from some of the harsher realities of life. Bruce's answer had been to hole himself away in an expatriate lifestyle in Cairo. Mine was an even more improbable reaction, that of hiding myself away behind the walls of the local refuse tip.

Despite only having a tiny boxroom in one of the halls of residence, Paul was in very high spirits the first time Dave and I ventured up the M1 for a weekend in Sheffield. On the outskirts, the steely towers and disused factories flashed past the windows of the bus. Some cities remain prickly and inhospitable, but despite the urban decay Sheffield seemed to welcome us with open arms. As we sipped our soapy pints of Tetleys (or the more palatable local brew Wards) Paul told us all about Sheffield's varied nightlife.

I re-acquainted myself with Sheffield's town centre, one that I had first espied on visiting my aunt and uncle as a child. It was here that my Beatle-obsessed cousin had introduced me to the fab four by taking me to see *A Hard Day's Night* at a local fleapit. Behind Sheffield's brick terraced facades were people with a genuine grittiness, counterbalanced by an unassuming friendliness. Or at least that's how it seemed to an insular and snooty Londoner like me. An added appeal to Sheffield was a truly radical local council. All bus transport was ludicrously cheap. In London, the GLC was trying to engender something similar but Mrs Thatcher was intent on teaching a particularly naughty schoolboy called Ken Livingstone a lesson.

By his second year, Paul had moved into a flat on West Bar. Initially he'd had a number of temporary homes including a few weeks in the Hyde Park flats, renowned not only for its ugly architecture but also high crime and suicide rates, not to forget a rare species of ant that had infested the heating system.

Paul had shed many of his initial mates in favour of increasingly hanging out with people from the local Sheffield music scene. He began to tell us stories about local personalities who were all involved in bands of different sorts. One day he played us this record by a local group that had just recorded their first LP. Called

Mix Up, the record was by Cabaret Voltaire. The name implied that here was a group prepared to wear their artistic pretensions brazenly on their sleeves. I was vaguely aware of the dadaist connection, but the name was also familiar to me due to the fact that they had played the odd concert with TG.

We sat in his flat with the windows wide open, trying to usher out a demonic, beer-induced fart. Once the odious gas had dissipated, I listened to the record above the sound of the thunderous traffic that rumbled passed his window. Unlike TG, who were still pretty much churning out Industrial noise or non-sensical nursery rhyme ditties, Cabaret Voltaire sounded like they were squeezing a similar idea out of a echoey fuzzbox. As ever, I was unrelentingly critical.

"Christ this sounds like it was recorded in a toilet. This is just amateurish bollocks," I rather haughtily sat in judgement.

"Oh, I think it has its moments," Paul smarted back.

"The trouble with all these drum machines," Dave chipped in, "is you just have to switch 'em on and go down the pub. Also, that guy can't play the bass to save his fucking life."

Paul battled on bravely, "That's not the point..."

I didn't want to hear the point, "Anyway, what sort of title for a song is 'Kirlian Photograph'."

Paul tried to compare them to TG.

"No way," I wasn't having it. "There's only one TG," I chimed in as if on the football terraces.

And so the banter raged to the general accompaniment of the p*ssssh* of ring pulls. It was just as well Paul's flatmate Haydyn Boyes-Weston, who it transpired had played drums on the LP, wasn't in. I guess I might have been thumped for my general smart arse-ishness.

I was altogether happier when Paul replaced it with the first record by the Human League, even if they were more New Romantic than Industrial. In fact, the Human League's promotion to Virgin records roster had been a relatively speedy one. Initially Ian Craig Marsh had got together with Glenn Gregory and

Boyes-Weston to form Musical Vomit. On meeting meet Martyn Ware they changed their name to the equally improbable Meat-whistle.

After Gregory and Boyes-Weston fell by the wayside, the Human League was born when the other two came across the distinctive looking Phil Oakey. A hospital porter with little ambition, Ware and Craig Marsh were convinced he exuded the star quality they were looking for and persuaded him to join their band. Once enrolled Oakey decided that most pop stars were distinguishable by their haircuts. Travelling on a local bus, he noticed a girl with an unusual lop-sided fringe and asked her where she had her hair cut. The next week Oakey's new image was born.

Originally they considered calling themselves ABCD (the first three letters would crop up again in the Sheffield music scene) and settled on the Human League taken from a science fiction board game called Star Force. Influenced by David Bowie and Roxy Music, the key defining moment for the Human League was Walter Carlos' soundtrack to *A Clockwork Orange*.

Their next move was to employ Adrian Wright as Director of Visuals. It somehow seemed very decadent to have a band member whose only job was to operate a slide projector. I was beginning to discover that Sheffield bands around the cusp of the eighties were all about the integration of arts and visual media with music. Film, slides and backdrops were almost as important as the music itself.

The Human League's first official show was at Bar 2 in Psalter Lane Art College in June 1978. Rather than hiding the fact that they used backing tapes, the tape recorder took pride of place centre stage. It was an essential ingredient to the band's perform-ances as they only ever played one track totally live – a minimalist version of Lou Reed's "Perfect Day" which allowed Ian Craig-Marsh to change spools on the tape player.

It wasn't long before the band had established a makeshift studio called Monumental Pictures and recorded a single called "Being Boiled" which was released on Edinburgh's Fast label. The band even appeared on TV with Oakey wearing a wedding dress (silly costumes were much in abundance in the late seventies Sheffield music scene). Gigs supporting the Rezillos and a tour with Souxsie and the Banshees followed – the band was apparently so wary of the reaction that they might receive at the hands of punk audiences that they considered employing motorcycle helmets and riot shields.

The early Human League was really a schizophrenic affair. Comparing their second single, the rather incredulously titled the "Dignity of Labour Parts 1-4", against their live rendition of Gary Glitter's "Rock and Roll Part 1" rather aptly highlighted this split personality.

When they were invited as the support slot to a European jaunt by Iggy Pop, the jealousy within the Sheffield music scene must have been palpable. There was also much merriment when The Undertones took the piss out of them in the lyric to "My Perfect Cousin".

With a charismatically goodlooking singer in Phil Oakey, and a general all-round pop sensibility, Virgin Records had been impressed enough to sign the band. *Reproduction* was the first major label success for a Sheffield band for some time. Paul impressed us with titbits he had picked up about the making of the LP, including a debacle over the sleeve. Attempting to capture people dancing on a glass floor of squashed babies, it somehow came out all wrong and the whole thing looked like an abortive mess even though it had cost a fortune to produce. Still, who cared? It was Virgin's money, was typical of the carefree Northern way of looking at it.

The Human League's reputation was considerably enhanced when they were asked to undertake the support slot on an early Talking Heads tour. In a piece of Kraftwerk-influenced jokery, they came up with the idea that they would send a taped support slot to be played at each concert – they themselves would stay at home in Sheffield. The promoter was not amused by the idea of a totally mechanised support slot and the tape machine was promptly thrown off the tour.

Nonetheless there was a definite buzz going around about T' League, and it was soon obvious that they were poised for promotion into the premier division. The press reported that David Bowie had turned up to see them at their London showcase in the gloriously sleazy surroundings of the much-lamented Nashville Rooms. Phil Oakey was not only a tall, imposing figure but a natural frontman. He was also the first person I'd heard of that had pierced nipples. Naturally squeamish, I baulked at what would make someone want to do something like that.

Once when we were hanging around Sheffield town centre, no doubt waiting for a pub to open, or turning our noses up at posters for all these boring heavy metal bands that endlessly played the City Hall, Oakey called out to Paul from over the other side of the road. Of course, "Hiya Paul", hardly constituted lifelong buddy-dom, but we were quietly impressed. It was evidence that Paul was making inroads into being accepted in the right circles. As a good guitarist, I guessed that it would only be a matter of time before he would be joining a band.

I returned to London thinking that the Human League might get somewhere – I even quite liked their version of "You've Lost That Lovin' Feelin" – but with the conceited belief that much of the rest was just provincial twaddle. A self-obsessed small town scene that was going nowhere. Or as one of the lesser lights on the Sheffield music scene put it; "The trouble with Sheffield is it's nothing but a one-eyed raincoat town".

Of course, I had mostly missed the point, not only about Cabaret Voltaire, but also about the Sheffield scene in general. You'd have thought that I would have learned from liking punk and TG, that playing the music was only half the battle. I was still trying to apply some old style standards of musicianship and was forgetting one of the primary rules of pop music; first of all it is important to look right and have the right attitude – technical proficiency only becomes a consideration later, if at all.

The obsessive determination that prevailed in Sheffield was to get somewhere no matter what – to break out of humdrum lives. It was something working class kids shared the world over, whether it was the black American kid dreaming of being a boxer, or the Andalucian kid wanting to fight the bulls. Working class kids from the North of England wanted to be footballers or pop stars. Martyn Ware summed it up when he said, "Sheffield engendered a certain desperation to get on with something different and creative, because there wasn't a lot of happening. It was a place of great depression at the time, because of all the factory closures. I was desperate not to replicate my father's life…"

In London, my answer to breaking out from the humdrum continued to be a determination to get down the pub for opening time.

messages received – "the Russians are coming"

By the time I headed for Sheffield again, Paul had launched himself onto the music scene and joined a band called They Must Be Russians. The Russians were a three-piece post-punk group whose name was derived from a *Sunday Mirror* headline that greeted the advent of the Sex Pistols. When Paul told me all about this new band, my initial reaction was typically cynical. But at least he was putting his plectrum where his mouth was – and I don't mean he was playing guitar with his teeth like Jimi Hendrix. Essentially, he was doing something constructive about playing music rather than talking about it. I was still shuffling pieces of paper around a desk, dreaming up names of bands that would hit the big time and naturally enough include me in their ranks.

They Must Be Russians was formed by Russell – a fellow student of Paul's from Sheffield University who had chubby hamster-like cheeks similar to Elton John's, which was a coincidence because Russell, like Reg before him, hailed from Pinner. My particular reputation in Pinner had nothing to do with music. I had the rather dubious honour of having been chucked out of every pub in the High Street. Not for anything more than looking scruffy or wearing a leather jacket, although there were also occasions when they considered me too drunk to serve. It is a bit of a shock when you're first shown the door with the customary, "I think you've had enough, mate". After a while you kind of get used to it and just look for a pub that is not so fussy about whom they serve.

The third member of The Russians was a guy called Tony. Posing around like some New York dude in wrap-around shades, his claim to fame was that he had managed to get himself declared medically unfit for work. Quite how, was the envy of many, myself included. Tony, like many of his Sheffield contemporaries, wasn't interested in run-of-the-mill music – noise was his thing. Eventually he quit the band because he was worried that Paul's musical competence was taking the group in an overtly commercial direction.

They Must Be Russians, or "the Russians" as they were known, were half-serious and half-jokey. Like the Ramones they had all adopted the same name, in their case Russian. So Paul became Paul Russian. They wrote songs about anything from nuclear fallout to a lecture on the differing forms of VD set to music. Of course it went without saying that they used slides as a visual backdrop. Other than Def Leppard, it was difficult to contemplate getting on a stage in Sheffield at that time without some kind of visuals.

Paul threw himself into this new musical project with characteristic enthusiasm. College lectures took a back seat as the three of them started playing gigs around Sheffield and recording demo tapes. In fact, as irony had it, Paul's first gig with the Russians was supporting Throbbing Gristle at the Sheffield University refectory. It wasn't that long since we'd rushed out and bought our first TG record, or since the film maker's co-op debacle, now Paul was sharing a stage with them.

Like many of the Sheffield bands, the Russians had a fairly fluid attitude toward instrumentation. They didn't have a drummer, preferring to play along with rudimentary drum machines. They were also not averse to experimenting with more exotic sounds – well, OK so they miked up a stylophone.

There was also a whole lot of other experimenting to do. The Russians had a penchant for dabbling with magic mushrooms, which as far as I could see involved a lot of crawling around the floor and occasionally throwing up. I was generally under the impression that magic mushrooms had gone out of favour when Steve Hillage left Gong. Just as Hillage was determined to leave flying teapots behind him, I wasn't about to revive any interests I had in hallucenogenic toadstools. Much better to get drunk.

There wasn't a pub on or around Sheffield's West Street that we weren't acquainted with. From the Grapes, to the Hallamshire, up the road to the Mail Coach and the Beehive (the centre of the music scene at the time) down the road to the Washington. In between the Washington and the Beehive was a pub called The Raven (later renamed The Hornblower). Nearing the end of a successful pub crawl – successful in terms of us reaching the end of West Street without falling over – Dave, Paul and myself staggered in for a final pint. We joked about being the beer drinking musketeers – all for one, one for all, and three for the road.

After picking a suitable table, Paul set off down the other end of the bar to talk to the hazy blur of a couple sat opposite us. Clearly they were not your average couple. He had a long dyed fringe that topped off an outfit of huge tartan baggy trousers and a leather jacket. His was the kind of distinctive face that made an instant impression. The eye-liner and plucked eyebrows gave him the air of post-punk glam. Sat with him was his girlfriend. She drank Guinness, he was drinking what looked like a Bloody Mary.

"Who are they?" I couldn't help asking on Paul's return.

"That's Richard, the guitarist from Cabaret Voltaire, and his girl-friend Lynne."

I was beginning to realise that being in a band in Sheffield instantly meant knowing everyone else who was involved in music. I was also already aware that They Must Be Russians shared the same rehearsal rooms as Cabaret Voltaire. I looked over again, they both smiled.

It is difficult to know why certain people can elicit immediate responses. Richard had an indefinable quality that I hadn't quite come across before. There was something about his whole demeanour that intrigued me. Almost instantly I got a strange feeling that his life and mine would somehow be linked. It was one of the few certainties floating around in a beer barrel of indecision. There was no outward reason to feel any kind of empathy. He was the guitarist in an aspiring industrial band that I didn't even think to be much cop at the time. I was an aimless individual from London who could drink quantities of beer in keeping with my surname.

taxi music – "calling the cabs"

Compared to my newly acquired stasis as clerk-in-residence down the local Depot, life within Cabaret Voltaire appeared to be one of constant movement. After my ever so brief encounter in the pub with their guitarist, I quickly endeavoured to catch up with where they had got to thus far. Paul helped to fill in some of the background details on the main players in the plot. I had already discovered that Richard H. Kirk had an air of charismatic translucence. Beneath the plucked eyebrows, his eyes could dart around a room in series of uneasy glances. A minute later and his face creased into a fit of laughter. The familiar Sheffield accessory, the long fringe, was in Richard's case tinged with a heavy dose of henna. An only child, he lived with his mother, his father having succumbed to a heart attack at an early age. Before his death, Rich-

-57-

ard's father had been a man of committed principles and was involved with the Unions and the communist party.

Musically, Richard's initial role was that of guitarist and occasional clarinetist. Coincidentally the same two instruments on which I was most proficient. However, it was safe to say that Richard was not acquainted with the second-hand blues licks I could churn out if pressed to do so. Nor, I suspect, did he have a Grade 5 musical proficiency certificate for the clarinet sitting at home in a drawer. To Richard, both instruments were a "sound source" rather than for playing in the conventional sense. Guitar notes and chords were almost a side issue when compared to the myriad of fuzz-boxes and echo units that could be applied to make it sound like anything but a guitar. However, whilst eshewing the rock guitar as such, he was nonetheless taken with the image of guitarist as gunslinger as portrayed by Keith Richards or Lou Reed. Hence, leather jackets, leather trousers and numerous pairs of shades were much in abundance.

The other ingredients Richard bought to the Cabaret Voltaire soup, were made up from similar flavours to those favoured by P-Orridge. So, enter again old Bill Burroughs with his cut-ups and Aleister Crowley with his potions and spells. Throw in a liberal sprinkling of James Dean, Bruce Lee, early Elvis and a fascination with pornography and military imagery and you would be close to where Richard's head was at.

Behind the second fringe, this time of the jet-black variety, was Stephen Mallinder. Known to all as Mal, he had a similar disregard for the bass that Richard had for the guitar. I was now becoming conversant with the idea that Industrial bands didn't really need to be able to play – in fact it was a distinct asset. Haphazard and rudimentary were two words that sprang to mind on first listening to Mal's bass playing. But Mal had another role, that of singer. Well, you guessed it. It wasn't really singing, more like a sergeant major barking out instructions. Outgoing, affable, Mal was dark-skinned and almost Mediterranean in appearance. He too, had been fatherless at any early age. Whilst Richard relished the role of subversive outsider, somewhere in Mal's make-up there was a latent popstar waiting to break out.

Richard and Mal had first met while making some extra cash working at a pork pie factory during the summer holidays. Legend also has it that they also hooked up with a gang of skinheads that hung around the city centre. This certainly explained their continuing liking for reggae and James Brown, not to mention a fascination with the type of ultra-violence typified by the film *A Clockwork Orange*.

By 1973, those kids in Sheffield that didn't buy into the whole heavy metal scenario tended to gather in clubs that played soul music. Letting their hair grow into soul boy fringes Richard and Mal became fascinated with the glam posturings of Bowie, Kraftwerk and Roxy Music. Add in some of the krautrock bands like Can and even cosmic rockers Hawkwind and you had somewhere near to a compendium of their respective record collections. By frequenting the Bowie nights that were held in the city's more happening nightclubs, they began to rub shoulders with other kids of the same age that were similarly fascinated. It is not inconceivable that had a tragic fire swept through one of these clubs, there would have been no music scene to speak of in Sheffield in the late seventies – well, OK there would still have been Def Leppard. Certainly many, if not all, of the city's pop glitterati were regulars in this scene. Names like Craig-Marsh, Oakey, Ware, Kirk, Mallinder, Fry, Coates (later Newton) and maybe Cocker (Jarvis, not Joe) would have been regular entries were anyone to have taken a role call.

But of course, the early Cabaret Voltaire wasn't just about two people – at the time there was a third side to the Cabaret Voltaire triangle. Altogether more studious was the tall figure of Chris Watson. Although adopting the long mac so popular at the time, Watson looked much less like the member of a pop group and more like a college lecturer. Watson's role within the group evolved to that of keyboard player and electronics manipulator. In a way he was the catalyst that cemented the whole thing together.

Watson understood all about the classical avant-garde, and indoctrinated the other two into notions that any noise could be music. He was neither a soul boy nor a rock 'n' roll freak, but much more of a theory man.

To the Cabs, or more specifically Watson, electronics meant surfing the airwaves for sinister snippets of spoken words or sounds that they could jumble up into their music. Convening in Watson's loft they started by splicing together these bits and pieces of noise and supplying a rudimentary rhythm to go with it.

For a while they had participated in a local band called The Studs, including a notable performance supporting one of Manchester's less distinguished punk bands The Drones. Playing versions of Lou Reed's "Vicious" and Iggy's "Cock In My Pocket", they were a riotous cacophony which succeeded out-droning The Drones.

The Studs were more of an unwieldy conglomeration than a band, and soon members Ian Craig Marsh, Martyn Ware and Adi Newton went off to form the Future, while Haydyn Boyes-Weston and Glen Gregory would crop up in later Sheffield outfits. For their part Mal, Richard and Chris detected that they shared a love for extreme noise and picked themselves the name Cabaret Voltaire taken from the Dadaist cabaret of 1916.

Their initial attempts at recording were greeted with ambivalence. They sent out a promotional tape which most record companies must have thought was distortional hiss and not music at all. It didn't take much to imagine record company bosses despatching the tape to the waste paper bin with a cursory, "Why?" Or, "What the fuck is this?" and quickly passing on to the next set of potential popstars.

Undeterred they sent out copies to various people like Eno. Not surprisingly the response to their tape was non-existent. But they must have sensed that they were on to something. Their little group was a strange melding of three highly different personalities and soon they had dreamt up a musical policy of sorts, which revolved loosely around the avant-garde weirdness of Stockhausen meets the leather jacketed wildness of the Velvet Underground. Like TG, they balanced out their instrumental incompetence with sheer energy and a stream of high brow and ambitious ideas.

A few early gigs were met with the type of hostile reaction often meted out to those confronting rather than trying to entertain an audience. The early blueprint for such confrontation had been set by the Stooges and the Velvet Underground, the mantle had then been taken up by certain of the krautrock bands notably Faust, and now the baton was in the hands of TG and Cabaret Voltaire.

Reaction to their early concerts varied from complete and utter disbelief to out-and-out violence. When the group hijacked a Science For The People disco, by claiming they played rock music and offering to play for free, the outcome was predictable. The ensuing violence saw Kirk fending off attackers with his clarinet whilst wearing a jacket covered in Christmas fairy lights. He then resorted to chucking his guitar into the audience, an action which Watson later admitted "hardly helped to calm things down". Mal meanwhile was dragged from the stage, chipping a bone in his back and had to be taken to hospital.

At another of their initial gigs, this time at Sheffield's Limit Club, supporting a rather dodgy band with fascistic flirtations called Molodoy, the three of them finished their set by leaving the tape running and marching out into the audience to watch the end of their own set.

The emergence of punk was really the catalyst that the three of them had been waiting for. It wasn't that the punks took to their music – their first concert at London's Lyceum supporting the Buzzcocks ended in a hail of missiles – it was more the whole infrastructure that grew in the wake of punk that allowed Cabaret Voltaire's ambitions to expand.

The whole explosion in small, independent record labels suddenly meant that bands like the Cabs could more easily find a way of making records. TG's answer was to form their own label, but the Cabs didn't have the funds for that kind of operation, so Watson decided to write to TG. The two bands immediately built up a rapport and TG responded by expressing an interest in releasing a Cabaret Voltaire record on their Industrial label. Already overstretched by bringing out their own records, P-Orridge explained that they didn't have the money to fund a Cabs record. But as a favour he recommended them to Geoff Travis who had just set up what was to become the daddy of all indie labels, Rough Trade. Travis took the bait and soon the ball was rolling. Collecting up their mass of oscillators, rhythm boxes and cheap guitars they promptly moved out of Watson's loft and into a Victorian factory building. Soon they had dubbed their newly rented rehearsal space Western Works.

Like them or not, they were beginning to develop their own unique musical way of looking at the world. Similar to the apocalyptic imagery of Burroughs, a Cabaret Voltaire record created a sense that the whole caboodle was spinning out of control. Burroughs felt that he could make more order from the confusion by splicing sentences together and rearranging them in what he called cut-ups. The Cabs too wielded their scalpels, but for them it was pieces of recorded tape rather than the printed page.

The more I read about the group, the more I realised that my initial naive reaction to their music had been very wrong. So whilst Paul had sung their praises, I had played devil's advocate more out of jealousy at Paul's newly acquired position within the Sheffield musical hierarchy than rational criticism. However, it wasn't long before even I had to admit that they had grasped a very thorny nettle. Burroughs had prophesied that technology, politics and drugs would become examples of control systems that no-one had control of anymore. The Cabs' music reflected this disorientation, where sounds collided and echoed to the point of aching monotony. The underlying tone was of some unforseen disaster or menace. Or as Richard so neatly put it in an early interview, "We want a Cabaret Voltaire concert to be like a bad trip."

Like Burroughs, Richard was a big believer in conspiracy theories. He seemed willing to be drawn into believing that people were plotting all sorts of mayhem through spreading viruses, disinformation or whatever. I was more of a sceptic. Although I could appreciate all the coincidences, paranormal phenomenon that fuelled these artistic endeavours, I simply couldn't take all of it seriously. I was far more convinced that those in the FBI, CIA or the Kremlin, however misguided their intentions, were not clever enough to control anyone. They were just trying to do their jobs, albeit rather malevolently.

It was difficult for music writers to ignore Cabaret Voltaire for too long. Jon Savage was the first to realise the group's potential and an early article in *Sounds* helped to give the Cabs a much needed boost. They then contributed two tracks to the Factory Sampler – the beginning of a relationship with Tony Wilson's label and his main act, the rather doom-laden Joy Division. But it was the release of an EP and LP on Rough Trade and a series of better received gigs that really put the group on the map. Then came the defining single "Nag Nag Nag". A perfect post-punk ball of fuzz, it summed up a kind of nihilistic desperation. After all who hadn't turned round to their boss, their teacher, their mother at some time or another and thought, "nag, nag, nag". Boy George was apparently so taken with the record that he used to have it playing on his answerphone.

Being someone who had no idea how records were made, I marvelled at how easy it all sounded. Paul amazed us with local Sheffield musical stories, the rehearsal rooms, the constant swapping of group members. Fanzines abounded with stories about the Cabs, Vendino Pact, Graph, Artery, 2.3, the early Clock DVA. The pubs were brimming with young kids with long macs and make-up, with brave but somewhat dark musical intentions. Endless discussions and swapping of musical ideas took place over a few pints. Back at our local pub in London, nobody apart from us cared much about music, industrial or otherwise. While we held our little musical debates in the seclusion of our favourite corner, most of the other punters were discussing shagging, drinking or fighting.

A year or so on and a picture of Richard standing outside Sheffield's main railway station, complete with customary long mac, was splayed over the cover of the *NME*. The accompanying article was a typical piece of Paul Morley writing – part astute insight, part endearing pretension. Maybe what Morley found so intriguing was the fact that here were three ordinary working class guys tackling music from a potentially very arty standpoint and with little compromise. Inflecting their sound with a staunch Northern stoicism they neatly stuck two fingers up at the London-centric music scene. Morley's article did much to announce their second LP called *The Voice of America*. I bought my copy from the local secondhand record shop. (I was still in the habit of constantly buying and selling vinyl to fund drinking bouts).

From the very opening snippet of a pre-concert briefing to US security guards, it was clear that the group's grip on the dynamic they were trying to project had tightened. Borrowing from the heavy echo of dub, the long spaced-out notes of Miles Davis, and the menace of tape loops and treated vocals, the LP was a much fiercer statement of intent than its predecessor. The rudimentary nature of early drum machines, rather than highlighting the group's musical limitations, only added to the general menace. Though one lyric went, "This is entertainment, this is fun", the group was clearly questioning what constituted entertainment. It almost went without saying that the LP was hardly a fun ride.

It was back in London that I finally got to see the Cabs when they played at the ICA in the Mall. They were every bit as spooky and menacing as I had expected. The intro and outro tapes were extreme in length and nature. At times the group were nothing more than three shadows projected on a wall. Mal would occasionally emerge from the gloom to the microphone and growl his way through songs like "Kneel to the Boss". Richard, hardly visible, was detectable by the sound of his heavily distorted guitar as it screeched and fedback. Chris Watson stood motionless at his keyboard. Behind them, films and slides compiled by Richard, reflected Nazism, pornography – you name it. As the repetitive extended outro tape started to drive people from the hall to the bar, it was clear there was to be no encore. There was really no need. People were stunned. Whilst TG were so extreme it was easy to dismiss it all as an arty joke to which you either got the punchline or you didn't, the Cabs were full of a more sexual electricity – straddling a number of musical genres and delicately poised between art and pop. For a brief period in 1980 they were it for me – a perfectly intoxicating mixture.

PART THREE

life slips by – "a change of vehicle"

By the end of 1980 I had fully accepted something that I had sus-
pected might be the case from the start – my Geography degree
was worth less than the paper it was written on. The fact that the
dustmen were earning twice my salary with not so much as an 'O'
level, seemed to gall everyone else more than it did me. It had
taken me twenty-four years to realise that it wasn't what you knew,
but who you knew that counted. I tried hard to convince myself
that I wasn't the archetypal under-achiever. But I also had to
admit I was hardly the epitome of the new Thatcherite Britain.

In truth, the Depot was now proving to be a convenient refuge.
Hangovers could be nursed away by wandering around the yard
with a clipboard, a few strategically arranged papers in my hand.
By giving the impression of knowing exactly what I was doing, it
was easy to become transparent.

A key defence mechanism was to keep on the move – it was
important never to sit at a desk for too long. An occupied desk
always became a sitting target for other people's unwanted paperwork. Of course there were always plenty of places to get lost.
Albert in the stores had the kettle constantly on the boil – the only
trouble was that Colin, his assistant, was known as "smelly". To
gain this monicker amongst such dirty company was an achievement in itself. You could also rely on Highways for a joke, Public
Lighting for a sit down, and Building Works for a moan.

For what it was worth, I was not only roving around the yard,
but I had also moved to a job in the vehicle repair workshop. This
was a promotion of sorts, in job title if not in financial reward. At
first I wondered about whether I wanted to actually change my

job. I had, in my opinion, a cushy number – albeit not a very well paid one. Did I want to jeopardise this position? But in the end I decided I really had to get out of the Transport office. A combination of Joe's pessimism and Margie's mumsiness was helping to drive me mad.

But in the rush of excitement (OK, a lukewarm meander) to get to my new desk, I had fallen foul of the oldest trick in the book. I had grabbed at the carrot of a new job title without settling on the monetary meat and potatoes to go with it. I had rather stupidly agreed to take on this newly created job on the promise that the position would be reviewed and upgraded once I had been in post for a while. Oh, how much I still had to learn. Paul had fallen foul of a similar broken promise, when I disbanded a pact I had made with him during a game of Risk with the words, "Aha, but there was nothing in writing, old chap!" Suffice to say, whilst it was months before Paul felt inclined to chance his arm at playing board games with me again, it was an even longer time before anyone came remotely close to acceding to my demands for my post to be re-graded.

The logic behind my move was explained to me by Ivan the Transport Manager.

"Look," he said conspiratorially, "We're getting a bit of grief from up above (meaning the Civic Centre) about the chaps in the Workshop. These time-and-motion guys are getting all huffy about the bonus scheme up there. They want someone up in the office to fill in the job times."

As he said this, he winked at me. I didn't quite know what that was supposed to mean. Was it that he knew that it was a hopeless cause? Perhaps he was in on some kind of fiddle as well. I nodded knowingly back. Knowing nods were much in abundance.

As the whole premise on which local government appeared to be based was depleting the world's forests, it came as no great surprise that the time-and-motion people had dreamt up a paper-heavy bonus scheme. Somewhat similar to the nonsensical and pointless petrol cards, my new job also revolved around filling in job cards – wherever you went in the Council there were never-ending piles of forms, card indexes and log books. Once filed and stored they were never referred to again. But who cared, just as long as all this mountain of paperwork was keeping us all in employment.

My sudden arrival into the vehicle workshop as a "technical assistant" was meant to have the fitters quaking in their muddy Council issue boots. The idea that such a small gesture somehow implied that management was getting on top of previously lax practices was laughable. I was met with that "Fuck you" look, clearly indicating that the fitters were going to continue recording whatever times they liked on the cards.

"Now, you're not going to give us grief are you, Micky boy?" said the shop steward as I tried out my new desk for size.

I was far too Depot-wise by now to have to ask what he meant. I knew exactly the reply required.

"Where's the kettle, I'll make a cuppa."

"Good lad," the steward smiled and started to roll a fag. He looked at me with a 'you'll do' kind of expression.

"The bonus that the fitters are paid is based on the comparison between the real time a repair job takes and the time we think it should take," explained the rather officious boss from Work Study with his ridiculous Kevin Keegan perm. I looked blankly back at him, amazed he'd braved the trip from the Civic Centre.

It sounded simple enough.

"So my job is to monitor the actual times against the estimated ones," I repeated.

He looked genuinely surprised that I had managed to grasp this basic principle so quickly.

"Exactly," he said, quickly scooping up all his calculations into a rather battered old briefcase.

I exchanged glances with the Shop Steward who was hovering rather menacingly in earshot. We didn't need to say anything, we were both convinced we'd never see him again.

Of course it made little difference what times I actually put down. I soon realised that the estimated times were ludicrously generous as the Union had been heavily involved in determining them. Most of the fitters rubbed their hands with glee come Thursday pay day. "Aaah, full bonus again," they would smile smugly. It was just this complacency that had prompted management to create my new post in the first place.

However, at very least my new job kept a record of what work was done to which vehicle. This, I was informed, was a legal requirement that had, up until this point, been swept under the carpet. Even though Ivan spent most of his time chasing the women drivers around, he was smart enough to want to keep his operator's licence.

With less understanding about the workings of a motor vehicle than the average two-year old, I was now in a working environment where people might as well have been talking outer-Mongolian. The hydraulic system of a dustcart consisted of all nature of flanges, seals and gaskets. I didn't really understand how the gears on my push bike worked. But the fact that I didn't know a big end from a universal joint was the least of anyone's concerns. A lot of the fitters seemed to find it difficult making the distinction themselves. Personally I was just glad to be away from being deskbound in an office with Joe, Jock and Margie and into a less clearly defined role. Being transplanted away from any kind of management control I could refine the art of marching around the yard without anyone questioning what I was doing. I was becoming one of the ghostly wanderers, lost like Josef K in a bureaucratic world with little chance of escape.

The fitters were a rag tag bunch that generally fell into two camps. Firstly, there were those that tended toward the criminally minded or the just plain stupid. This included some of the older fitters employed since the sixties, a time when working in a vehicle repair workshop merely called for knowing what a spanner looked like, not necessarily what to do with it. They had hands covered in calluses and welts of hard skin acquired from years of trying to crank some life back into the fleet of rusty old heaps. Amongst their number was Mario, the Italian, who had a chip on his shoulder the size of MacDonalds lorry. Fat Burt made the tea and chain-smoked St Moritz menthol cigarettes, while Vince cleaned the loos and that was about all. Lofty recharged the batteries if you were lucky, and John washed and steam-cleaned the vehicles when he wasn't tending to his own little vegetable patch which he had planted out in a remote corner of the yard. I shouldn't forget Alfred, the guy with only one testicle. This came as no surprise, I was already fully aware that having two of anything was an unusual occurrence at the Council.

The second camp consisted of the younger fitters who had all done the appropriate apprenticeships. Generally, it was this nucleus of under-30s that did most of the work. They simply accepted that it was unwise to give anything too technically taxing to the older brigade. In the morning, a couple of them would sit in my office shuffling the pile of job cards like they were expert poker dealers, allocating out which job was best suited to whom.

This should really have been done by the chargehands, both called Bob, but they were both from the old guard. Bob with the beard had something similar to Alzheimer's and was on occasions pushed to even remember his own name. The other Bob was a likeable guy who spent most of his time covering for his namesake. The Supervisor was Tim, who all the fitters called Captain Birdseye because of his similarity with the character in the advert, white beard and all.

"You see, Mick," Tim explained in his thick Bernard Matthews Norfolk accent, "I just told him to pull 'em all out."

He was in fact referring to his teeth. Tim had taken the extraordinary decision some time in his youth to have his complete set extracted. The weird logic behind this seemed to be that false teeth were less of a bother.

At least in my new environment, there was some point to the whole exercise. The Council vehicles did need servicing and repairing, even if the vehicles often returned the same day with the same fault apparently unrectified. For my part I sat in the Workshop office overlooking the shop floor, and answered the telephone.

"So what's the matter with your vehicle?" I shouted, struggling to hear the reply above the sound of revving engines and welding torches.

"If I fuckin' knew that, I would fuckin' fix it m'self," came the muffled reply. "I'm in the middle of fuckin' town and I'm holding up all the soddin' traffic."

And so, more often than not, a ticket marked "dustcart broken down at 10.30" was affixed to a job card, and that was pretty much my bit of the job over with. The Union rep made sure I was never the subject of any demarcation dispute.

Two or so hours later, a grubby job card would be flung back on my desk. "Topped up hydraulic oil – one hour call out". All times were rounded down. Essentially, the quicker a job was completed, the more bonus the fitters received. However, it was two weeks before the bonus found its way into the pay packet. Normal pay, one week in arrears; bonus pay, two weeks in arrears. When it came to working out holiday or sick pay, it led to all sorts of confusion.

Even though I knew I was a million miles away from living the kind of life that the fitters led, I tried to get on with the general atmosphere of blokishness. A couple of the younger fitters were even remotely interested in music and would browse through the *NME* or *Sounds* I would bring in with me on Thursday mornings.

In general, it was simply no use getting prissy about anything. It was accepted that everything was covered in grease and dirt. Merely putting a digit in the phone dial produced a finger the colour of coal. The noise was often deafening, the office cold and drafty. The worst days were those when the back end of the dustcart needed welding. The welder who was called Frank Rust – I kid you not, that was his real surname – would light up his acetylene torch and prepare to go to work. The pall that hung in the air as he burned off years of trapped and congealed refuse can only be described like a million rotting eggs being fried in a pan. To this day, thinking of it turns my stomach.

Not that you'd let that kind of weakness show. These were a tough bunch that drank and fought in the local pubs, had tattoos right up to their armpits, and stank continually of engine oil and Swarfega. Mostly I would sit up in the Workshop office and do the crossword until the next job card needed filling in.

Provided that I wasn't overturning any applecarts, no-one gave a fuck. It was best to turn a blind-eye to the fact that many employees were at best using the situation to their own advantage, or at worst ripping off the Council in some fashion or another. I fell into the former category, the length of my lunch hours gaining me considerable respect amongst my new workmates. I was also responsible for monitoring my own flexi-time sheet – an act of trust by the management verging on plain stupidity. The fitters couldn't care less whether I was in the office or not – they probably preferred me out of the way – so no-one was going to tell any tales. Again the unspoken code of cross-covering for respective backsides generally worked to everyone's advantage.

"Oh he's not here at the moment, he's out collecting spares," was a stock line. It covered a multitude of sins.

wait and shuffle – "doin' the Hula Kula"

On a visit to London, Paul proudly played me a copy of They Must Be Russians' first proper demo tape. The best track "Nagasaki's Children" was truth be told, not a classic – but fuck it, at least it was an attempt. I was begrudgingly learning to be less cynical. The demo was produced by Mal at Western Works – even I had to admit that this was obviously a plus. I took a day off sick to accompany Paul to Rough Trade to see if they were interested in releasing it. The Rough Trade shop/label was a dingy and noisy hovel in Ladbroke Grove. Nevertheless Paul and I waltzed passed the sadly outdated mohican punks flicking through the record racks, and into the packaging room at the back of the shop. We played the tape to Geoff Travis who informed us that he couldn't release it, but gave Paul a pre-prepared handout on how to go about pressing up a single. If they did this, Travis said he would help with distribution. Which is duly what happened. The first They Must be Russians EP was self-pressed and available through Rough Trade's outlets. All I could think was, "Fucking hell, Paul's going somewhere. The little shite."

It was once we were back in Sheffield for one of our customary boozy weekends that I spoke with Richard for the first time. To some it might seem strange, considering my initial impressions, that I can't remember when or where this was. Those more acquainted with the lack of recall associated with drinking benders will no doubt empathise. My guess is that it must have been in the sizeable saloon bar of The Beehive. As Paul was now hobnobbing with many of the musicians in Sheffield, it was only a matter of time before Richard and I would be rubbing shoulders to get to the crowded bar.

I guess Richard and I must have hit it off in some fashion. My initial concerns that he might be a rather serious and gloomy individual were quickly dispelled. He was quite the opposite and full to the brim with witty quips. As we sat around a table in the Beehive, Richard would lower his chin, screw up his eyes in laughter, and launch into a routine.

Looking back on it, I think the real crux to becoming increasingly tolerated within Richard's orbit was down to his girlfriend Lynne. She was a down-to-earth type who looked with scepticism at the shallowness of many of those running round the Sheffield musical racetrack like headless chickens. We were merely Paul's mates with whom they could have a laugh and get drunk, without worrying about keeping up appearances. I was not connected in any way with the Sheffield musical hierarchy. We had no hidden agenda. We didn't want his patronage, we didn't want to use the studio, borrow equipment. We simply wanted to drink beer.

Also, Lynne and I both worked for our respective local councils. She knew all too well the bureaucratic nightmares involved. We agreed that thinking up the title for an LP was small fry compared with having to struggle back to work having binged away a million or so brain cells in a weekend.

If getting to know Richard broke a musical duck of sorts, then Mal was a like batting on an easy wicket. Mal was almost over-friendly. He would saunter along with a wide grin and greet everyone as if like they were his long lost brother. It was obvious that he had the sort of personality ideally suited to the music business. Pressing flesh and buttering up the right people was not a problem. Mal was a fashion conscious, quick-witted, rather flighty individual. Not quite the hardened drinker that Richard was, but he could hold his own on a good night out and still look cool.

For his part, Paul well and truly secured his position within the local music scene when he took a room in one of its more notorious hangouts. He bundled up his possessions and moved them into the spare room of a large Victorian house on Upperthorpe in Walkley. Had *The Addams Family* been filmed in Sheffield, his new abode would have provided an ideal location. The family, such as it was, was Mal, who had the main upstairs room. Then there was Ron from Sunderland, his geordie compatriot Alan Fish (my namesake, no relation) and Mark, whose room, even by student standards, was an Aladdin's cave of clutter and junk.

The house itself was nicknamed the Hula Kula. Only five guys sharing could name a house after an obscure Roxy Music B-side. Ron, Mark and Al had gone one step further and formed a group called Hula. The first time I lugged my bag through Hula Kula's hall, there was a dank smell associated with houses where it is simply impossible to exorcise the cold. As a result it was freezing even in the middle of summer. Things got considerably worse come winter when I can clearly remember waking up one morning on the floor of Paul's room only to find that his goldfish tank had frozen over.

If the air was icy, the atmosphere was kept warm by a devil-may-care bonhomie. In Paul's new residence, the levels of hygiene and cleanliness were questionable (the kitchen particularly would have benefited from female intervention). The kitchen was also the place where one was most likely to bump into the two house cats – Morticia and Greta. The cats roamed around unchallenged as did the strange creatures that would often wander down for late afternoon breakfasts. "Who's she?" people would mouth at each other. Welcome to Bohemia – Sheffield style.

The standard of the jokes was exemplary. For a bunch of guys who were all involved with groups playing doomy music, individually they seemed to be a never-ending barrel of laughs. Conversely, I assumed that the Barron Knights were probably a bunch of manic depressives of Hancockian proportions.

Mal and Paul made a good double act – Paul had even affectionately re-christened Mal as Malcolm. Mal, took all this in his stride and was not above taking the piss out of Cabaret Voltaire. Richard's sense of humour, although well developed, did not stretch to jokes about his group's music.

The general merriment within the Hula Kula was in the face of constant adversity. Everyone was permanently skint. Especially Mark, who was so convinced he could make it as a painter that he refused to sign on the dole. In true Van Gogh style, the fact that he had hardly sold a single canvas wasn't about to deter him in his quest for artistic purity.

The living room was adorned with Mark's attempts at painting. One notable picture featured a large dark canvas with just a pair of eyes, a painting that Mal re-titled, "Black man in a coal cellar". By the time the new title had done the rounds, a final version of "Sammy Davis Junior in the coal cellar with a black cat on his lap, both eating licorice" was decided upon. Another of Mark's efforts was a still life of an orange on the carpet. This particular picture had such a strange grip on perspective that the piece of fruit appeared to hover above the ground like an alien spacecraft from the planet Jaffa.

All the cooking was done within the strictest of budgetary limits – one of Mark's more memorable efforts consisted of rice, a heated up tin of pilchards, topped off with brussels sprouts. This was all for the benefit of his friend Beaker, one of the strange characters that would sometimes make an appearance at the Hula Kula. Named after the character in the Muppets, Beaker would always greet Mal with, "So, how's things in the music business?" in a voice that sounded like Fred Scuttle from the *Benny Hill Show*.

In the living room a gas fire battled bravely to keep the temperature above freezing, but in general, everyone was kept warm by the fact that they were involved in some kind of artistic endeavour that was going to change the world. This enthusiasm, although naive, was infectious. All kinds of musical instruments, cassettes and videos were strewn around the place. Everyone had their own stereo that blared out strange hybrids of Northern funk.

Of course, all the guys were happy to go along with the sort of laddish priorities which dictated that the fridge only ever contained half-empty tins of baked beans whilst they had nonchalantly hired the most up-to-date video recorder.

The Hula Kula was shrouded in its own mythology. Almost predictably, it was haunted by a ghost – a certain Henry – a previous resident who had died in one of the rooms. Incidentally this turned out to be Paul's room. (The rest of the household had democratically allocated it to Paul prior to his arrival. Only later did they reveal the room's history to him). I never caught so much as a glimpse of the ghost itself, but even I had to admit that it was rather strange that one of the cats would never set foot in there.

But it didn't end there. Another previous resident, a doctor called Mark, was found dead in his car with carbon monoxide poisoning. Unlike Henry who had left his spiritual residue, Mark had donated something slightly more tangible to the household – a cellar full of his home made wine. One night drunk as ever, having failed to persuade Alan Fish to open up a sentimental bottle of whiskey he had been saving, we cracked open a bottle of the dead man's vintage. It was actually quite palatable.

The cellar also doubled as Hula's rehearsal room and on occasions a dull thunderous sound would waft up into the living room as we tried to watch TV. One time Hula decided they should make a little film – I was already more than conversant with the idea of Sheffield groups taking every opportunity to film something arty for a visual backdrop. So they hired a camera, got together with local film-maker Pete Care and dreamt up a surreal plot based around the house and its overgrown garden. One scene featured a table full of jellies, another some wriggling maggots. Luis Bunuel would no doubt have been proud of them.

One of their scenarios necessitated a long tracking shot of a convoluted indoor carnival parade. This started with everyone crowded into the bathroom, then slowly working their way down the long flight of stairs and ending up in the basement kitchen. Everything went fine until they reached the last few stairs into the kitchen where they bumped into Mal, who was playing mother, making his way to the living room with a tray of teas. "Tea, anyone?" he said into the lens, leaving them to huffily shoot the whole sequence again.

On my next trip to Sheffield they were still editing this particular footage down. In fact, Alan seemed to be forever splicing bits of Super 8 together, or scratching the surface of the film to give it that arty texture. All this went on even at the breakfast table.

Many weekends were spent drinking in their Walkley living room. Odd incidents occasionally resurface like acid flashbacks, including one afternoon where we all sat and watched the Argentinians attacking the HMS Sheffield appropriately enough. Or the time we were all sat round watching the wrestling on the telly and someone called up from the kitchen to say that William Burroughs was on the radio. Mal, instead of rushing to hear his group's mentor, merely shouted back down, "For goodness sake, not now, Bad Boy Bobby Barnes is on!"

Most nights we would all toddle off up the road and catch the bus to West Street. The rest of the passengers would look askance at our rag tag crowd with its assembled leather trousers, eyeliner and flouncey post-punk clothes. If we were out of place on the bus, then we would be right at home in the saloon bar of the Beehive. More often than not we would meet up with Richard and that's when the serious drinking would begin.

Drinking with Richard was an altogether different experience. He not only had an unnerving ability to stop a conversation with a perfectly timed witty remark, he also had a never ending selection of drinks appearing in front of him; Guinness, Bloody Mary's, bottles of Pils, Brandy, Tequila. In those days, Lynne usually matched him drink for drink and had the broadest Sheffield accent I'd ever heard. This involved saying the word "like" a lot.

As the Beehive was merely a stone's throw from Western Works, its saloon bar was Richard's second home. No matter how crowded it was, Richard and Lynne always somehow managed to get seats. But Richard always had to be seated with his back to the wall and seemed genuinely unsettled by the notion that something might be going on behind him. Travelling on any form of public transport was another particular phobia.

Aside from these odd foibles, and let's face it we've all got them, Richard was genial with even the most persistent of hangers-on (myself included). He wasn't in the least snobby or affected. He would always spare a few minutes conversation for the bloke who collected the glasses – the ubiquitous fat Cyril.

Mal would rarely make a full session, but time his entrance perfectly for nearing last orders. Later evidence indicated that the previous hours had probably been spent performing a grooming ritual. Always immaculately turned out, he would swish past the amassed throng of long macs with a Polish ship worker's hat perched on his head, throwing out the odd, "Hiya" to people he recognised.

Chris Watson would sometimes put in an appearance, more often than not accompanied by his girlfriend Margaret. But for some reason our paths never really seemed to cross. In fact, I can only remember a few occasions off stage where I saw all three band members together. But from the amphetamine glances that darted around the Beehive, it was detectable that most of the Sheffield scene was rightly jealous of all three of them.

I wasn't so much jealous, as worried about where the next drink was coming from. As the wretched clang of last orders rung in my ears, any concern for avant-garde music theory was quickly replaced by the burning issue of where were we going to drink after closing time?

just fascination – "the sound of Sheffield steel"

Achieving the right balance between the experimental and the populist is something that few bands achieve for long. But to remain credible in the pop industry requires an element of both. Some bands start off like The Beatles with pure pop intentions and then take on board more radical ideas. Others start with the wild ideas and try and then temper it with a pop sensibility. Most of the Sheffield bands fell into the latter category, but from whichever end you started, it was really the crossroads reached halfway that tended to produce the most rewarding music.

The Cabs were very taken with those bands that had managed to successfully mix avant-garde arty ideas with pop music dynamics. This was a balancing act that was difficult to maintain. The Velvet Underground hadn't lasted long enough to sabotage their credibility, whilst both David Bowie and Roxy Music had blown it by stretching themselves too far. For the moment Cabaret Voltaire had only started to edge down the road towards pop. But the stepping stones were clearly there; Mal had the looks of a Ferry, Watson the off-the-wall ideas of an Eno, and Richard the sardonic wit of a Lou Reed. The one question mark remaining was whether the music could crossover.

"The thing about the Doors," Richard would pontificate, "was that Morrison was all arty and pretentious with all that poetry stuff, but they still threw in pop tunes." As a big Doors fan I wasn't disagreeing, but refrained from pointing out that he had raised the nub of the problem within his own ranks. If they were serious about making further inroads into a pop market, the odd tune wouldn't have gone amiss.

What obviously appealed to Richard was that the Doors could be intimidating as well as popular as in "pop", and most importantly they sold a truck load of records *and* appealed to women. Traditionally these were two things that experimental bands were spectacularly bad at doing. For their efforts, the only audience that the Cabs had really been able to capitalise on, consisted mostly of twenty-something males with serious muso tendencies in search of the doomy and macabre. Much as I didn't want to admit it, that cap was fitting me rather well.

For his part, Richard's favourite types of listening ran the full gamut from the most extreme avant-garde noise to the comparatively light relief of "Roadrunner" by Junior Walker and the All-stars. Which, by the way, was one of his all-time favourite singles.

Something he talked less about was his fondness for the Stones, although I thought buying their excruciating *Emotional Rescue* LP was stretching that loyalty a bit far. Despite what people thought, much of the Cabs' rock 'n' roll attitude came not only from punk and krautrock, but also from bands like the Stones. What impressed Richard most, was that the Stones were obsessed with everything black. Black music, black magic, not to forget painting things black.

Of course, Jagger and company weren't alone in idolising black music but they were pretty much the first white pop band to dip their feet into the muddy waters of the occult. They had also, for a crucial period in their career, created an elusive screen behind which it appeared they were doing something quite shamanic and dangerous.

This was very appealing to Richard, particularly the tales of drugs and debauchery. With his collection of shades and leather jackets, like many musicians of his generation, he mimicked this rock chic. Both the Cabs and TG in some way attempted to recreate the same aura that the Stones had crafted (P-Orridge later wrote a song called "Godstar" which eulogised Brian Jones' apparent mystical quality).

So, Richard and Mal became Sheffield's miniature version of the glimmer twins with Mal playing the outgoing upwardly mobile Jagger role, to Richard's attempts to match Keef's iron constitution. I guess Chris Watson was the sensible one – the Charlie Watts of the band.

Certainly the Cabs were very aware of the hierarchy in which they were placed. In Sheffield's incestuous music scene, maintaining one's cool was all important – especially toward outsiders. Once, when Richard strolled down West Street to escort a rock journalist back to the station, they bumped into Gary Wilson, the drummer from Artery, who promptly addressed the pair with the remark, "Hiya, how'ya diddling?" It was the wrong remark at the wrong time. These sorts of things worried Richard's idea of rock 'n' roll decorum.

For my part, I was undeniably being drawn further and further into a musical web where the spiders were the main players in Sheffield music scene, Richard and Mal included. As an insignificant insect entangled in its silky spun web, for a while it seemed to me like whole musical universe was now centred around Sheffield. In the early eighties, the music press was filled with stories about the Human League and Cabaret Voltaire. Even if I was forever doomed to fester down the local Depot, at least I vaguely knew, or had hung around in the same pubs, as some of the people they were going on about.

Of course, it wasn't long before the press would turn their attentions to Manchester and Factory, onwards to the Liverpool scene centred around the bands on Zoo records, then to Glasgow and the Postcard bands, Newcastle and Kitchenware, then back to Manchester and Factory – it all went in circles. It was a whole period when the music press was playing that game of "Guess the next city". Such was the quest of a scribe in search of discovering a scene. The one thing the Sheffield scene lacked was a locally based record label, (until the later emergence of Warp).

Having been converted to the charm of the Sheffield musical world, it was becoming increasingly easy for me to understand why there was such press fascination with the whole myriad of groups and personalities that were at its core. Richard constantly denied there was a scene at all, but from the outside it was painfully obvious to me that it was a thriving melting pot of cross fertilization.

In London the whole post-Bowie world was all about the flouncey trouncey world of The Blitz Club and the nascent Culture Clubbers, while in Birmingham it was centred around the hedonistic narcissism of Duran Duran. It was all too camp and silly for me. Boy George was turning everything he touched into a Danny La Rue sketch, Duran Duran were obsessed with turning music into a one long Martini advert, whilst in the London suburbs Wham! were perfecting their brand of 18-30's style disco.

In time, bands like the Human League would become as fluffy and throwaway as their London counterparts, but initially they too were immersed in a world that was more down-to-earth. In London it was all too easy to become lost in the incestuous music business world. With A&R men flapping around, a band like Spandau Ballet could easily lose sight of its objectives before it had even started. In fact, when the Kemp brothers' combo made their first *Top Of The Pops* appearance I laughed so hard that my stomach ached. All of a sudden, being in a band had degenerated into a bunch of style junkies dressing up in kilts and wailing on about cutting long stories short.

Much of what was beginning to happen to the music business was a portent of the decade to come – a victory of style over content. After the "anybody can do it" mentality of punk, a form of cultural elitism was creeping in. A whole new brash bunch of image conscious youngsters had bounded upon the scene. They didn't want revolution or rock 'n' roll. They wanted to party. The *NME* was replaced by *The Face* as the young people's bible and journalists lorded it over their readers by trying to dictate rather than reflect what was new, hip and trendy. The media in general loved these new style junkies. Brash and clothes-obsessed individuals like Boy George immediately became ideal tabloid fodder. As a result many of these bands were swept up into the establishment almost before they had got going.

Certainly the whole musical axis was shifting. Kraftwerk had started the drift toward the general acceptance of backing tapes in live performance. With the emergence of MTV, live performance would in parts become redundant, or at least an irritating distraction. Most of the Sheffield bands were very much part of this drift. Certainly the Cabs disdained the idea of rock 'n' roll touring in favour of short bursts of gigs, followed by long sojourns back in their Western Works bunker.

The Cabs' saving grace, at least for the moment, was the fact that moving to London was no longer a foregone conclusion for an aspiring band. In fact it was a disadvantage. The Cabs had been horrified by Rough Trade's suggestion that they join the pseudo-socialist co-operative of Scritti Politti and The Raincoats in London. To be a member meant generally mucking in with everyday duties at Rough Trade. "I'm not fucking selling records in that dingy shop," was Richard's understandable response. In fact, the more the Sheffield music scene turned its back on London, the stronger it seemed to get. They egged each other on and positively attacked the music world with the Northern swagger of a soulboy hitting the dancefloor

Also, up North there was an altogether darker agenda. Somehow, in places like Sheffield and Manchester it was difficult to ignore the spectre of the Yorkshire Ripper or the Moors murders. It wasn't surprising that many of the journalists considered that Northern music was more at the cutting edge. As a result the music press were forever sending their best journalists up from London to delve into the early synthesizer scenes that were multiplying faster than yoghurt culture. Suddenly the North was the place to be. In Manchester, Joy Division cast long doomy shadows, in Leeds Marc Almond had acquired the arrogant boy slut attitude that would be central to Soft Cell. In Liverpool, the collective egos of Burns, McCullough, Cope and Wylie were starting to assert themselves.

As a result the Sheffield scene still reverberated with the news that anyone could do it. With the Human League on a major label, the Cabs on Rough Trade, suddenly there was an army of long macs queuing up to follow them. If you really wanted to, you just upped and did it. And at the centre of all this "up and doing it" was the social life of the Beehive, the culmination of the traditional Friday night pub-crawl we called the West Street Shuffle. True, the Guinness was better in the Mail Coach, the Hallamshire should have had a greater appeal as they occasionally put bands on, and The Saddle boasted the newest computer games like *Missile Command* and *Asteroids*. But it was in the Beehive's lounge bar where all the serious drinking was done. The place positively buzzed with musical gossip and innuendo. By the end of a Friday night, it would be packed with arty and exciting looking people – all dressed up to the nines and plastered in make-up. Everyone you talked to seemed to be in a group: Artery, I'm So Hollow, Graph, 2.3, Clock DVA, The Stunt Kites, Hula – oh yes and Pulp. The list was endless. All these people seemed so busy with all their musical projects, their trendy clothes and hanging around looking cool.

On subsequent weekend trips to Sheffield we started to get invited back to Richard and Lynne's house after the pub. They had moved into a Bohemian garret perched at one end of Sheffield's red light district. They had painted the living room walls a bright red, the shutters were black and never opened. In the corner of the living room a TV endlessly flickered videos of anything from Bunuel to *Quadrophenia*. Posters for *A Clockwork Orange* and horror movies adorned the walls. After hours drinking would accelerate with more and more beer, the evenings got later and later. Marijuana and speed were much in evidence. I'd lost interest in smoking joints and I had yet to acquire a taste for amphetamines. I also had this notion that it was somewhat uncool to indulge myself in other people's drugs – an inhibition I lost later. Like a bunch of all night Chinese gamblers leaving an opium den, we would wend our way back to Paul's place in the sharp spikiness of the morning light. Only to get back to the Hula Kula to crack open some more cans. It seemed like I could never have too much beer.

whip blow – "bill and the boys"

The other guys that made up the Transport Department management at the Depot mostly resided in a Portacabin outside the vehicle workshop. To this day I am not exactly sure what they did in there, but I had to be particularly careful to avoid the used teabags that were regularly flung out of the door. Entering their Portacabin was to sign up for an education no academic establishment could provide. Here were guys idling their final working days at the last bus stop before retirement. Finding out about the intervening stops on their respective journeys made it easy to understand why they were happy to be ending their working days at the Council. Sometimes it seemed like everyone I met was either ex-army, ex-coppers, or an ex-something. As their backgrounds unfolded I can only say that I was happy to remain a very peripheral part of their lives.

There was Henry, the man who continually picked at his hooter and kept a blackened towel in his bottom drawer. This mildewy item would be ceremoniously pulled out every Friday night as he marched off to the fitters' showers.

"Why waste your own hot water, when you can shower at the Council's expense," was his reasoning.

Then there was Roy and Les who were always bickering light heartedly with each other. But best of the lot was Bill, a man who had accumulated enough blue stories to put any working men's club comedian to shame.

"You see," Bill would smile, "I had a few decent blow jobs during the war, but the best I ever had was from another bloke in our mess."

Bill would lean back in his chair and chuckle. You never really knew whether all these tales were true. But his descriptions of fucking his way through the brothels in Italy were so lurid and detailed it was like you were there with him. He was like a surrogate uncle who told you all the extra "facts of life" that your parents had conveniently omitted. Paul would always ask me for stories from "Blowjob Bill" as we referred to him.

Bill had an owlish face, an infectious laugh and only nine fingers. On making a hasty exit from a bombed-out tank, the ring on his middle finger had caught on the tank lid and promptly ripped the digit from its owner.

"It was a bloody expensive ring as well," was typical of Bill's take on life.

Bill's knowledge of sex and pornography was so encyclopaedic that he dispatched his titbits with almost academic zeal. He was like an elderly professor in the carnal arts. One day he would be holding forth on the practices of those people whose fetish it was to have sex with amputees, the next day he was preaching about prostitutes with slack fannies, the shared condoms, sloppy seconds and the desperation of squaddies fucking like that day might be their last. My eyes were being opened to an even stranger world.

Bill, like many others at the Council, actually had a lot more diverse talents than he liked to let on. Certainly he took great relish in having more technical car maintenance expertise in one of his remaining fingers than the rest of the Workshop had put together. He could also whip the pants off me when it came to finishing any crossword. He would nevertheless always look surprised and slap me on the back when I got the solution to a clue he had probably solved ages ago.

Bill was typical of some of the old timers for whom working at the Depot was only a secondary diversion, in his case running his own car repair business from home. One of the refuse drivers owned a coach and fairground equipment firm, another drove a licensed black cab in the afternoons. Some earned so much from these extra activities that they had invested in second homes abroad. There was a never-ending supply of moonlighters. Old Steve in Building Works with the Bobby Charlton hairstyle was good for plumbing – any carpentry needed doing, see Charlie. And so it went on. The overriding opinion was that the Council was a bottomless pit of money – nobody spared much of a thought for the poor ratepayers that had to fund such gross mismanagement. Almost daily I would learn of another character who had some bizarre money-making scheme on the go.

If a lot of attention was paid to these extra-curricular activities, then scant regard was still being made toward hygiene. Just when I thought I had seen it all, along came Fred the sewer man. Here was a man who would wipe his sewer rods with his bare hands and then eat his sandwiches. Wash his hands? I don't think so. Even Bill and the other guys in the portacabin were appalled by this disregard for cleanliness. It was made all the worse, by the fact that Fred was a burly but tactile kind of guy. On being slapped on the back, one could only hope he hadn't left too much of a residue behind.

On visits to the canteen it was best not to pay too much attention to what your fellow diners were up to. The sound of munching huge greasy breakfasts was enough, without looking at the toothless holes that the food was being shovelled into. I had to wonder if these people behaved so badly in their own homes. Sometimes it felt like time had suddenly been frozen in the era of the Dickensian workhouse. But just as the workhouses were inevitably reformed, so the forgotten inmates of the Depot were soon to be discovered by the outside world. A certain lady called Margaret Thatcher had already got her iron eye on us.

the set up – "western workings"

Unlike London, where rehearsal space was expensive and difficult
to find, Sheffield's industrial decline offered no end of disused factory space ideal for up-and-coming bands to vent their musical
spleens. The Cabs were now well settled into their own studio,
Western Works, which was essentially two rooms – one doubling
as a sitting room/office and wasn't that different in appearance to
my office in the Council workshop. The other was a rehearsal
room/studio. Richard, Mal and Chris had been smart enough to
realise that using a commercial studio to noodle around in would
have been economic suicide. Also, being hugely influenced by
Can and Kraftwerk, both of whom had their own studios, it had
seemed like the decent thing to do to follow suit.

At first the Cabs had shared the studio space with a number of
other local groups, but as their popularity grew, they invested in
more and more equipment and took it over full time. Like everything else in Sheffield, excepting the pubs, it was a cold and
draughty place. However, somehow the atmosphere seemed just
right for the kind of music they were concocting. It had that feeling of being a nerve centre of something exciting.

On my first visit to the studio, Paul was still in They Must Be
Russians and we plinked and plonked around on some of the
instruments. On leaving Mal was sitting rather studiously reading
some correspondence in the office, and looked up and smiled.

"What's Mal doing?" I turned to Paul, "dreaming up a fourth
mantra?" referring jokingly to the fact that the Cabs had just
released a 12" single called "Three Mantras". The record only had
two tracks on it, both verging on the self-indulgent in my humble
opinion, but it was a good joke title nonetheless.

Paul however didn't think my remark funny. He looked at me rather icily, "At least they're getting somewhere, rather than the load of crap we were playing." His comment was of course directed at our jam session that had gone precisely nowhere. But he might as well have been talking about my life in general.

Getting somewhere was exactly what the Cabs were doing. They were fully in charge of their own destiny. They had a record company in Rough Trade that made no demands on them, all they had to do was deliver the final tapes and a couple of months later there was an LP sitting in the racks. They had a growing reputation for live performances and they had their own studio. What more could anyone possibly want? Regularly I was told that such and such a journalist had just been in to interview the group and I would often read the results a few weeks later.

Being interviewed on home ground was a big advantage to the Cabs. Down the pub, the journalists' home environment, it was easy for everything to get unfocussed and for guards to slip. At the studio, Richard in particular, felt more at ease. Also, journalists were no doubt impressed with the way Western Works buzzed like a home industry. Posters for gigs adorned the walls and music thumped away at all hours of the day. The only damper on proceedings was when those in the clothes sweatshop downstairs banged on the ceiling by way of complaining about the continual industrial beats.

In terms of the recording process, it all seemed so advanced. I was amazed at how much equipment they had managed to amass in a relatively short time. I had visions of the three of them sitting up there, dropping acid and wreaking havoc on the strangest array of instruments.

Certainly, Richard's lysergic experiments were central to the group's early output, most notably the visual accompaniment. Apart from it causing him to miaow all through a screening of *Cat People*, Richard was capable of constructing visual backdrops that were like psychedelic flashbacks. The random effect could be like witnessing the whole world's media flashing before ones' eyes within the matter of a few seconds. With the advent of satellite television, enhanced video techniques and MTV-like computer graphics this has now become a cliché. But in the same way the Cabs use of snippets of found voices pre-dated and predicted sampling, so Richard's splicing together of visuals predicted much of the pop video-making that followed.

Anyone flirting with psychedelics for too long runs the risk of playing desert island discs with Syd Barrett. Safer for the sanity, but not necessarily for the general paranoiac disposition, is to allow oneself to be attracted by the pull of faster and less sedentary thrills. It was the white powders of sulphate and cocaine that were generally fuelling the Sheffield scene by the time I found myself on its periphery. For the moment I was able to decline the centrifugal lure of the mirror and crisp tenner. I felt I was lucky enough to be flitting around something exciting, without needing enhanced chemical stimulation.

When it came to drinking beer, it was an altogether different story, and it wasn't long before sessions moved on after closing time in the Beehive. One favoured destination was the twenty or so yard stagger up the road to the studio's sitting room. Armed with limitless supplies of drink we would all sit up in the Western Works office and watch videos. On the first visit, as Richard slipped a video-tape into the machine, I readied myself for the possibility of an arty movie. It was somewhat a surprise when Russ Abbott's chirpy face beamed out of the screen at me. Just about as funny – but not intentionally so – was the splendidly titled horror movie called *The Living Dead at the Manchester Morgue*. Finally when the sun began to rise over the silo outside the window – the very same silo that was to become their label Doublevision's logo – we knew it was time to get some kip.

jazz the glass – "white souls in black suits"

Somewhere in between marathon drinking sessions, Paul had left They Must Be Russians and joined Clock DVA. His final concert with the Russians and his first with Clock DVA was on the same night at the ICA. He came off stage with the Russians with the retort, "Thank God that's over, I've left". He then had a quick haircut so as to give the impression he might be a different guitarist and took to the stage with Clock DVA.

The ICA concert was not the best initiation for me to the live sound of Clock DVA. The previous night I had been to a wedding and just for a change I decided to celebrate the occasion by seeing how much beer I could drink without falling over. No amount of paracetamol washed down with more beer could halt the revenge of the hangover from hell. I emerged from the ICA with one of those headaches that stretches from one ear to the other. Clock DVA's music hadn't really helped my ailing situation. Cacophonous Beefheartian rock is not exactly what doctors recommend for this type of hangover. In fact, the softest of chamber quartets would have probably sent me over the edge. Nevertheless, others with clearer heads than my own seemed to appreciate their sonic attack. I was, however, distinctly impressed that they had attracted P-Orridge and some of his hangers-on to turn out for the occasion. For his part, Paul had obviously moved up a rung of Sheffield's musical ladder and was rightly chuffed about it.

Whether the promoters were so excited by the scene backstage is another matter. After the gig, certain members of Paul's new band had decided that the ICA's black backcloth would make rather fetching curtains. A handy pair of roadie's scissors made short work of cutting it into the necessary pieces. The ICA naturally enough assumed that the group was also responsible for nicking their mirror ball. "I wish *we'd* thought of that," was the general conclusion back in Sheffield when they got the ICA's letter of complaint. Not that the journey home hadn't passed without incident, when the group's singer Adi Newton had filled the van with Derv rather than petrol. I had to smile to myself. Perhaps pop stars weren't that perfect after all. It was a regular mistake made back at the Depot.

Clock DVA was very much Newton's baby. Previously, along with Paul Bower from 2.3, he had edited *Gunrubber*, Sheffield's answer to *Sniffing Glue*. Punk had spawned a host of photocopied, cut-and-paste fanzines, the other two front runners at the time were *NMX*, started by an ex-member of the Russians who still wrote under the name Martin XRussian, and another that had the rather splendid name of *Modern Drugs*.

After trying his hand at self-publishing, it was soon clear that writing about bands was not enough for Newton. He wanted to front a band – be a star. After all, Newton (real name Gary Coates) had already been in a number of bands including The Future with Martin Ware and Ian Craig Marsh.

So, just as Mark Perry had abandoned *Sniffing Glue* in favour of ATV, so Newton formed the first configuration of Clock DVA. The name was an amalgamation of the first syllable from *Clockwork Orange* with the Russian for two. The Anthony Burgess novel used a language constructed from various different European dialects, and this was Newton's attempt to mimic him. I thought the name was rather good, and initially it was pronounced Clock Dva (Dvay as in the Russian pronunciation) and not Clock D-V-A as they were later known.

Their initial musical outpourings had been very influenced by both Throbbing Gristle and *Low*-period Bowie. It was all harsh electronic landscapes. One of the troubles with this early incarnation was that TG and the Cabs were doing the same thing, only better. So, Newton decided to collect together a group of local musicians to re-interpret his romantically-doomed vision of the world. So, in came drummer Roger Quail, saxophonist Charlie

Collins, while Jud, the only surviving member of the original band, bravely tried to play bass. The resulting unit, like the Cabs, were already in contact with TG, recorded a tape and sent it down to Industrial records who were impressed enough to release it – they had also by now released a collection of Richard's solo material called *Disposable Half-Truths*. The Clock DVA tape revelled in the rather splendid title of *White Souls in Black Suits*.

The record also featured a guitarist who was a junkie. Most successful bands can put up with the unreliability of junkiedom for a while, but for an aspiring band to have one your number so afflicted is the kiss of death. And that's where Paul came in to plug the group's punctured arm, so to speak. On joining, Paul was asked to contribute to material that was a considerable move away from the sound of *White Souls* and closer to Beefheart and Joy Division. Although generally considered still part of the industrial scene, they were now more like The Pop Group than Throbbing Gristle. This shrewd move actually set them apart from the other arty synthesizer bands in Sheffield.

As a singer and performer, Newton obviously had a Bowie fixation. The Newton part of his name was even derived from Bowie's character in *The Man Who Fell To Earth*, whilst the Adi bit was supposed to be a kind of shortened version of Adolf. Apparently having dyed his hair black he resembled a certain well-known dictator. Live, Adi was a compelling spectacle, mixing a Beefheartian growl with a kind of Ian Curtis menace. Off stage he seemed so obsessed with appearing cool to the point of being cold and distant.

His sidekick, Jud (Turner) the bass player, was in equal measures unmusical and unpredictable. He drove the band's van, despite having no driving licence. However, he was a far better driver than he was a bass player – tuning up was a particular problem. He also had a penchant for stealing things, probably fuelled by the fact that he too had acquired an on-off smack habit. The sax player was a bearded ex-alcoholic council gardener called Charlie who I rightly guessed was into Ornette Coleman. The drummer was young Roger who not only worked for the Coal Board, but was also a mine of encyclopaedic musical information.

And of course there was Paul – my mate. I was no longer jealous. By now I reckoned that if being involved with modern music meant getting up on stage to create the unholy racket they did, then I guessed I wasn't really up to the job.

And boy could they kick up a racket. They were truly an abrasive and strongheaded bunch. This was a band fuelled by tension. Their rickety little rehearsal room often echoed to both types of discord – both musical and verbal. Sometimes Adi and Jud would not turn up to rehearsals at all, and when they did, Newton had often forgotten the key. Then there was the time they all arrived to find that the door had been nailed up. Someone had forgotten to pay the rent. Arguments raged over everything from money to musical direction. It was the sort of growing pains that had to be overcome if they were going to last more than a few short months.

PART FOUR

Premonition – "shirts and ties"

At Central Depot, the first sign that the whole mismanagement issue was beginning to be tackled came when distant rumblings of the word "privatisation" could be heard coming from the Civic Centre. For those who were starting to see storm clouds gathering over their safe-haven this was a worrying expression, for others it was quite simply outside of their vocabulary. But no-one was really exactly sure what it meant.

Initial reactions were that this so-called "privatisation" would surely never extend as far as the Depot. It was soon clear that this was far from the case. Margaret Thatcher, as well as being hellbent on breaking the power of the Unions, was also determined to castrate local government and throw the whole thing open to market forces.

The first sign of real turbulence arrived in the form of Mr Evans. On his first day he marched around the yard like Livingstone discovering Africa's interior. Never before had the Depot seen someone with such a grand title as Assistant Controller. At first, the news of his arrival was greeted with the usual, "Oh, we'll soon get him into line". But as he gave a brief introductory speech in the canteen to all the Depot staff, it was obvious that here was a man that had been on management courses and whose brief was to get tough. The invisible sign around his neck read "New breed of manager – beware!" He was small in height, but he made up for it by walking tall with the fire and brimstone of a new religion called accountability. With his snooping mentality, it was obvious that the days of being left to ones' own devices were numbered. It wasn't long before John's vegetable patch had been dug over, Lofty been offered early retirement and one felt Bert's days of simply making the tea were surely in danger.

More worrying for me was that he had got wind of the fact that I was a graduate who, in his opinion, was wasting my talents holed away in a godforsaken corner of the Depot workshop. His impression was strengthened when one day he sneaked up the back steps to my office and caught me struggling to configure a tricky anagram in *The Guardian* crossword. He may well have been impressed by my highbrow choice of newspaper, but by the disapproving look he gave me, it was obvious he considered my education should be applied to Council matters.

A few days later I was cycling up the yard on my bike, when I heard the voice of the "Welsh Wizard" – he'd only been at the Depot a few days but he already had a nickname.

"Mike (only the fitters called me Mick), I think it might be an idea if you thought about wearing a shirt and tie".

"AARGGHH", was my first reaction. Then that line of CJ's from *The Rise and Fall of Reginald Perrin* came to me. "I didn't get where I was today by wearing a shirt and tie." Then I realised that I hadn't actually got anywhere. In the end "Yes, OK", fell meekly from my lips. Mr Evans was not the sort of guy you could say "no" to. Before I knew it he had also conned me into doing some kind of part-time business course. He simply couldn't believe that as a graduate I didn't want to advance myself in the Council's ranks.

He obviously hadn't bargained for the fact that I looked worse in supposedly smart clothes than I did in jeans. And anyway the Depot with its greasy chairs, oil-stained canteen and muddy pathways was hardly the place to be showing off the latest Armani collection. So, wearing a half-hearted stab at a shirt, a tie I took off most of the time, and a jacket I had bought for a fiver in the local market, I wandered down the local tech to sign in looking vaguely like Mark E Smith circa 1978. Most of the other people on the same course were naturally enough entering into the spirit of the eighties and power dressing to the hilt.

It went without saying that my fellow students appeared to me to be loathsome individuals who had grand ambitions of getting on at the Gas Board or wherever. I was still convinced there must be more to life than that. But just exactly what, I couldn't quite put my finger on. I think everyone thought I was some kind of weirdo as they turned their gaze toward me and I gave my little speech to introduce myself. When it came to my interests outside work, for some reason, "I like reading stuff like Dostoevsky" blurted from my lips. What a thing to say! Naturally I was met with vacant stares. At that moment in time I'd have signed a pact with the devil if he'd have just had been so kind as to whisk me away from it all.

I couldn't believe that after leaving the whole sorry business of exercise books and essays behind at University, somebody had so easily conned me back into a lecture theatre again. As this new course progressed, I couldn't really work out what the fuck most of it was supposed to be about. We played silly games like imagining we were all stuck in a sinking hot air balloon and then having to debate why we should not be the one thrown out.

"If I were stuck in a balloon with you fuckers, I'd be pleading to be the one chucked out!" I felt like saying.

Back at the Depot, the fitters would laughingly ask, "How's college then, Mick?" knowing damn well that I hated every minute of it.

Mr Evans, however, seemed well pleased that he had got my career prospects back on track. "You can never learn too much," he informed me.

He then proceeded to bore me with the details of how he had attained all his qualifications by correspondence courses. "Well, bully for you, you Welsh cunt," I thought. Did he actually think I was supposed to be feeling grateful that he was putting me through this shit?

About half way through the course was a residential weekend at some godforsaken hotel in South Mimms. This little weekend might as well have been dubbed "hell on earth" as far as I was concerned. Two days beforehand, the phone rang. It was Paul.

"What about coming up this weekend and having a right old session?"

"You fucking bet." This was just the excuse I needed. I walked straight into Mr Evans' office and said I was jacking in the course. I explained that the whole fucking caboodle was a sham, run by a load of wankers who didn't know what the fuck they were talking about. Not in those exact words, of course, but that was the gist. Whatever I said, I must have appeared convincing.

"OK as long as you are prepared to explain to the college head all your complaints," he said.

For a weekend in Sheffield, I'd have jumped around stark bollock naked in front of him if that's what was necessary. My future as a business executive chucked away for a weekend in Sheffield. It seemed like a fair swap to me.

I returned the following week and accounted for myself with some aplomb by rather eloquently relating the course's shortcomings. I never really did fathom the basic contradiction inherent in business courses. Surely, anyone remotely good at business would be out there making vast amounts of money in industry and not teaching it at the local tech for a paltry salary. As it turned out, the previous year someone else at the Council had resigned from the course for the same reasons as me (well, probably not the bit about a weekend on the piss in Sheffield). Two weeks later the head of the business courses at the local tech was sacked for fraud and incompetence. I prided myself that I might in some small way have played a part in his downfall. Go rot.

Anyway I didn't need any business course, because it was only a matter of time before I got out of the Council and into something involved with music. "Why couldn't I be in some band, just like everyone in the Beehive?" I kept thinking to myself. I was like some spoilt child who couldn't have its packet of sweeties.

Stranded in London I finally realised that the only way to get involved in something to do with music was to try to emulate the same home recording ethic that the Cabs had tried. As a result, Dave and I invested in a small Teac four track recorder and tried to write some songs. Over the past decade Dave and I had both travelled the bumpy road from Clapton to the Clash, from the Dead to Devo, so we set about trying to construct a sound that in some way ignored and embraced this increasingly lengthy musical journey. Locked away with our Teac we recorded a tape of songs, spurred on by the fact that the Cabs now had a successful recording career that started off with recording a tape in Chris Watson's attic.

Unsurprisingly, the results were more song-orientated than Cabaret Voltaire. After all, as we could play our instruments, it was stupid to try and pretend to be some kind of noise terrorist band. We wanted a jazzy feel to the music so Dave borrowed a trombone which he attempted to learn in two hours, and I dug out my old clarinet. It was a laugh and added to the ready-made feel of it all.

Now what? Try and think of a name. Where else but down the pub. We sat staring at our beer going through the usual list of silly names.

After four pints, I thought my suggestion of the Spanking Bottoms was an inspired one. That day, Bill and I had been sitting around in his Council portakabin reading out loud sections of a spanking magazine that someone had salvaged from the back of a dust cart. One article had been delicately titled "Spanking Bottom" and was accompanied by pictures of rather flabby buttocks being paddled until red with welts.

"We could call the tape Second Anal Report," I persisted.

Blank looks all round.

"Well, what do you want to call it," I said getting exasperated, "the fucking Serious Arts Foundation or something." We all laughed as someone got some more beers in.

The tape was released (if you could call it a release) on our newly established Serious Arts Foundation label. We even set up a PO Box number. We printed up some cassette covers, and sent out a kind of press release that was full of self-important twaddle. We were aware that there were a number of people distributing cassette music, so we sent out press releases to them. Next we sent a copy to *Sounds'* Cassette Pets page which reviewed bedroom efforts like our own.

Rather naively we included a sentence on the bottom of the bulletin inviting people to "tell us what you think". If I'd been a researcher for *Points of View* I could no doubt have warned against this folly. Fancy inviting people to tell us what they thought. What stupidity! In the end we received complaints we were selling the tape too expensively, weird notes from people who evidently never left their bedrooms, some moderately interesting pieces of mail art from Italy, but mostly bitter expletives. Here was a sadder world than that which I had to put up with during the day.

We quickly decided we didn't want to exchange tapes and correspondence with pathetic, small-minded people. Mal had warned me that this would be the outcome. He himself had become tired of receiving letters from sad fuckers who were perhaps taking what they were doing a tad too seriously. Sure Richard and Mal were serious about producing noise terrorism, but they were also in it to have a rollicking good time along the way.

When the *Sounds* review dropped on my doormat it said, "definitely a window to watch". This obviously warranted a few extra pints that night to celebrate the fact we had made such a huge splash across pages of the music press. In truth, the entry barely competed with the size of a postage stamp, but we were still chuffed. The next week our tape peaked at number 4 in the Obscurist Chart and we sold about 30 copies. We even got some response from leaving a few leaflets around in the Oxford Walk Virgin shop. For some reason this shop always seemed to stock the most weird records. This, we later found out, was due to the shop manager being one Jim Thirlwell (then known as You've Got Foetus On Your Breath). Mal and I chuckled over the fact that his bank account was even in that name.

One of the LPs that sat proudly in Thirlwell's Virgin shop was *Thirst*, the latest LP by Clock DVA. The Clocks had signed a deal with a label called Fetish, the brainchild of an Irish guy called Rod Pierce. Fetish, like many small labels, ran on tight budgets and the band was given just a week at Jacob's Farm Studios in Surrey to commit their own particular brand of post-Beefheartian rock to vinyl. With some excitement Paul related every detail about its recording, including the fact that U2 were in the adjacent studio. It was all very rock 'n' roll, down to the mandatory line of coke while listening to the playbacks. On being asked if he'd like some, young Roger had endearingly anticipated a can of soft drink.

Some of the ideas on *Thirst* were a bit rushed, and in places it suffered from tinny production. (Apparently it is never good to agree any final mixes on coke.) Nonetheless, it sounded like a major victory and a minor classic. Others were similarly impressed and come that December it was only pipped by Japan's *Tin Drum* as "album of the year" in the opinion of at least one *Sounds* writer. Rightly so, *Thirst* was a brave and aggressive piece of vinyl. It also had sleeve notes by Genesis P-Orridge and a cover by the fledgling Neville Brody. At the time, that was a good enough endorsement for me.

Possibly muted when compared to a live performance, at least the LP gave listeners the chance to hear Newton's haunting lyrics set against the angry duelling backdrop of Paul's guitar and Charlie's saxophone. However, Paul was soon to find out that making a good LP was only part of the battle. In the post-punk eighties, merely sticking out a record and hoping people would latch on to it was no longer enough, even if it did receive good reviews. To truly win the battle, it was becoming increasingly necessary to employ a whole army of stylists, hype merchants and pluggers.

One of the main problems with Fetish was promotion. Like many indie labels they were falling apart due to lack of organisation and money. They simply couldn't play the same games as the majors without overstretching themselves. Whilst in punk's heyday, labels like Rough Trade could just about do what they liked and still remain solvent, now it was getting increasingly competitive. As the "me decade" wended its merry way forward, being businesslike was becoming the name of the game.

over and over − "the mission is terminated"

The Fetish label's crowning glory was undoubtedly the *Fetish Night Out*, when TG, the Cabs, Clock DVA, Boyd Rice and Z'ev played to a packed house at London's Lyceum. It was not so much the beginning of the Industrial era but a closing celebration. Far from being a miserable wake, it was a memorable evening. But to be honest all that industrial music on the same bill was a bit hard to bear. At the bar I overheard ex-Skid and soon-to-be "media personality" Richard Jobson telling someone how much he hated the Cabs. The dislike was mutual. A favourite game back at the Hula Kula was to sit around laughing at Jobson's recently released poetry LP. Requests for repeated plays of particularly hilarious couplets were commonplace.

The end of the Industrial era was well and truly confirmed when Throbbing Gristle played their last ever gig in San Francisco in June of 1981. TG, by now dressing in army fatigues and pretending to be a close-knit terrorist unit, were in reality like any other group − a mess of conflicting egos and musical differences. The delicate symmetry that had held them together was now in shattered pieces. In their typically bombastic fashion, postcards were sent out which announced that "The Mission Is Terminated".

It was a shame. TG's last two LPs had unearthed a band developing into something more than just an unholy row accompanied by some controversial imagery. *Twenty Jazz Funk Greats*, mainly under Chris Carter's influence, had lacked their usual jackbooted aural thuggery. Parts of it almost verged toward disco, pissing off many of their hardcore fans in the process. This commercial shift was probably worthwhile for that reason alone. Likewise, their final studio LP *Heathen Earth* showed them taming their raw noise but maintaining the overall feeling of unease. Essentially a live recording at their Martello Street Industrial studio, the group demonstrated that they were capable of handling dynamics and atmospherics in a much more crafted way.

As a final release, the group's four Industrial LPs were packaged together with a live recording of their San Francisco appearance in a lavish limited edition box-set, released by Fetish. I duly went out to the Virgin Megastore to purchase my copy, only to find that the contents were incomplete. On returning to the shop, the staff had to open up at least 10 boxes before they could find a set that included all the right contents – i.e. five different LPs, the booklet and the badge. It was no doubt these sorts of things that helped Fetish to go under.

Pumped up by the success they had achieved as TG, the various factions lost no time in splintering into two new groups. Cosey switched musical and romantic allegiance to Chris Carter. But it soon became clear, that without P-Orridge's mischievous intent, Chris & Cosey were too tame an outfit to confront, nor were they able to display any pop potential despite becoming friendly with the Eurythmics. Nevertheless, their first LP *Heartbeat* had its moments.

Meanwhile, Genesis and Sleazy formed Psychic TV together with P-Orridge's new American wife Paula who took up the Yoko Ono role. In the following months all sorts of manifestos about psychic rituals started appearing in fanzines like *Flow Motion* and *Vox* (nothing to do with the later rock publication of the same name). Without the dynamics of a democratic group, clearly P-Orridge's ideas were running out of control.

P-Orridge had apparently decided that what the eighties needed was his own little cult. By replacing f with v as in ov, and adding an e to the, Thee Temple Ov Psychick Youth was born. I, for one, couldn't be bothered with it all and I quickly lost interest in trying to disentangle the mass of information. Other former TG fans might have been prepared to search for meaning from these muddled manifestos and half-baked conspiracy theories, but not me. There was only so much time I could spend pondering the number 23, or staring into dream machines and reading about the group's sado-masochistic rituals. P-Orridge was getting sidetracked up an alley with those who were into body piercing and mutilation. I too found it mildly amusing that there were people around who had extended their scrotum to enable them to stuff their balls up their arse, but really it was nothing more than freak show antics. It was hardly surprising the music press were beginning to find it difficult to take him seriously.

Mal and Richard tried in vain to explain to me the general philosophy behind Psychic TV. They had both remained commendably loyal to P-Orridge and his new venture. But I sensed Mal, in particular, was having the same reservations as me. One night arriving back at the Hula Kula after a particularly heavy session in the pub, we found Mal in the living room with a couple of Psychic Youth sidekicks (it may have been Stan Bingo and his group Last Few Days). Sleazy had sent them up to Sheffield to put a soundtrack to one of his films. Things were all very intense as they sat in their army fatigues and listened to a tape of the music they had been recording at Western Works. Being an inner member of the Temple of Psychic Youth apparently involved not drinking – a cardinal sin in our eyes. In short, it was no different from being the member of any other cult – in other words miserable.

In any event, Paul wasn't about to let them take over the communal living room. So we staggered in, turned on the telly, and broke open the four packs. Dave was so drunk he sat on a wicker chair which promptly tipped over backwards. However he twisted and turned he just couldn't seem to upright himself or the chair. He steadfastly refused to let go of his can of beer. All credit to him, he never spilt a drop. To us, here was a man who clearly had his priorities in order. To the psychic paratroopers, here was one drunken arsehole. Finally we managed to get Dave back to a vaguely upright position and for half an hour we generally belched and giggled while Thee Psychic ones looked on with disdain. In the end we decided to leave them to get their beauty sleep and dream of Charles Manson, Jim Jones or whoever. We, on the other hand, voted in favour of continuing drinking in Mal's room upstairs.

"Thank fuck you arrived," Mal turned to me, "I've been busting for a drink all night."

seconds too late – "trouble at mill"

As with most of the early eighties Sheffield scene, arty pretensions were never far from the surface in Clock DVA. They, like many others, used slides as a backdrop, and even sometimes appeared with a friend Bob Baker who was known to do a bit of performance art under the name Prior To Intercourse. On one memorable August night at Sheffield's Leadmill club, Baker had set up an elaborate performance piece where he crawled through some plastic tubing whilst loud industrial music throbbed away. The crowd watched Baker making his tortuous progress toward a black plastic sack suspended above the stage. On emerging from the end of the tubing, Baker lunged at the black bag with a knife sending the contents, which as it happened was a load of rotting pig and sheep offal, gushing over the stage. The piece ended up with Baker rolling around in the entrails to the stunned amazement of the crowd.

This was of course all very well for Baker, but it was hardly Paul's idea of rock 'n' roll to have to pick his way through rotting offal to get to his position on stage. He took up the matter with Newton, having noticed a particularly unsavoury lung lurking by his amplifier. Paul insisted that he wouldn't go on until it was cleared up. He reasoned that, as Baker was Newton's friend, the singer should clear away the mess. The singer wasn't inclined to help with clearing away the equipment, let alone offal. Finally, after Baker himself was located and with the offending mess cleared away, the concert got underway.

Not that the band's performance passed without incident. Half way through the frenetic set, in an attempt to liven up an ambivalent crowd, Newton decided to throw his snare drum stand into the audience. The singer would quite often angrily bang away at this drum in time with his vocals. Luckily the discarded stand hit no-one. In fact it was promptly returned to the stage by Tim Owen from the Naked Pygmy Voles (a local band whose music didn't live up to their rather splendid name).

More successful at upsetting the crowd, was the band's decision to set off no less than three strobes at once during their last number. Rather predictably, the result was that a member of the audience went into an epileptic fit. (It is now a well-known fact that strobes have the tendency to do this if used indiscriminately). At the end of the evening they were summoned to the club owner's office and instructed to get their act together or they would never be asked to play there again. As the Leadmill was then run by right-on types serving vegetarian food, no doubt having a stage covered in offal was not their idea of fun.

The band was unrepentant. They were unconcerned about causing ructions. It was typical of the way that Sheffield bands looked towards putting on something special by way of a show. Never afraid of mixing up visual imagery, performance art and music, it might have been pretentious but it was never boring. In truth they launched themselves into these arty kinds of happenings with an endearing naivety which would have been difficult to get away with in London.

However, it was apparent that this line-up of Clock DVA was having problems ironing out their personal differences. There was much rehearsal, but concerts tended to be few and far between. (the Human League and the Cabs weren't exactly touring machines either). One gig Clock DVA did play was the Futurama festival in Leeds along with Siouxsie and the Banshees and a host of other doomladen groups – a kind of gothic Woodstock. Highlights of the concerts were broadcast on TV, and they played a storming version of their most commercial song "Four Hours". For a moment it seemed like they were becoming a striking force.

Another notable gig was at The Clarendon in Hammersmith. We missed The The (we were in the pub) and arrived in time to see Martin Fry and his band Vice Versa. Fry's first stab at pop was much more in keeping with the rest of the experimental scene in Sheffield. Even so, it was easy to detect a keen pop brain at work. Clock DVA and Vice Versa sometimes shared a van on jaunts down to London. Clock DVA being a slightly rougher bunch would play tricks on Fry and his cohorts like pretending to drive off without them at the service station. On the way home from another joint gig at the Moonlight Club in London, the rest of Clock DVA returned to the van to find Martin Fry and Stephen Stapleton discussing the idea of gold lamé suits and working through routines which included Smokey Robinson's "Tracks Of My Tears". Clearly they were about to give birth to ABC.

Clock DVA's Clarendon set was somewhat eclipsed by headliner Fad Gadget who split his head open by bashing it against a snare drum. A short interval ensued as Fad was rushed to a nearby hospital for stitches. Once he resumed the set, the whole evening began to resemble a scene from a David Lynch movie as Gadget pranced around the stage with a huge white turban of a bandage around his head.

This incarnation of Clock DVA played their fair share of support slots. When playing second fiddle to Bauhaus in Heaven, Paul was walking across the hall with his guitar during a sound check, when he overheard Peter Murphy's girlfriend say, "Oooh Peter you have your own guitar tuner, how cute". Paul smiled to himself, Murphy wasn't even the guitarist in Bauhaus. What a load of bullshit the music business could be at times.

Clock DVA were a band fuelled by tension. They could be anything from exhilarating to diabolical. On a good night, just like The Birthday Party, they were capable of conjuring up a post apocalyptic brew of dark terror. They were the kind of support act that could blow anyone off the stage if the mood took them.

On other occasions they really needed their wits about them. Supporting Killing Joke on a short tour that included the Kilburn National was hardly most people's idea of a dream booking. In fact, arguments raged back in Sheffield about how wise it was for them to be accepting the gigs at all. The Joke had a reputation of relishing their support acts being thrown to the mercy of their baying fans. Some lasted a couple of numbers, the more timid like Aztec Camera lasted about 20 seconds. Clock DVA didn't pause long between numbers, so as not to encourage hecklers, but they completed their set without so much as a bottle being thrown – the odd lighted match maybe. It seemed they could even survive in front of Killing Joke fans. That wasn't just cool, it was fucking brave.

the damage is done – "industrial decline"

TG had dissolved, Clock DVA were experiencing growing pains, now cracks were also beginning to appear in Cabaret Voltaire's veneer. Chris Watson had suddenly announced that he was temporarily upping and leaving the group in favour of a job as sound man for Tyne Tees TV. Was the man off his head? The idea of someone quitting a band in favour of a nine-to-five sounded like pure lunacy to me. I'd have signed a pact with the devil to escape from my particular nine-to-five. Surely, the Cabs were riding on a wave. They had already released *Red Mecca*, their most critically acclaimed LP to-date, as well as playing to packed venues at home, in Europe and on the West Coast of America.

Red Mecca continued in a similar vein to *The Voice of America*, but displayed a group clearly thinking about a more musical direction. As drum machines improved, so the beats became more four square. This shift worked admirably on the LP's masterful opening instrumental "A Touch of Evil", but tended toward more monotonous grooves as the LP wore on. Tracks like "A Thousand Ways" clearly outstayed their welcome.

Musical differences had never been mentioned as a reason for Watson's departure, but clearly they were moving in a more conventional direction.

"Well, he always said he'd leave if he wasn't enjoying it anymore," Richard told me in his usual matter-of-fact way.

Typically he wasn't going to let his disappointment show through. Initially it seemed like Chris might at some stage return, but soon it was evident that they were permanently down to two.

As time went on it became obvious that Watson's input, although less tangible, had been important and would leave the band exposed as a two-dimensional entity. Mal, ever the more open, admitted that being a duo felt strange.

"Christ, I suppose that makes us the Simon & Garfunkel of the industrial scene," he joked as he squeezed in alongside me at our crowded table in the Beehive.

And so it was, that Mal began to play "Art Garfunkel" singer to Richard's "Paul Simon" composer role. Initially the two of them carried on pretty much regardless, going up to the studio and generally hanging out in Sheffield. Record sales were still healthy enough for them to continue in the rock 'n' roll lifestyle that they had become accustomed to.

Even so, it was noticeable that they had lost the internal democracy inherent in being a three-piece. There was now a growing rivalry between Richard and Mal created by Watson's departure. They were in some respects too similar, Chris Watson had been the perfect non-rock 'n' roll foil for the two of them to bounce ideas off. In the resulting jockeying for position, they were also rather wary about each other's solo material. Neither should have worried that much – being even less commercial than the Cabs' material (yes, you read it right, *less* commercial) it was hardly going to rival Duran Duran or whoever was then riding the top of the charts.

Nevertheless, as the Cabs prepared for 1982, life in Sheffield was generally still going rather swimmingly. They had set up their own label Doublevision, the initial remit being to get involved with video. Paul Smith, an enterprising guy from Nottingham (as is his namesake the fashion designer), was brought in to oversee all the administrative duties. Some indication of his abilities were amply demonstrated when he miraculously managed to get Doublevision's second video release *Johnny Yesno* distributed through the W.H.Smith chain of shops.

This short feature film was directed by film maker Peter Care, who had quickly fallen in with Richard and Mal, and together with his Irish girlfriend became regulars on our drinking jaunts. After failing to get a big band soundtrack for *Johnny Yesno*, Care had settled on accompanying music by Cabaret Voltaire.

What was becoming increasingly clear to anyone with more than a passing interest in industrial music, was that there were now a lot of other groups picking up on what TG and the Cabs were pioneering. Firstly there were those who were going even further into translating these ideas into a more commercial framework. Initially the Cabs associated themselves with these newly emerging bands. 23 Skidoo trundled up to Western Works to record, and Richard and Mal went down to London to help produce Test Department. The latter was an experience that left them jaded. After spending a whole weekend endlessly re-mixing tracks, Test Department finally brought out their own mix. It was all very well being seen as the Godfathers of Industrial music, but it was also all too easy to be swallowed up by the competition. After all, even those nice boys from Basildon, Depeche Mode, had started to metal bash.

Despite Mal's obvious reservations about the direction in which the whole industrial thing was going, for a while their Doublevision label expanded from video and started releasing records by all sorts of like-minded groups. Ignoring Paul Smith's intuitive nose for a winner, Richard and Mal immediately demonstrated their failings as label bosses by turning down the first record by Sonic

Youth. This left Smith no option but to set up his own label Blast First.

At the other end of the scale there were those intent on pushing industrial music into ever more extreme corners. As a result the whole industrial scene was becoming a parody of itself. Richard told me horrifying stories about groups that he corresponded with who were trying increasingly gross things to attract attention to themselves. SPK had even allegedly made a video of simulated oral sex between a dead body and a severed penis.

Then there were groups like Whitehouse emerging who were hellbent on out TG-ing TG. Suddenly being an industrial band meant musically celebrating the actions of Yorkshire Ripper Peter Sutcliffe and generally being as objectionable as possible. Whilst TG had their moments of bad taste – such as their reported press release on the death of John Lennon which simply stated "Give Guns A Chance" – the impression was that tongues were placed in cheeks. Now other bands were picking up on the bad taste and not on the humour. Obviously it was time to move on.

As a result the Cabs slowly began to disentangle themselves from these Industrial extremes. Their answer was to record an LP that went further down the road that *Red Mecca* had signposted. This turned out to be their last record for Rough Trade. It was a record that many regarded as the crowning glory of their early years – *2x45*. Named because it was a double 12" that played at 45 rpm, some of the tracks were left over from sessions featuring Chris Watson. For the rest of the double LP they augmented their line-up with extra musicians – most notably Eric Random (with whom they had already recorded a live LP under the name the Pressure Company) and drummers Nort and Alan Fish. Certain tracks were positively funky and clearly locking into a Can-type groove, whilst "Yashar" aped Middle-Eastern musical scales. *2x45* generally benefited from the fact that saxes, guitars and keyboards were used in a much more conventional fashion to create riffs and melodies. Clearly they had learned to layer their sounds in a much less abrasive way.

As I sat in an isolated London orbit, the gravitational pull exerted by planet Cabaret Voltaire was becoming ever stronger. As a result Dave and I recorded and released another tape. One side was an ambient atmospheric noise kind of thing, not really very good. We were falling into the same trap as a lot of the Sheffield groups we were drunkenly eager to take the piss out of – we were beginning to sound like a bad Cabaret Voltaire. Side two concentrated on the fact that we could actually play instruments and conjured up a form of muzak from around the world. Thus one track was Japanese sounding, another had a flamenco groove, another was a spoof of a Jacques Tati soundtrack and entitled "Monsieur Le Supermarche" – a track which we described as "music to shop by". There was even a track where an Irish friend of ours played a mandolin reel over our backing track. Fuck knows if it worked or not, even Richard thought it sounded weird. We guessed he was in a position to know.

We released the tape under the name of *The Sound of Concrete*. In the end it outsold our first tape by 20 copies. Once again it was reviewed in *Sounds*, an event that prompted another early visit to the pub.

split second feeling – "the day the clocks stopped"

It was only a matter of time before something happened within the unstable cauldron that was Clock DVA. The first inkling of irreconcilable differences appeared when the rest of the band found out that *Thirst*'s LP sleeve, instead of featuring a co-production credit for the whole band, just featured Newton's name. It was obvious the singer didn't want to be in a band, he wanted a backing band. It was an all too familiar story of an ego out of control. The other members, particularly Paul and Charlie had egos of their own to contend with, and weren't prepared to let Newton run roughshod over them in that way.

Newton was also thinking about changing the musical direction toward something altogether more funky (a constant Sheffield obsession). On the way back from a gig he had announced his intention to make the band sound more like A Certain Ratio.

"Did he really say that!" Paul and Charlie turned to each other in disbelief.

"A Certain fucking Ratio! God help us!" Paul muttered under his breath. His dislike for their tepid funk was well known. He didn't know whether to laugh or cry.

One of Newton's new lyrics was the appropriately titled song "Bone of Contention". That's exactly what the newly proposed direction became. "We're not fucking playing that sort of stuff," was the reaction from the rest of the band. Newton, being from the same Sheffield soul boy clique as Oakey, the Cabs et al, was still obsessed with white boy funk. It was obvious that there was no way Newton was going to drag Paul or Charlie away from Captain Beefheart and towards James Brown.

The end, when it came, wasn't so much a firework display of temper as the fizzling out of a spent sparkler. "Oh look, we've got a gig in Brighton," Paul noted on browsing the music papers. What the singer had in fact failed to tell them was that Clock DVA did indeed have a gig, but that a whole new band of musicians were being invited along for the ride. "Well, I guess we've been sacked," they mused. Paul was philosophical, but underneath it all I knew it smarted.

Having discarded the jazzier shackles of his previous line-up, Newton put together Clock DVA mark III. In his efforts to exert absolute control, he even dumped his bass playing flatmate. In any event it made little difference, as a few weeks later Jud was pronounced dead from a heroin overdose. Few people were that surprised.

For the new line-up Newton collected together a more compliant bunch of musicians from the Sheffield scene, including John Caruthers who was later to join Siouxsie and the Banshees, and David Palmer who went on to play with ABC, Yellow Magic

Orchestra and eventually joined Rod Stewart's band. Newton managed to persuade Polydor that his new band was a good prospect, and the resulting LP *Advantage* was much more commercial. Also, in places, it was rather good. Understandably, Paul and the rest of the sacked band couldn't bring themselves to say so. Instead they re-grouped with a new bass player who, unlike Jud, could at least tune his strings. They settled on the name The Box and it was business as usual.

The Box tried a number of singers, one whom sort of whooped like a Red Indian chief but couldn't sing in tune. They even played two gigs with Mal on vocals – a marriage of styles that was quite successful in its own way. For their concert at Heaven, supporting another new tepid funk outfit called Shreikback, they were advertised as "Cabaret Voltaire and Clock DVA move on" – Richard apparently was not amused. He had flatly refused to attend the only other gig of this line-up at The Marples in Sheffield. Richard also nixed Mal's idea that Paul should add some more professionally adept guitar playing to some of the Cabs' material.

The Box eventually advertised for a singer. By far the best response came from Pete Hope from Hertford. Vocally somewhere between Tom Waits and Howlin' Wolf, he moved up to Sheffield with his young family. Hope was a good singer and useful lyricist, even if he somewhat lacked Newton's arrogance and stage charisma. In truth, although Newton could be awkward and unpredictable, they were also missing his leadership. As a newly established co-operative the material was beginning to become so angular and discordant that at times it jarred like a dentist's drill. Paul did his best to keep things together when a track sounded like it might implode under the weight of its own atonality. But it was soon clear that if it was going to happen at all, it was going to be an uphill struggle.

eddie's out — "all changing houses"

Drinking sprees in Sheffield carried on unabated. Every couple of months, I would hurriedly throw a few clothes into a bag on a Friday night and head off to Victoria bus station. So as not to waste valuable drinking time I would down a greasy burger at Leicester Forest, and then watch night descend over the disused steelworks as the bus turned off at junction 33. Arriving in Sheffield in time for a good few rounds in the pub, we'd then pick up some afters supplies and onwards we went.

The rest of the weekend was spent catching up with the local gossip. Who was now in what band. What the main players like the Human League were up to. We would regularly reconvene with a whole bunch of characters like John Clayton, former bass player of 2.3 who had played on the Cabs' "Three Mantras". He looked like a young Geoffrey Boycott and could spit out the word "bastard" like no-one else I'd heard. Then there was always the perennial Ron and Alan, the geordie boys. Their band Hula was still endlessly rehearsing and re-rehearsing down in the Hula Kula cellar. But duck and dive as they might they just couldn't break out of the shadow of Cabaret Voltaire.

However, increasingly I detected that the pivotal axis was shifting. Symbolic of this shift was the day that we were greeted by Paul only to be told that the Beehive was now off limits. Essentially, the place had been redecorated and rechristened something trendy like Busby's. The landlord had decided to pick up on the early eighties entrepreneurial vibe. His idea was that he would capitalise on the pub's success as the centre of the music scene, thereby attracting an even bigger crowd by turning the place into some kind of theme pub. Of course he shot himself in the foot. When a whole gaggle of Northern Sharons and Tracys moved in, the music crowd moved out. After some exploratory work on the part of Richard and Paul to find an alternative hostelry, everyone changed locations. The winner in all this was the landlord of The Washington, an old fashioned boozer with a sizeable collection of teapots.

However, the buzz of the Beehive was never really recreated in The Washington, even though the whole in-crowd was generally partying on regardless. Everyone was still applying the eye-liner – hair styles still changed almost weekly. But, whilst all the budding musicians had swarmed around the Beehive's long lounge bar, the new venue was more of a family-type pub. Rather than moving from conversation to conversation, people huddled into different groups. What was once a scene full of people talking about how their group was going to follow in the path of the Human League or the Cabs, was now replaced with the realisation that perhaps their band wasn't going anywhere after all. (Although, after over a decade of trying, Pulp for one did finally make it and their drummer, Nick, philanthropically bought The Washington pub to prevent its "redevelopment" along the lines of the Beehive).

Richard, as well as changing locals, had also moved to a new house. Following a number of break-ins he had become nervy about living in the crime-infested red light area and no-one could blame him for wanting to get out. His new house was a comfortable three-storey terrace house and he and Lynne were as hospitable as ever. Richard had even taken to playing me advance tapes of the group's latest recordings and asking me what I thought. Very flattering! But what the fuck did I know?

Generally, upheavals seemed to be the name of the day. Everyone was tired of tolerating cold houses that leaked heat like sieves. As a result Mal, Paul, Ron and Alan, decided to uproot themselves from the Hula Kula and leave Henry the ghost to his spooky goings-on. Mrs Thatcher was endlessly whining on about England becoming some property owning utopia, so Mal decided to buy a house. Actually the suggestion had been Paul's – the plan was that Mal, as the only earner, would pay the mortgage while the rest of the guys rented rooms off him. As a result, they packed up the mass of junk, equipment and general musical memorabilia and debunked out to a house in Hillsborough not far from the football ground.

Hillsborough is a close knit community that doesn't take to outsiders with much relish. The joke goes that interbreeding is rife. Their welcoming committee took the form of anonymous phone calls. "Fuck off queers", announced the voice at the end of the phone. Having espied four blokes sharing, those hiding behind their twitching curtains had jumped to the wrong conclusion. As the never-ending parade of girlfriends started to show up at the house, so the calls dried up.

One of the features that had so attracted them to their new house was the bar that stood like an altarpiece in the middle of the living room. Made from large blocks of stone, it was complete with optics and glass mirrors. "Mal has taken out a mortgage on a bar with a house attached," the others quipped.

As my appetite for booze bingeing remained undimmed, I was obviously as thrilled with their new bar as they were. When not taking turns to play barman, much time was spent in The Castle, a local pub where the landlady looked like one of the McWhirter twins. She had the strange habit of rationing the ice cubes, "one lump or two?" she would ask. Maybe it was this pettiness that had prompted her husband to stab her. In any event we were informed that he was residing at Her Majesty's pleasure for attempted murder.

The other patrons in The Castle looked askance as our overdressed, leather-trousered and heavily made-up brigade marched in to order an alarmingly exotic array of drinks. The locals would look into their pint glasses and chuckle to their mates with a general "look at the state of them" gleam in their eye. True, we were a bit incongruous with the surroundings, but I liked it in there – it was a pub after all. The jukebox even had a version of "I Can See Clearly Now" by the visually challenged Ray Charles – a joke that kept us amused for hours.

On returning from The Castle we would always fix ourselves more drinks. One night Mal and I decided to make cocktails out of any old ingredients we could find. Whilst someone else loaded up the uncensored version of *Caligula* into the video machine, Mal and me amused ourselves by gauging people's reaction to sipping our mixture of Vodka, Pernod, Hazelnut Yoghurt and the juice from a tin of grapefruit segments. Not recommended by the way.

In general, the Hillsborough house had a more sedate air to it than the Hula Kula. Not only was it centrally heated, but it was more tastefully decorated with pot plants and large black blinds. Mal was more talked about than seen, as he had the top floor self-contained flat complete with bathroom and large stereo system. However, the real reason he was an absentee landlord was because he was spending much of his time in London.

Paul, Alan and Ron were all by now on the dole, so money continued to be tight. Despite all the excited chatter about records, advances, record companies and the like, only Mal was able to make a living out of it all. The others would look jealously as his PRS statement clunked onto the doormat. The Cabs now had accountants, equipment budgets that they could offset against tax. The rest of them would have given their eye teeth to be in his position.

As Paul's chance of making a living from music was receding, Dave and I used to march him into the job centre. "Isn't it about time you found yourself a proper job?" we would jibe. As the eighties progressed, unemployment had begun to spiral out of control, especially in the North. All that seemed to be available were the weirdest collection of jobs. I doubt whether Paul could have qualified for "Shepherd wanted for farm just outside Rotherham". Better recompense could be had from "Aeronautical engineers required for Saudi Arabia". However, I couldn't quite see Paul advising a Sheikh on which private jet to buy. Which guitar maybe.

bad self – "starting to gather speed"

For the poorer members of the Hillsboro household, the favourite night out was to go down to Penny's on a Monday night where all drinks were 25p. Typical of the trendy clubs that would spring up from time to time, Penny's was a transient "place to be seen". Less official, were the late night drinking/dancing events organised by an enterprising individual. With a late licence, a few loud speakers, these were early versions of raves. One such night, in a club named Cleos, Dave and I helped everyone to drinks by leaning over the bar and pouring out pints while the barman wasn't looking. As a result we got drunker than ever.

Richard would jump onto the dancefloor every time James Brown came on, but always refrain from taking off his overcoat. I meanwhile chatted to Lynne, a fellow non-dancer. She continued to like Paul's friends from London as we weren't in a group and jawing endlessly on about our next record, or how we were going to make it big.

Another evening we all made our way up these rickety stairs into a disused warehouse where a couple of Hell's Angels guarded the stash of beer cans that were on sale. The music was so loud that the old dilapidated floorboards creaked under the strain of those dancing. Unlicenced and unauthorised, I guess the authorities would have had little sympathy if the whole place had caved in and crushed the lot of us.

More ominously, I was now happy to engage in hoovering powdery lines from shiny surfaces. Having spent the last couple of years watching the Sheffield scene buzz around on amphetamines, the call of the sulphate was just too much to refuse. Very quickly I realised that for me this wasn't going to be an occasional pick me up – in a flash I had seen the blazing light of a new religion in the shape of a little pile of white powder. As the speed surged its way through my bloodstream, I wondered why I had wasted all those years smoking dope. Here was the kind of high that I was finally looking for. The rush had a tingle that was almost sexual. One sniff and I was hooked. I might as well as had "instant speed freak" tattooed on my forehead. "Just add lager" the recipe read.

With speed there was none of that "Awhh, OK, yeah man" of dope-speak, it was all "Come on, let's fucking go for it". Now the general silliness and giggling that accompanied a good session of spliff seemed all the more tame and childish. Also, with speed I could drink even more than ever. Whoopee, come on, let's fucking go for it!

As a result, weekends in Sheffield were now putting my body through increasingly rigorous excesses. The moment we arrived in Sheffield on a Friday night the drinking and snorting would begin, and finish with aching limbs as I collapsed into Victoria bus station on Sunday night. Monday morning I would wonder how the fuck I could clear my head and slow my heart rate down.

Back in London I lost no time in procuring a regular supply and after a couple of months I was rarely without a couple of grammes burning a hole in my pocket. On speed I acquired a sense of self-confidence that I had so far lacked. The whole sensation of being superhuman for a brief 4 or 5 hours appealed to me. Amphetamines were also very cheap. Of course I knew all about pop stars and their expensive coke binges in nightclubs. My Depot wages could only stretch to speed – the rougher the better. I loved the whole thing about it; the mirror, the chopping, the snorting, the taste, the jangling arms, the beating heart. At last I had found my poison.

spies in the wires – "trouble at the yard"

As the clock got watched and one arduous day followed another, to say that I was getting to be part of the furniture at the Council was an understatement. I could now find my way around the Depot's treacherous and machine-ridden pathways almost blindfold. Certain corners of the yard were so cluttered with old road sweepers, tractors, highways and parks equipment that it was like an industrial graveyard. In amongst the scrap iron, the Council's cats – maintained at ratepayer's expense to keep the yard's rat population down – roamed at will. There was also a large rabbit that had built a home under one of the prefabricated huts. The whole place was a little ecosystem with a hierarchical structure of both the animal and human kind. I had pretty much found my place in the human pyramid, buried deep in the tomb of the Transport Department. By 1983 even my parents had stopped enquiring of me, "When exactly are you going to find yourself a proper career?"

Mrs Thatcher's Conservative government was coming to the end of its first term. To those of us less than convinced about the direction she was pushing the country, her determination now looked unstoppable. The Falklands factor seemed set to return her to power on a tide of jingoism. But Local Government was proving to be a more lingering thorn in her side than the Argies had been. Although she had already made some noises about bringing all these "Loony Left" Councils into line, it was yet to become a reality. She was convinced that Local Authorities were over-manned bureaucracies run by inefficient and corrupt regimes. The Conservative publicity machine started going into overdrive as they dragged up scare stories to discredit the left-wing town halls.

As if to prove her right, certain corrupt practices at the Depot were being brought into the glare of the spotlight now shining down from the Civic Centre. Some meticulous auditor had uncovered a fiddle that was being operated in the very same workshop I worked in. Of course as my over-powdered nose had been buried in the crossword I hadn't noticed a thing. So oblivious was I that I barely noticed as the Controller of Engineering marched through the workshop's massive sliding metal doors to announce that one of our number was under suspension. Like many, I was still surprised that any of the Civic Centre bigwigs could find their way into the yard.

It transpired there was a major discrepancy. A whole load of vehicle spares; specifically batteries and tyres remained unaccounted for. During the following weeks scrawny and miserable looking faces from the Civic Centre swarmed over my office, taking away bundles of paperwork with them. The end result was that one of the fitters and Ivan the Transport Manager were sacked. A few others, like Cap'n Birdseye, left the sinking ship before being swept under the rising tide of suspicion. For my part, I was surprised at the scale of the scam they had uncovered. Amounts varied depended on which person I talked to, but noughts were being added to estimates almost daily. People in other departments kept pestering me for juicy details, but I really couldn't tell them anything. Not surprisingly, I hadn't been approached to take part in any misdoing. Exactly what was I supposed to do with a load of old car spares?

It was a further indication that certain people at the Civic Centre were finally waking up to the idea that the Depot existed. Put simply, they realised that something was going to have to be done about this ungovernable principality in the Borough's kingdom. Names that up until then had just been entries in the internal phone book now started showing their faces. Their expressions were stern and unforgiving.

The advance guard, in the shape of Mr Evans, wandered around the year with a smug, "I told you so", expression on his face. For the first time, Union officials looked genuinely concerned about their ability to cover this one up. Even the main Union power base of Ernie the rottweiler, and Gladys, a grandmother who smoked roll-ups, seemed impotent in the face of such a flood of interest in the happenings down the Depot.

It was now assumed that everyone was on some kind of fiddle, we were all guilty until proven innocent. But no matter how much they pried they couldn't dig up much more dirt. A lot of acts had been cleaned up very quickly. The shock wave caused by the auditors' invasion of the workshop proved to shore up many of the remaining leaks. "It's not worth getting sacked for," was the general conclusion.

All this rather neatly coincided with the dawning conclusion that sooner or later the Council was going to have to fight off the threat of impending privatisation. If they'd wanted to stage a coup, or pick out a couple of scapegoats, they couldn't have timed it better. The management was getting to grips with the idea that they could actually sack people. However much moaning the Union did, there was little they could do about it. Shop stewards were already talking about the "good old days" when the Council chamber was invaded by Union members and committees buckled at the very thought of a refuse strike. The real result was the free-and-easy attitude that had prevailed over the last four years was now replaced with a nervous uneasiness where everyone watched their backs.

Of course there were those who took little heed of the warnings that were being passed down from on high. As the new Conservative mentality was beginning to grip the country, some Local Authority employees still considered themselves immune. It would take a while before many Council workers realised they couldn't hide behind the safety screen of public service forever. There was a gung-ho spirit around that believed that however bad things got, it would be a while longer before the Tories and their evil initiatives could get at us in our hidey hole. Or perhaps

Arthur Scargill and his heavy brigade would come riding over the hillside with a last minute cavalry charge.

For my part I was scared that venturing into the outside world would mean being swallowed up by a new breed of superhuman vultures known as Thatcher's children. To the kids now leaving school, punk was a thing of the past, let alone the love, peace and freedom of the sixties. They didn't want to know about stupid idiots wallowing in utopian misapprehensions. The new intake, the class of the eighties weren't particularly interested in LSD or Timothy Leary. They wanted their drugs in the shape of a *Wall Street*-like flurry of cocaine, and their drink by way of expensive bottled lager. Like an army of miniature American Psychos they were riding a new capitalist tank already showing signs of careering out of control.

Times had moved on. The music business was now a grown up leisure industry. Many of the mavericks and oddballs that had proliferated in the late sixties and seventies were either dead or forgotten. The success of Virgin Records very much typified the tide of change in the eighties. From spending much of the seventies championing alternative bands, running a mail order operation and generally subverting the norm, they were now concentrating on bland marketing campaigns for benign monoliths like Phil Collins. Richard Branson had met the challenge of the eighties head on and come out grinning like a cheshire cat.

In my own small way, it would be dishonest to claim that I hadn't been dragged along with the times. I had been promoted again. Hanging around in Local Authority service for any length of time meant getting shoved up the ladder merely by default. Whether I liked it or not, I seemed to be working my way up the Council hierarchy. I think a lot of the time they felt it was simply easier that they chose the devil they knew rather than import a "troublemaker" from outside.

My move away from the vehicle repair workshop, Blowjob Bill and his pornography collection, was back into the main Transport office where I was to take over the reins from Alec who was retiring. Jock had already preceded him. Joe had left in a fit of pique no doubt connected with being told to truncate his tea breaks, and even Margie had finally retired. Typical of the re-organisations that were afoot, three people were now expected to do the work previously done by five. So, whilst Alec had bathed in the luxury afforded to him of four members of staff, I was in charge of two newly appointed clerical assistants.

However, neither of the staff I was presented with was in keeping with the new broom sweeping across the yard. Wilfred was a deeply religious 60-year-old with a heart condition. He was typical of those still looking at the Council as a pre-retirement home. David was more typical of the old maxim that it isn't what you know, but who you know that counts. He had been dropped on our department from on-high because he happened to be a Highways Supervisor's son. David's main interest in life was reading *Angling Times* and he also had the rather disturbing habit of wheeling his bike into the office and parking it next to his desk.

My shift upwards meant I was no longer one of the minions whose only concern was opening their pay packet at the end of the month. It was made clear to me that I was expected, along with my dynamic two-some, to shoulder some responsibility and take an interest in the way that Council affairs were being run.

"You might be taking over Alec's job, but we don't expect you to mimic his working practices," I was told by the new acting Transport Manager. I took this to mean that I wasn't expected to go walkabout up at the Civic Centre.

As I donned a remotely smart jacket and tie, I tried to kid myself that I wasn't being swallowed up by an increasingly alien world. Nonetheless I couldn't help imagining Maggie and her odious cohorts rubbing their hands at the sight of local government workers like myself finally being drawn into their efficiency drives. Members of the dustmen's Union that had once shared a joke with me in the yard, now assumed that I had crossed some imaginary picket line and become part of the management. They still chatted with me but there was now a distance between us that precluded me being let into their innermost thoughts. "Micky boy" soon became "Mick", some were even addressing me as "Mr Fish". In my new role as manager, they squinted at me with "you used to be alright" looks on their faces.

Indeed, I was being forced to see the whole affair from the Civic Centre's side of the fence. I regularly attended meetings in committee rooms I had previously only heard about through reports in the local press. I was also being included at the bottom of memo distribution lists, not to mention mainly redundant and yawn-inducing training courses.

It was symptomatic of the fact that the top guns at the Civic Centre were finally beginning to wake up to the threat of private competition. Certain members of the ludicrously top heavy and overpaid Administration Department were now jumping around on hot coals, predicting doom and gloom. Early retirement was becoming a particularly attractive option. The new officers who were brought in as replacements attempted to crank some get-up-and-go into the rusty old machine. Many of these were tough nuts from the world of private enterprise. Unlike their predecessors, they were not scared to get their hands dirty and come down to the Depot. No longer could we orbit like a disconnected satellite.

Many people at the Depot looked horrified at the way things seemed to be going. They talked in hushed tones about new Departmental heads with worse reputations than the Gestapo. In a series of panicky knee jerk reactions, there were now more new brooms at the Council than at a witches' convention. A typical example of just such a bristling newcomer was my administrative counterpart in the Cleansing Department.

"I'll be at the Depot for a maximum of two years." Steve told me as he brushed aside some loitering dustmen and made his way to introduce himself.

Apparently, this would be enough time to get things sorted out, then it was onwards and upwards. It was not that I disliked Steve – even though he had already negotiated two grade rises for himself

– I don't think I understood him. He might as well have been talking Bulgarian for all I knew. But it was soon being made very clear to me that this was a language I was supposed to be learning and I was meant to be aping Steve's attitude and commitment to change.

Part of my new job was to oversee the payment of a myriad of bonuses, inclement weather supplements, tool allowances, man short payments, task and finish times and overtime rates that made up a refuse driver's pay. The whole ludicrous system had built up over the years, whereby instead of negotiating basic pay rises that they couldn't justify to Council committee, they upped a person's wages by adding on all sorts of little incentive payments. In short, the whole thing was a mess and a throw back to the days when the Union ruled the roost. If Maggie Thatcher needed any persuading that she was right to be curbing local authority power, then filling in a driver's weekly timesheet was it. With such a maze of Council personnel regulations and payments to fathom, the chances were I might have to do some work!

Those in control at the Civic Centre were no longer happy to let budgetary control run amok. To put it bluntly the never-ending well of finance was running dry. Every week there were rumours of re-organsations and assimilations, whatever they were. Every department was tightening its belt. But more than that, out-and-out squabbling was beginning to break out between departments about who was wasting the most money.

"Why should we pay for your expensive and badly maintained vehicles?" was typical of the accusations being levelled at us by departments like Building Works.

"Yeah but your drivers are mistreating the vehicles, and anyway your building maintenance charges are outrageous," we would hit back in return.

Everyone began to gripe that they could get the same work done cheaper by hiring contractors from the private sector, which of course was just what Mrs T wanted us to do. The reason why outside firms could do everything so much cheaper was because they didn't have the same overheads as we did. To put it bluntly we were still paying for all those fuckers sitting around in their over-heated Civic Centre offices. Of course pointing this out to top managers was tantamount to signing our own death warrant.

Not only were my lunch hours beginning to shrink into non-existence, but the whole workforce was declining before my eyes. More often than not, when someone left, their post was not re-advertised. Slowly the workforce of broom-pushers, weirdos, alcoholics and misfits began to dissipate into the ether. The question of where these people would find alternative employment was not our concern. The Conservatives were snipping the strings to all the safety nets, thus guaranteeing many would be washed like excess effluent down the borough's drains.

The only choice for those of us left was to learn to swim. I was advised that I had the choice of going with the flow and using the changes to my advantage, or hang onto old working practices and drown. Whether I liked it or not, it was months since I'd even looked at a crossword, and I was being drawn into meetings where we were continually discussing ways of fending off the impending threat of privatisation.

With what money I had accumulated – my previous regrading had finally come through in the form of a backdated lump sum – I took the plunge and signed up for a mortgage on a small two bedroom flat. After all, I had already donned a tie, I might as well go the whole hog and get mortgaged. Everyone was talking about what a great investment property was, and house prices were beginning to rise steadily. "Get in while you can" was the wording, writ in letters 10 feet tall.

At first, my new neighbours looked upon me rather warily. One of them had introduced herself to me after finding me slumped at the bottom of the iron stairs to the flats, nodded out drunk. Day-time I would stroll off to the Depot, my Council-issue donkey jacket covering up a shirt and tie, whilst in the evenings and week-ends I would don leather trousers, eyeliner, and sniffing rather profusely head off down the pub or off to a gig. In truth I probably looked a right cunt in both. I was far too skinny and weedy to carry off even the smallest of workman's donkey jackets, whilst the whole leather and eyeliner thing was of course influenced by the Sheffield scene. If all these Northern guys could get away with traipsing out to the pub with eyeliner on, then so could I. But underneath it all, I knew I just couldn't wear it with the same aplomb. I was also scared that in the rush to get to work on Monday morning I might forget to wash under my eyes. My fellow workers at the Depot thought I was strange enough already without having that to contend with.

the crackdown – "everything goes pop"

Paul's band The Box had not so much had their hopes dashed as had the lid closed on them. Just as socialism was being abandoned wholesale, so anyone trying to make it with such patently uncommercial music was having a hard time of it. The indie/punk launch pad that had lit the Cabs touch paper was now firing off more blanks than rocketing anyone into the charts. Even Rough Trade, the godfather of the indie labels, was beginning to show signs of strain. When run like a small co-operative, they had been a happy little ship. The growing pains of expansion had left the ship open to financial shipwreck and even worse, internal mutiny.

Bands like The Box looked more and more like they were fighting some kind of rearguard action. Just like Arthur Scargill was being lampooned for his views, so anyone making defiant music was beginning to be looked on as some sort of pariah. Nonetheless, they had got themselves a record deal with a guy called Andy MacDonald who had just set up his own label Go! Discs.

I had first encountered MacDonald a few months previously at the Hula Kula, when I had wandered into the kitchen to find the very odd sight of this guy in a suit, drinking tea and listening to Marvin Gaye on his walkman. This was not exactly the usual type of visitor to the house. My initial reaction had been to run upstairs and warn the guys that the landlord had come round to repossess the kitchen table. As it turned out MacDonald was up in Sheffield to scout for talent for his new label. In the end, The Box were his first signing and I wondered at the sense of a man who really thought that he could make a success of their harsh racket. However, he was a man of considerable nous and The Box soon had their first session on Kid Jensen's Radio 1 evening show. Anyone who could organise that was obviously going somewhere as the later success of Go! Discs proved.

In the April of 1983, Dave and I put our Teac, guitars and drum machines to one side. We had tentatively started recording some more commercially-orientated songs with the view of producing a demo tape. But the events surrounding the possibility a publishing venture had hijacked our attention. In the weeks following my speed-racked conversation with Mal that night in Heaven, we sat down the pub to think about how to realise a book about Cabaret Voltaire.

I sat in my newly acquired flat, trying to imagine how on earth anyone went about writing a book. My surroundings weren't providing me with much inspiration and the lack of any central heating usually sent me scurrying for the warmth of the pub.

The Cabs were still riding relatively high. As a more established entity than The Box, the mainstream seemed ready to embrace them. Tired of being seen as typical of the indie scene, they genuinely seemed ready to make a stab at the big time. This was helped by the fact that Mal was now regularly commuting down from Sheffield to stay with his new girlfriend Karen in a flat off the Finchley Road in north-west London. As a result he could keep his fingers on a bigger pulse than simply what was happening in the small incestuous Sheffield scene.

The Cabs' ship was still holding a steady course when it was blown onto an even faster track by a transatlantic trade wind. "Yashar" from 2x45 had been picked up and re-mixed by John Robie in Arthur Baker's New York studio and released on Factory.

The fact that a hip dance producer had seen some dance potential in one of their tracks chuffed them both to bits. It was easy to see their brains churning over the prospect of entering a whole new musical universe. Finally, here was the passport out of "indie country" they had been looking for. The first tentative building blocks were now in place for the bridge between experimental music and the dance-floor. It was a melding that would spawn such a musical rave explosion a few years on.

But it was also the death of the old Cabaret Voltaire. As two Northern soul boys at heart, they had always been obsessed by dance music, but as "non-musicians" they had never really had an inkling of how to go about it. This chance remix gave them the opportunity to redirect their music away from the avant-garde and toward the dancefloor. Richard and Mal hardly gave a second thought about making the switch. Had Chris Watson still been around it might have been an altogether different matter.

So, by the time I started work on the book, it was all change in the Cabaret Voltaire camp. They had severed their ties with Rough Trade (not difficult, it was an album-by-album arrangement) and signed up with Stevo as their manager. After starting the Some Bizarre label, Stevo had rocketed to success on the back of Soft Cell's "Tainted Love". Very quickly he had become a sort of Machiavellian svengali for Industrial music. At the peak of his activities he could actually boast a roster that included Psychic TV, the Cabs, Einstürzende Neubauten, Test Dept, The The, Foetus, and of course Marc Almond.

It was certainly a coup on a grand scale. Not because he had managed to entice these groups into his management set-up, but because he went on to procure considerable mainstream media coverage for what was essentially uncommercial music.

In any event, Stevo was notorious for the unconventional way he conducted his business. Contract negotiations could be hammered out at railway stations at midnight, additional clauses might contain anything from bubble cars to teddy bears. For a while he seemed to have the Midas touch and it wasn't long before he had found the Cabs a deal with Virgin Records. Richard proudly showed me the brand new CD player that had been thrown in as part of their deal. The only snag was that there was still little for him to play on it. OMD's *Architecture and Morality* was not Richard's idea of home entertainment.

Another of Stevo's funnier ruses was to have a limited edition set of bronze dildos cast, with the names of some of the major labels with whom he'd had dealings engraved on them.

"Umm, very nice," I said, as Richard proudly handed around a bronze dildo for our inspection. I couldn't help thinking what a strange business the record industry was becoming.

As well as a deal with Virgin for the Cabs, Stevo negotiated a 6-album option for Psychic TV with CBS. This particular contract included a year's worth of free baby food for P-Orridge's new baby. Gen had presumably had a complete change of heart from the time when, backstage at the Fetish Night Out, TG were overheard singing, "Who do we hate, we hate Stevo" to the tune of "We Are Devo".

Stevo had persuaded CBS that there was some commercial potential lurking within Psychic TV's ranks. As a multi-national record company they had failed to detect the direction in which P-Orridge's new outfit was heading. They could be forgiven for this misunderstanding, it was difficult enough for TG fans like myself to disentangle the magickal and nonsensical gobbledygook attached to their music. The resulting albums were on the whole incomprehensible – even japery like getting a choir boy to sing a Charles Manson song just didn't seem funny any more. Not surprisingly CBS dropped them after just two LPs. After managing to part acrimoniously with Chris & Cosey, P-Orridge now fell out with Peter "Sleazy" Christopherson. The latter went off to form Coil, whilst P-Orridge soldiered on with Psychic TV as a kind of one-man crusade. Quite what he was crusading for or against was pretty much anyone's guess.

Virgin obviously saw Sheffield as a rich seam that they could mine. They stumped up in the region of £50,000 for the Cabs having reaped rewards from two of Sheffield's other bands, the Human League and Heaven 17. The Human League had by now split into two camps. Phil Oakey had picked up Susanne Sulley and Joanne Catherall in a Sheffield nightclub called the Crazy Daisy and gone wholeheartedly pop. The other two, Martin Ware and Ian Craig Marsh had formed Heaven 17 with a suave looking singer Glen Gregory and had also adopted a pop agenda. Heaven 17 may have been another name taken from *A Clockwork Orange*, but there was little to confront in their music. People in Sheffield were very taken with their minor hit, the anti-Reagan single "We Don't Need This Fascist Groove Thang". Although its heart was obviously in the right place, I thought the record stank to the very end of its final groove thangey. Ware's comment that, "We've got all the talent, they haven't," seemed all the more disingenuous when Oakey's new outfit started having hit after hit. Heaven 17 eventually had some hits of their own, but they struggled to catch up with the likes of "Don't You Want Me Baby".

Finally there was ABC who had also jumped on the pop band-wagon. They were now riding high with their sophisticated pop symphonics, produced by Trevor Horn and championed by Paul Morley.

The first real surprise of the Cabs' Virgin deal was that some shrewd individual had enticed them out of their Western Works shell to record their new LP at a commercial London studio. The fact that their new record company was prepared to pick up the tab was an obvious incentive. I couldn't help thinking that this was a good move. At Western Works everything was getting very insular and claustrophobic. If their sound was to develop, what they needed was some fresh surroundings and maybe even a pro-ducer to entice a pop element out of them. Being familiar with Richard's protective attitude toward his "baby", it surprised me that he agreed to this change in working practices. For a while it looked like they were prepared to make the kind of compromises that would catapult them truly into the limelight. Of course, I was delighted. The book would come out just as they hit the big time. Great timing!

I was beginning to view the book idea as a good opportunity to look back at the last 5 years of the old indie band as well as heralding the arrival of Cabaret Voltaire the radical new dance act. Their old muckers New Order were also shadowing similar moves (as it turned out, much more successfully). Richard and Mal were still friendly with their Mancunian counterparts – the Cabs having played gigs with both Joy Division and New Order. They had also attended Ian Curtis' funeral.

The dilemma that faced both bands was essentially the same as that which had faced the white mid-sixties R&B groups – i.e. that old chestnut, can white men sing the blues? Or to put it in a more up-to-date setting, could they credibly incorporate essentially black idioms and musical ideas into white pop music? Both the Cabs and New Order saw it as an ideal opportunity to take their long macs to the jumble sale and shuffle onto the dance floor.

talking time – "the tape is rolling"

As I got down to thinking about how to compile a Cabaret Voltaire book, I conducted the first interview with Mal rather than Richard. Mal was not only in London a lot of the time, but he was so much less guarded about protecting the group's legacy. Thus I thought it might be easier to obtain background material from him first. But as I sat in my new flat transcribing the interview I had just conducted, it became more and more obvious that a straightforward biography was out of my grasp. About ten minutes into the interview, Mal was straying unchecked and we were digressing off the subject at hand. I was totally naive as an interviewer and had absolutely no idea how to keep someone on the subject. The telly was on, we were drinking and taking the piss out of some pop video or other. The conversations rambled on about everything and anything.

I then decided, if that was the case, then so be it. If I couldn't shape the book I would let the interviews speak for themselves, warts and all. The final book would be a collection of interviews on different subjects that I would collect under broad headings. With this in mind, and a couple of grammes of speed in my wallet, I was Sheffield bound once more. I decided I would try and get Richard to stick to the same topics broadly speaking that Mal had waxed so lyrically about. This gambit worked. Richard had been keen that the book adopt the tone of one of our chats down the pub anyway – he even wanted to do the interviews out of our heads down the boozer. (We never did get that together but I often wonder what sort of book it would have turned out like if we had). In the end, the main interview was done at Western Works with both of us somewhat groggy from the previous night's indulgence. Richard stared distantly out of the window in a pair of shades, I nervously peered at my recording Walkman, praying it was working. I was fucked if I was going to have to do this again. A supply of beer cans was never far from reach.

Even though I had aligned myself to the idea of rambling conversations, I had fully expected that, once we got down to talking "on the record", the Cabs would be full of high falutin artistic ideas. Most of the time, this was really far from the case. Everything seemed to happen by accident or luck. In true Dadaist fashion they often stumbled upon things and then chucked them willy-nilly onto a track. Naively my expectations had been that they would fire off grand schemes about what they were trying to achieve. Of course, what they were really trying to do was be in a pop group and have a good time. After all, they were two working class club-wise guys and not music theory students.

But once I realigned the book to reflect Mal's incessant bubbliness and Richard's paranoiac defensiveness, everything started to come together fine. I ditched what I had already written as an introduction, and concluded that it would be much better to reflect them as personalities, rather than trying to squeeze them as being conceptually somewhere between the Velvet Underground and Kraftwerk. After all it would be a bit stupid to give the impression that I knew more about their music than they did. But in my typically conceited way I still wondered if it weren't the case.

In any event, whatever finally made it onto the printed page, I was much happier with the idea of doing something other than recording and releasing home-made tapes. I even strolled around with the misguided impression that Sheffield's poperati were viewing me in a whole different light. No longer just Paul's pissed mate – but also, Cabaret Voltaire biographer.

The rest of 1983 should have been spent finishing the book, but mostly the call of the pub was too enticing to resist. In spare moments I pasted together the interviews and realised that I hadn't enough material. I was going to have to do a second interview. (Yes, I really thought I could write a book by conducting one interview with each member). However, by now the Cabs were getting busy and it was becoming difficult to pin them down to doing more interviews. The results of their two weeks in a London studio surfaced as *The Crackdown*, an LP that was greeted with almost universally good reviews. As they prepared for TV appearances, Mal perfected his pop star pout while Richard armed himself with a suitcase full of dark glasses.

Part of the glistening success of *The Crackdown* was down to the music itself. The squawky sax and scratchy guitar of *2x45* had been replaced by programmed beats and synthesiser patterns. Mal's bark was now more of coaxing rasp. Accidentally, their gambit to try their hand at dance-orientated material had worked, due in part to the help of Dave Ball who was at a loose end after the split of Soft Cell. But as it turned out, *The Crackdown* succeeded in doing something that they were only rarely able to repeat. And that was to produce a major label LP that was both danceable but also still carried along with it some of that old Cabaret Voltaire mystique. Mal's rudimentary attempts at singing and

Richard's first stabs at melody were rather engaging. On their first visit to the pop racetrack their form was looking promising.

Even so, their jump towards commerciality was not universally greeted with approval. Chris Bohn, writing in *Sounds*, risked the group's wrath by describing their new sound as approaching that of Simple Minds. Mal and Richard, who were used to being championed in the music press as pioneers, were hurt and very sensitive to this sort of criticism. I was actually quite surprised that in five years in the recording business they hadn't developed tougher hides.

But credit for their increased profile must also be laid at the door of Stevo. His confidence in being able to manipulate the media was growing. I remember watching him swan up and down the aisles looking very pleased with himself at an event called the Final Academy at the Brixton Ritzy. This four-day extravaganza was co-ordinated by P-Orridge and featured readings by Burroughs and Gysin, supported on different nights by various groups, poets and film-makers that had all been influenced by them. The Cabs played a low-key "ambient" set with back projections that worked quite well. Psychic TV on the other hand were in the middle of promoting some scam called holophonics. Genesis P-Orridge strutted around with a load of his sidekicks who all dressed like him and had the same shaved head with pigtail. They looked like some kind of silly psychic boy scout troop. Nevertheless, the Final Academy was some achievement and credit must go to P-Orridge in being able to pull it off at all. As for Burroughs, his readings were sublimely humorous – a man in full charge of his self-created comic routines. Hunched behind a small desk, he positively charmed his audience in his own inimitable St Louis drawl.

"Great sit down comedian, that bloke," Richard said to me afterwards.

He was right, of course, although I'd never really thought of it that way before. I'd always thought of him as a great literary figure rather than comic raconteur. In truth, he was both.

"I could have sat and listened to him for hours." High praise indeed from Richard in a seated venue with no bar.

So, whilst the Cabs were undoubtedly benefiting from appearing with Burroughs and from Stevo's patronage, there were other reasons for the Cabs adopting a higher profile. One of these was the fact that Mal had become rather adept at courting certain members of the music press and as a result a succession of journalists fell under their spell. Over the years a whole range of writers passed through their orbit. Paul Morley who had been quick to become a champion for the band, even described Mal as the "best looking man in rock". Evidently, Morley's former girlfriend Karen thought so too, as she switched romantic allegiance from Morley to Mal.

animation – "on the road"

By the end of 1983 I still hadn't done my second interview with either Richard or Mal, and it looked like the book idea might never get further than the starting blocks. Anyway, The Box were going on a short European tour (their second) which was going to take in a night at The Paradiso in Amsterdam. Dave and I jumped at the chance to go. By a happy coincidence the Cabs were playing the very same venue, the following night.

It was a bitterly cold December day when we met up with The Box's tour bus. (OK, their battered old transit). They were nonetheless buoyed up just to be out on the road in Europe. They had been well received in Berlin, Vienna and Prague. Their tales of playing secret gigs behind the Iron Curtain made us green with envy. Perhaps it was going to happen for them after all. They had good reason to be happy, at least they were out there gigging.

Pete Hope was altogether more easy-going than Newton had been. He was getting the hang of being in a group and was starting to adopt an alarming array of strange haircuts – follicular arrangements previously denied him in day jobs. His crop at this time consisted of having his head shaved with the exception of a sculpted oval of hair. This was referred to by the rest of the band as the "khazi cut", as it resembled a furry toilet seat placed on top of his head.

Pete had a cockney chirpiness and did his best to soothe the fraying tempers of the rest of the band. Still, some of the same arguments that raged through their short time in Clock DVA were once again resurfacing. By the time they reached Amsterdam, Paul was obviously uptight with certain members of the band, having had to suffer every musician's nightmare – namely being cooped up in a small transit for a couple of weeks. It was the sort of confinement that would have tested the most loyal of married couples, let alone a group of musicians from such diverse backgrounds.

Having noticed the ever prominent sign of Ausgang (Exit) on the German autobahns, the bass player commented on what a large city Ausgang must be. Paul's eyes, not for the first time, went skywards. The same fellow had also taken to asking Paul what time the soundchecks were going to be, or where the dressing rooms were, before they even got inside the venue.

"Look, I don't even know if the gig is going to happen at all, let alone if there was going to be a fucking dressing room or a soundcheck!" Paul's temper was getting shorter and shorter. Playing behind the Iron Curtain in those days wasn't an exact science.

In the end, the Prague gig did go ahead, but as it constituted an illegal gathering, the promoter had instructed the audience not to clap. If anyone in authority turned up they could then explain that they were just watching a rehearsal. Mind you, it was not the first time the band's music had been met with a stony silence.

The afternoon before the Amsterdam gig, they did an interview with a journalist from the Dutch music press. It had been common practice during the Clock DVA days for the various band members to let their musical differences spill over into interviews. That afternoon, Paul and Charlie raged into each other about the direction their music should be taking. Sentences like, "That's absolute bollocks and you know it," flew around. Their Dutch interviewer was stunned and could hardly get a word in edgeways. Not quite the "Well, our new album's out on Monday," sort of stuff he was used to.

The Paradiso turned out to be an old converted church near the centre of Amsterdam. For The Box, however, this was an ambitious booking and the place was about a quarter full as they hit the stage. Still, they acquitted themselves well and the tour had obviously smoothed off some of the rougher edges. Needless to say we needed little encouragement to help them polish off their rider.

Back at their hotel, I had a conversation with Charlie the sax player over a bottle of blue label Vodka. The conversation inevitably came round to the Cabs. He told me that many musicians in Sheffield had initially been very wary of them because they considered them to be a bunch of fascists. When one of the first tracks they released was called "Do the Mussolini Headkick", I guessed it was an easy conclusion to jump to. However, it said something of their initial impact that even their closest musical allies had wanted to keep their distance.

The following night and we were back in the Paradiso and by now it seemed like everyone wanted to get to know Cabaret Voltaire. The place crammed to the rafters with Dutch punters and the sweat was running off the walls. It was difficult not to assume that the Cabs had well and truly arrived. Outside of their dressing room the band greeted us in a somewhat irritated fashion – they had been locked out and were none too pleased with whoever was responsible. We bided our time reading some of the graffiti left on the walls. To our surprise by far the most lewd and disgusting remarks were attributable to the Paul Young band.

Once we were all finally let into the dressing room, the Cabs regaled us with their "on the road" tales. These were far different from those of The Box, and included sell-out dates through Germany and France, five star hotels and drugs of chemical purity.

Everyone attacked the considerable rider with a vengeance. Band favourites like gold label Tequila were stacked up in a fridge in the corner of the dressing room. Richard had walked straight in, opened the fridge door and turned around and exclaimed, "No fucking Vodka, where's that fucking tour manager?" It was the closest I ever saw either of them throwing a rockstar-like tantrum.

We sat around and discussed other important tour minutiae, like how all the sitting around in the van had given Mal piles. Nonetheless he was on good form and was keen to know what had been happening in *Coronation Street*. The whole Len Fairclough scandal had just broken. Looking over at Dave and I, Lynne commented, "Good to see Gilbert & George could make it." We all laughed.

The set was comprised nearly entirely of material from *The Crackdown*. From the moment the intro tape of stripper's music started they were mesmerising. That summer in Sheffield they had played a rather disappointing showcase, with a stage set designed around a bank of televisions. However, half the TV's didn't work and the band themselves seemed to be running on half steam. Perhaps the pressure of Stevo having bussed up a load of journalists from London had got to them. Certainly Richard never ventured out of the dressing room. At the Paradiso in front of a couple of thousand of pissed Dutch punters there was no such pressure.

The only hitch came when a glass thrown by a member of the audience nearly hit Richard and sprayed beer over his synthesizer. For a man who said virtually nothing on stage, I was surprised by his offer to punch the guy's lights out. Mal, in true back-up fashion shouted "wanker" through the microphone, but immediately looked a bit embarrassed at having done so. In any event, the guy in the audience declined Richard's offer of a bout of stage fisticuffs and the Cabs slipped back into their set.

The combined effect of the music and films obviously impressed the Dutch, and the group played two encores. If they carried on like this, I surmised, the only way forward was international success, world tours, the whole bit including a best-selling biography. Of course I was getting carried away. Certainly a world tour was out of the question. This tour, like all their others, had been a relatively short one. About ten dates to be exact. The official reason for this was that each concert was an event and it would ruin the effect if they repeated it too often.

The real reasons were less artistically motivated. Firstly, Richard nearly always travelled with Lynne. As she had a full time day job, most foreign tours had to be arranged around her holidays. Secondly, Richard (like me) disliked flying. "It's not natural, is it?" we both agreed. As a result jaunts that included too many flights were discouraged. There was also the issue of the intake of stimulants before and after a show. At the prevailing rate of consumption, more than about ten dates at a time would have tested the most hardy of constitutions. Concert dates had to be liberally spaced with days off in between to recover.

The evening of the Paradiso concert we finally bade farewell to the Cabs as they held court in a smoky nightclub. Richard had just settled down to nursing a Bloody Mary. Mal was charming anyone and everyone. They were soaking up the attention and praise. I saw the promoter hand them a wad of notes by way of a cash bonus for selling out the venue. As we said our good-byes and made the long walk back through the deserted and cold streets to our hotel, Dave and I discussed how huge the Cabs were going to become and how many copies our book we would sell.

The following night, I decided it was high time to lose any inhibitions I might have had about cocaine. OK, so it was a drug for all those rich wankers that were now making fortunes on the stock exchange, but the whole point about the eighties was that no-one had any principles. I soon discovered that, whilst a line of speed or a black bomber could last a whole evening, a coke habit required continual visits to the bathroom. That night I became fully acquainted with the toilets in a rather strange nightclub called The Fizz.

your agent man – "bringing it to book"

Sometime in the alcohol-soaked Spring of 1984 I decided that come hell or high water I was going to finish the Cabaret Voltaire book. I interviewed Richard and Mal again, this time at their respective houses in Sheffield. As we sat around drinking in his living room, Richard stared at the ever flickering television. It was a Saturday afternoon and the golf was on. He seemed to enjoy being bombarded with imagery, even golf. It was almost like he was re-enacting Bowie's character in *The Man Who Fell To Earth* – trying to assimilate the world's culture by watching non-stop TV.

As I asked my vaguely mapped out questions we passed round a bottle of Polish spirit, the effects of which burnt all the way down into my stomach. I could almost feel an ulcer coming on. As ever Richard answered in his dry Yorkshire monotone – but this time around I was getting better at coercing the answers I wanted from him. I even tried to prompt further qualification of any answer I thought was too vague. Just watch out Melvyn fucking Bragg, I was getting the hang of this lark.

Mal's interview was done in his Hillsborough living room and went well enough. His answers were a mixture of erudite comment and gossip. He was ever careful to drop one or two things into the conversation that could be construed as mildly controversial, a standard music business trick in dealing with the press. "Always give them a quote they can extract as a headline," the rock 'n' roll instruction manual should read.

"It is a very cosmetic point about the Nazis, but it is still true that however much you hate them, they still had style!" Mal would throw back his head and laugh, and then light up his customary Rothmans. It was a fair point, right wing imagery always seemed to have a much more powerful effect on people, something both the Cabs and TG knew all too well. When Test Department tried the same thing with left wing imagery it just didn't seem to have the same impact.

But increasingly I got the inkling that Mal was adopting a kind of pose. The more he did so, the more I liked him. I'd ring him up and he'd say cool as hell, "Oh, I was just going to ring you this week," when I knew damn well he hadn't the remotest notion of doing so. But that was just fine by me. "Let's just go out and have a few drinks," I'd say. Mal loved invitations. If it happened to be a quiet evening, the answer was usually "Sure".

Mal especially loved all the faux-glitzy excitement of hanging out in nightclubs. I assumed that was why he was spending more and more time in London. It simply had bigger and better nightlife. Underneath it all, I sensed that he would have quite happily traded in some of the group's notoriety in exchange for a touch more celebrity.

So, I persevered with my questions, my tape recorder filling up with Mal's rapid banter. There was the odd interruption, like Alan Fish's insistence that he water all the houseplants during the course of the interview. Alan was smarting after his summary dismissal as drummer. Having toured with the group on a number of occasions, he had decided to ask Richard and Mal if he could perhaps be considered a permanent member. The reply was distinctly, "Thanks, but no thanks". There was no lack of other drummers in Sheffield that they could employ.

With the second interviews typed up, I decided that I had enough material. To be honest I didn't really know what I had. But something swimming about in my increasingly amphetamine-addled mind was willing me to move onto something else. That was the thing with speed. I was always rushing around, "Must get on, got things to do". But in reality I was just like the White Rabbit in *Alice In Wonderland*. I was chasing my own tail, and hence getting absolutely nothing done at all. I had read about people taking years to write books, endlessly researching facts and figures. I wasn't even sure that I'd even heard all the records the

Cabs had made. A constant amphetamine intake was never going to allow me to concentrate on anything for that long. I was starting to worry that sooner or later I would go cold on the idea and merely return to my normal position as "drinker in residence" down the local pub.

In one of my more lucid moments it occurred to me that it might be quite a good idea to speak to Chris Watson – after all he was a founding member of the group! I got his phone number from Richard and taped an interview. I then sent off a letter with some further questions. A few weeks later a tape of answers arrived at our PO Box number. Chris was open and rather appealingly matter-of-fact. The tape finished mid-sentence with what sounded like a whole load of books falling off a shelf – then nothing, silence.

In Newcastle, Chris had started recording again with a guy called Andrew McKenzie under the name The Hafler Trio. McKenzie for some reason had been so rude about the two remaining Cabs that Richard had sworn to punch him, or at least that's the version Mal told me. Nevertheless, The Hafler Trio's first LP was released on Doublevision, to rather indifferent reviews. In truth it was rather difficult to have an opinion about the music – if indeed that's what it was – but I won't get into that argument. Both the Cabs and TG were living proof that such distinctions were meaningless. *Bang! An Open Letter* isolated the snippets of noise and cut-ups that Watson had inserted into the Cabs' music to the point where it was almost like spinning the dial of a radio. It was an exercise in sonic manipulation that I found hard to get excited about.

Far easier to take objection to was the stupid scam they had dreamt up that there was a third member of their "trio" – a sound theorist called Dr Edward Moolenbeek. Undeterred the duo (oops sorry, trio) compounded their felony by weaving a totally incredible fairy story about them continuing the work of a Swedish sound scientist – a certain Robert Spridgeon. It was difficult not to assume that this gimmick was directly nicked off The Residents who had a similar imaginary mentor – one Nigel Senada. Whilst I could chuckle at the way The Residents (also a duo posing as a group with a greater number of members) were always contorting themselves through mythical scenarios, The Hafler Trio's po-faced attempts to convince people, including Richard and Mal, that Moolenbeek and Spridgeon existed, verged on the childish. "I can't believe they're trying it on us of all people," Mal laughed dismissively.

Luckily, Chris Watson's interview did not allude to this fictitious concoction of sound theorists, which I assumed meant the idea had been Mckenzie's. In any event, shortly after Watson himself left McKenzie to represent the trio alone. Watson's interview covered his time in Sheffield, and then his decision to work for Tyne Tees Television.

As it turned out Chris also had a rather curious fixation about recording the sounds of bird noises. It was all rather more Johnny Morris than Johnny Rotten. It was clearly going to be difficult to place him within the rest of the book so I decided the only thing to do was to give him a section of his own.

By the summer of 1984 things were gelling nicely. I mixed together Richard and Mal's answers and interspersed them with some expanded questions. Satisfied that I was close to finishing, I headed off to Spain. After soaking up the sun during the day and soaking my liver in vodka until three in the morning, I came back looking a bit like a tanned but shell-shocked alcoholic.

a thousand ways – "the presses are rolling"

Back in London I was getting involved in a speed-induced wildness (maybe wilderness is a better word) of my own. The result was that the drinking had generally moved up a gear, and from just cruising along on beer and wine, I had stepped on the accelerator and moved out into the spirits lane. My chosen poison was clear spirits like vodka or tequila. I couldn't share Richard's love of bourbon or brandy. In sober moments, I set about thinking how I was actually going to bring to book this loose collection of Cabsisms.

A guy at Dave's work had a printing press in his garage and we decided that we would print up a page at a time. Each printing plate was made from a pasted up page of typewriter script – typesetting wasn't an option for us. (Bear with me. I know this sounds like madness, but we really didn't have a clue, or any money for that matter). We bought a bulk load of cheap paper and every night we went up to Nigel's garage in Watford to see how he was getting on. We sat and shivered in his cold garage watching page after page coming off the small press. Nigel danced around to Madonna's "Like A Virgin", saying things like, "Who the fuck are Cabaret Voltaire, anyway?"

"Yeah, and why are we bothering to publish a fucking book about them?" I joked. Why indeed?

"Money, my old chap," Nigel quipped.

He was surprised that our only concern seemed to be about the artistic principles behind putting a book together. Nigel had acquired a typical eighties entrepreneurial ethos which dictated that he always had some money making scheme on the go.

"Sorry, can't do any more," he'd say, "I've got to print these invoices for a mate of mine."

By the end of November we had 110 double-sided sheets printed up. We set up a number of decorating tables in Dave's bedroom and over the Xmas break we hand-collated 2,000 sets of 110 sheets. A total of 220,000 individual repeated actions – so much for automation. We just got dizzy going round and round those tables. The hand collated sets were then passed on to a bookbinder. In retrospect it was complete craziness. But to us it seemed like the most natural way in the world of producing a book.

By December 1984 the Cabs were briefly touring in the UK. Very briefly as it happens – they were now down to 4 or so dates at a time. This little frenzy of activity was intended to promote their newly released LP called *Microphonies*. What they couldn't quite grasp was that the eighties idea of promotion involved doing a bit more in the way of public appearances than Richard at least was prepared to countenance. Unfortunately, Maggie's ideas were even beginning to infiltrate the record business and it was all getting to be like hard work, that is if you wanted to survive.

Microphonies wasn't a bad LP, but it lacked the commercial polish of *The Crackdown*. Paul risked Richard's wrath by suggesting that a track called "The Operative" had a kind of Stones' groove to it. Whilst Richard was still willing to admit his liking for the Stones, particularly the video for "Undercover Of The Night", he was less than chuffed to be musically compared to them.

"The Stones used to be alright when they used a 4-track," Richard observed.

"Yeah, so did you," Paul retorted risking even further anger.

Microphonies had the feel of a band having second thoughts about commerciality. By recording under their own steam again at Western Works, it meant a return to the rougher more home-made approach of their earlier material. Obviously in Paul's opinion this was not altogether a bad thing. He tended to prefer the idea of the Cabs as a kind of electronic garage band rather than a dance act. But many others viewed it as a step backwards. It seemed that after a flirtation with the big time, they were still hovering on an island of indecision between the indie and mainstream seas.

However, indie music was moving into an altogether more guitar-orientated phase as typified by the emergence of The Smiths. Andy Macdonald at Go! Discs was, as always, keen to stay ahead of the pack, and rather than signing up more bands like The Box, opted for the more commercial guitar-driven music of Billy Bragg and The La's. The Cabs however, had all but abandoned the idea of guitars – at this late stage Richard was hardly likely to try and learn what an augmented ninth was. Likewise, Mal was rather relieved at no longer having to plod away at the bass. As a result he became more of a front man in the band – the lead singer. Maybe Mal summed it up best when he said, "Maybe that's what Cabaret Voltaire is all about.... Two people who've spent seven years trying to play and still can't do it."

The Cabs' four feet were now clearly plonked one side of a divide that was opening up between those who thought there was mileage to be had from the old guitar, bass, drums format, and those who believed technology-driven music as pioneered by Kraftwerk was the way forward. The Cabs were now so firmly entrenched in the latter's school of thinking that reverting to a "Nag Nag Nag" style thrash was out of the question.

It would be another few years before their decision to abandon guitars was vindicated by the emergence of the techno and rave scenes, demonstrating that keyboards were back in fashion. The problem was really that Richard and Mal had become so completely obsessed with seeing themselves on the cutting edge that they had almost forgotten where they had come from, or where they were heading for that matter. Having access to the equipment was one thing, doing something useful with it was another.

It was almost like the last five years had been a honeymoon period. Now some of the age-old problems of being in a band were coming home to roost. Stevo had launched them into the music business at a level where the mainstream was now craving complete commerciality. Big labels wanted quick returns on their investment or they would bale out. Long term nurturing of acts was less of a consideration than in the past. The Cabs were lucky that they were on Virgin, a label which then still employed enough of the old guard to care a bit about artist development and were on the whole sympathetic to, if not understanding of, experimental music. After all Virgin had started by releasing records by the likes of Tangerine Dream, hardly the biggest singles band of all time.

Ever keen to help consume the free beers, Dave and I freeloaded our way into the dressing room of the Top Rank in Leicester. I searched out Richard from behind a haze of spliff smoke and hangers-on to do a bit of hanging on myself. We chatted away amicably enough and Richard looked at the leaflet that we had printed up and were handing out to punters. We had travelled up specifically from London to let the good people of Leicester have news of our soon to be released book. Our leaflet had a picture of the cover to the book. It was a grainy image taken from a video still which didn't make Mal look more prominent, so I think Richard was quietly pleased. All too often their new record company promo photos would show Richard lurking around as the mysterious one in the background.

"Of course," he said laughing, "You've got to realise that most of our fans can't read."

It was a neat one liner, but it couldn't have been further from the truth. Most of their audience still looked suspiciously like they had a copy of Jean Paul Satre's *Nausea* hidden under their coats. This was the very same long mac brigade that Richard and Mal felt they had outgrown. Now they were fervent about appealing to club-goers. In the end, they lost out on both counts. The long macs got pissed off with the commercial direction of the music, whilst the clubbers – well, they remained in the clubs. To them Cabaret Voltaire remained avant-garde shite. The craze for ambient and chill out rooms was still a way off in the future.

The band could still deliver a pretty powerful blow to the solar plexus, but in places I sensed that they were now hiding behind a live set which was becoming too dependent on a taped backing. It was a sign of the times. Electronic bands were increasingly turning up to act out PAs rather than playing live. Ever the luddite, I thought that this was a bit of a cop out. For me it was just too easy to turn the tape player on and let the backing track do the hard work.

We stuck to the idea of leafleting as the best way of letting people know about the book – an odious task but one which seemed to work nonetheless. After leafleting the London concert at the Hammersmith Palais, we sat back to see what the reaction was. To our surprise, within a month we had sold 200 books.

Then *Sounds* (yes that paper again) ran a feature on the book and we were in business. They described it as "an essential and lively read". Eventually a few other papers and magazines reviewed it, but none were quite as enthusiastic. Nevertheless, exporters started phoning up. When one said they would take 600 copies, I nearly fainted. Obviously I had to rush down the pub to celebrate. A German exporter even came over to London and asked us what other books we had in the pipeline. Of course, we didn't have any. People even started phoning us up and asking if we had any jobs going.

hallucination sequence – "new year, what new year?"

For the new year we set off for Sheffield once again, where we presented Mal and Richard with their complimentary copies of the book. They seemed genuinely flattered, not to say surprised that the book had actually come out – so were we. No-one could blame them for thinking it was never going to happen. The whole weekend was an unmitigated success as far as I was concerned. It was New Year's Eve – also the eve of Mal's 30th birthday – and there was a party. Mal and Karen celebrated the event with more costume changes than pantomime dames, as was increasingly becoming their way. At the final count they had both sported at least three different outfits in as many hours.

I started the night by celebrating in a far more powdery fashion. Gathered around the now customary mirror, first a line of coke, then a line of speed – important to take them in that order so I was informed. We then drank some wine, went down the off licence and headed off to Mal's. I continued to sniff sulphate all night and drank and drank. One of my grammes of sulphate was brown and tasted funny. Up at The Castle, every time I tried to take a gulp of my drink it was like I was suffocating in my pint glass. "What is this?" I vaguely remember thinking. "Heroin?" To be honest I was passed caring. After a while, a feeling of queasiness was replaced by well being and I was off drinking again.

1985 had started with a bang as far as I was concerned. In retrospect, perhaps the cocktail of coke, speed (possible heroin), wine, beer and vodka in one night was over doing things a bit. I considered that now I was a rock biographer (my term, not others), the only decent thing to do was to live the same lifestyle as those I wrote about. I was hardly the first to make that mistake.

All this meant that rolled notes were increasingly being applied to my nostril and I didn't go out without the assurance of a regular supply of alcohol. No bar, no go. In my confused state, the drunker I got, the better time I was having. I had now been drinking heavily for longer than I cared to remember. As a result I was losing sight of why I liked drinking in the first place. It was when spirits started entering the equation that the whole business was being thrown into a sharper relief. I was playing in the big boy's league now.

My problem really revolved around a complete inability to say "No". Like many others I laughed my arse off at the naivety of the "Just Say No" campaign against drugs, but underneath it all I should have paid more attention to the message. For me, perhaps they should have tried the slogan "At least try to say 'no' once".

"Fancy a few pints tonight?"

"Yes"

"Another pint before last orders?"

"Of course"

"Just one more line of speed?"

"Oh, go on then, chop 'em out"

Leaving a pub before closing time was a physical impossibility. Why have some speed burning a hole in your pocket? Much better take it now!

But it was becoming increasingly obvious to all but myself, that the drink and drugs were skewing my personality out of shape. By mid 1985, I was still drinking every night (something I had done since I was 16), I was also taking sulphate all weekend, every weekend. A good night out wasn't complete without speeding out of my box, and then drinking myself into submission. However obvious it might sound, whilst in the midst of the haze it is not evident that anything is at all wrong. The trouble was that I thought I was having such a great time that I didn't want to be told anything.

In May 1985 I was back in Spain with some friends. We even smuggled some sulphate through customs – some nerve, more like madness. Every evening, the drinking would start at 5 or 6 with beer and cheap sparkling wine and a line of speed, then onwards until 4 or 5 in the morning, usually ending up with vodka cocktails. I was getting so drunk every night that I would forget to pay at the bar and get chased down the street by irate bar owners. Spain was cheap, and resorts like Sitges offered endless opportunities for staying up all night partying. An odd sober moment was spent in Figueres, visiting the newly opened Dali museum. We also hired a car and drove up to Andorra – a duty free paradise. Great idea! Generally, one day blurred into the next.

war of nerves – "back at the yard"

The Cabaret Voltaire book had sold well, and by the end of 1985 it was nearly sold out. To make things worse, we'd done no budgeting, taken little account of discounts. The book was under-priced. It had taken two years to get together and what little money we'd got to show for it had disappeared up my nose.

It was looking increasingly like I was destined to rot away with the piles of refuse that blew around the Depot. Finally at 65, I would walk out the gates having idled my life away at the Council. At least I might have a decent pension to show for it all. As I sat at my desk, nursing a virtually continuous hangover, it had been all change in the Transport Department. My two assistants had both deserted me. Wilfred had finally had the bypass surgery he so urgently needed and taken early retirement. David had taken a leaf out my old routine and started going walkabout all the time. Whilst five years ago I could get away with it, now the bosses had noticed his absences.

I was given the task of telling David to shape up. It wasn't without a touch of irony, not to say hypocrisy, that I berated him for the very same actions that I had taken some years previously.

"Look, if you don't pull your socks up, you're going to get sacked. It might not be easy to find a new job if you have that on your record." I could hardly believe this was me talking.

I think I convinced David and he decided to bail out before he was thrown out. Whether I had convinced myself about my new authoritarian role was another matter.

If hiring and firing is a sign of responsibility then I had acquired it. I was told to find replacements for my now non-existent staff. The resulting interviews were depressing. I was going through the whole routine, "So, why do you want the job?" I just couldn't put my heart into it.

Eventually I found one replacement, Sandi a rather officious and bossy Indian woman. The second replacement was foisted upon me. In my naive and precarious position as boss, I was persuaded that there was an intelligent and wasted talent pushing a cleansing barrow around the yard who should be given a chance in an office environment. As Janet lolloped into my office one Monday morning, I realised I had been duped. It was soon obvious that she wasn't just incapable of sweeping, the poor girl was just plain incapable. She was one of the last remnants of those round unemployable pegs that the Union was still trying to fit into square holes.

Perhaps it was natural justice. I had struggled to uphold the belief that the Council should try and provide employment for the underprivileged and handicapped – it was their social responsibility. But not in my backyard! Janet's hearing aid meant it was virtually impossible for her to hear people on the phone. Other people couldn't hear her because of her speech impediment. She stared at my computer printouts like they were drawings done by creatures from Mars. Her old sweeping mates would come and ogle at her through the window, laughing at her sitting at her desk, then laughing at me struggling to answer two phones at once.

"You got that Janet working for you," some smelly individual stopped me as walked across the yard. "Give her a drink and she'll get her tits out for you!"

"Great, just what I need," I thought.

It transpired that a favourite game on the sweeping round had been to take Janet to the pub, where the poor girl, so desperate for recognition and friendship, would bare all. Political correctness was a directive on Civic Centre notepaper, it wasn't a Depot reality.

Things came to a head when I had a day off and my boss asked Janet to type up a letter. The resulting effort was more difficult to decipher than the Dead Sea Scrolls. In the end, Janet escaped the cull and she was welcomed into the Civic Centre photocopier room.

Janet's replacement Tricia was a paragon of efficiency and looked a bit like a young Penelope Keith. The only problem was that she and Sandi took an instant dislike to each other. Neither of them liked me. I was beginning to realise that bosses weren't there to be liked. The two of them protected their respective areas like brooding hens. They argued about which way round their desks should be positioned. When one had a day off, the other would surreptitiously reorganise the filing. The other would then complain to me about it.

"Oh, who cares," I felt like screaming. "Bring back Janet!" In fact I was being far too accommodating. "Stop fucking bickering," was what I wanted to say. In fact, "OK, let's all try and get on, shall we?" was about the best I could manage. I was genuinely trying to be the reasonable boss.

So, it was not a particularly happy office. Some of the blame for this must also be put at my door. Not only did I have monster hangovers to contend with, but I was now beginning to experience the effects of amphetamine-induced paranoia. As I was taking speed all weekend, every weekend, it was some time into Tuesday before my body equilibrium was stabilising to anywhere near normal. This meant I was increasingly moody and unpredictable. Some days I could be alarmingly jumpy. The loud bangs that were a common occurrence at the Depot made me literally leap out of my skin. I was living in a kind of tunnel vision, praying for the weekend when I could get out of my skull again.

My paranoia wasn't helped by the alacrity with which things were changing at the Depot. Not only had my staff changed, but the management had also embarked on a never-ending game of musical chairs. Bill, Les and Henry had all gone and their portacabin now stood empty like a monument to the good old days. Bill had actually suffered a stroke. It had been a sad sight seeing him hobble back to work, his speech slurred and barely able to finish a single clue in the crossword. You could literally see the frustration in his eyes as he realised his faculties would never be the same again. Naturally enough, it wasn't long before Bill's name was added to the ever lengthening list of early retirements and redundancies.

Ernie the new Transport Manager, ex-army and consequently rather starchy and formal, was trying his best to tackle the thorny issue of privatisation. The government had had enough of the fannying around. They had put a definite deadline on the Council's services being opened up for competitive tendering. The rest of Ernie's team comprised of Clive (also ex-army) who was in charge of the workshop, Jim who followed him around like a little puppy dog, Jerry and Martin who looked after the drivers, and me who was in charge of admin and computers. As a strike force we weren't exactly going to rewrite the book of business acumen. Predictably, all this talk of privatisation had made everyone wary of their respective positions. All sorts of rivalries and petty jealousies were beginning to surface. Ernie had decided that every Monday morning we should convene in his office to define some new initiatives. To me, words like Monday morning and initiative were hardly compatible.

We thrashed out a few ideas, some of which were more successful than others. Clive, being the Sergeant Major type, had weeded out a lot of the dead wood in the workshop. Twenty guys were now doing the work previously done by forty. Eric's attempts to do the same with the refuse drivers had met with Union opposition. Some elements within the manual workers' Union were simply refusing to face the obvious. Anyone would have thought that the abject failure of the Miners' strike would have taught them that they were in a no-win situation. If Arthur Scargill's impersonation of King Canute hadn't done anything to turn back the conservative tide, then a few dustmen were hardly likely to succeed either.

But succeed they did – at least partially. This was because the management at the Council was displaying exactly those qualities that Maggie was bleating on about. Namely they were unused to playing the game of harsh business realities. All the old structure of Council procedures was still very much in place, and there was real confusion as to how to react to all these changes at once. The Union took extreme pleasure at all this confusion and more often than not came up with more sensible and rational ways of saving money and cutting budgets than those supplied by management.

For my part, I wasn't as worried about the consequences as most. If I got made redundant, so be it. I had a mortgage to worry about, but that was about all. But why worry when it hadn't happened yet. Perhaps some saintly assassin would put Maggie out of action so things at the Council could get back to normal. Some hope.

In November, Dave and I decided to head off to Germany. It proved to be a Busman's holiday. Rather than laying off the beer, we tried to visit every possible keller on the way. Strolling along Hamburg's Reeperbahn was like diving headlong into a Cabs video as flashing lights and flickering pornographic images whizzed past us. Things got even blurrier as we staggered from one dodgy bar to the next.

On waking the next morning to espy the flaking paintwork of our Turkish flophouse, we worked out we had spent a week's beer money in one night. Even more worryingly, my last few travellers cheques had been stolen. It was going to be an expensive week. Our instincts were confirmed when we hit Berlin and everything seemed twice as expensive. We resigned ourselves to eating at road-side Imbis bars by day and drinking tinnies of beer on the street by night.

With a beer in one hand and a curry wurst in the other we passed the hotel that the Cabs told us they stayed in when they played there. It only went to highlight what a large gulf there was between the band and their biographers. We guessed that they knew a Berlin that we could only dream of.

On our last night back in Hamburg we dispensed a hotel alto-gether, having found a bar that was open until 8 in the morning. We spent so long (near on 8 hours) in the place, the owner decided to bring us free Cherry Schnapps chasers. I assume we got back to London, I can't remember the journey at all.

why kill time (when you can kill yourself) – "falling apart"

1985 rolled into 1986 and it felt like I was still nursing the hango-ver from our night down the Reeperbahn. I thought about doing music again, or putting on some kind of event, but mostly I just thought about going down the pub. So that's exactly what I did.

Mal was living in London most of the time by now, so every now and then I would meet up with him and catch up with what was new in the Cabaret Voltaire camp. A party at Mal's London flat meant rubbing shoulders with New Order, Mark E. Smith, Paul Morley and various assorted hacks, trendies and hasbeens. And of course, never-was-in-the-first-places like myself.

Mal gave me the impression that the whole Sheffield music scene was running out of steam. Unlike Manchester where it was going from strength to strength, Sheffield's scene was lacking in staying power. Mal was probably right to be tired of its small-minded mentality. He was also mistakenly labouring under the misconception that he could keep up Cabaret Voltaire's profile in London by hanging out with a drinking set that included members of the Jesus and Mary Chain, Rob from the Cocteau Twins and his new mate Pete Wylie. Other regulars in this rock 'n' roll clique were Paul Rutherford from Frankie Goes To Hollywood and Mick Jones now fronting Big Audio Dynamite.

"Basically a bunch of people who used to be good at making records, but are now a lot better at drinking and taking drugs," was one friend's rather cynical opinion. I nodded along hypocritically. I hadn't even bothered with the making records side of this equation.

Mal's move south was swiftly followed by Paul. In the end The Box had made two LPs for Go! Discs (and a live album for Doublevision) before deciding to call it a day. Both the studio LPs had their moments but there was the sense that they couldn't quite get the balance right. Just as a track started to swing, it was thrown off kilter by some obtuse idea. I sensed that Paul realised that it was never going to gel in the way that he wanted. There were too many people pulling in different directions to achieve the symmetry that the name The Box implied. Perhaps The Dodecahedron would have been a more accurate name.

The Box played a farewell concert at The Leadmill in Sheffield and they positively ripped their material apart in the knowledge that this was the last time they were going to be playing together. Not a pretty sight, but captivating nonetheless. It was a Tuesday night and I remember bumping into Richard as he staggered around in his overcoat (however hot it was he never did take it off). He was trying to juggle two double brandies – one in each hand. Still ebullient as ever, he looked tired. As I juggled my never-ending supply of half-finished beer glasses, God knows what I looked like.

In the end, the split in The Box was amicable and they all went their separate ways. Pete Hope did some recording with Richard, whilst the bass player eventually joined the Comsat Angels. Charlie, the sax player, has recently resurfaced in Pulp-offshoot band Vendini.

Also the general camaraderie and laddishness that made weekends at the Hillsborough house such riots of humour, had palled. They were all getting older, I supposed that they didn't want to carry on getting drunk and mucking around like the Young Ones forever. The fact that Ron had nearly torched the whole household by leaving a joint burning in his room was just the tip of the iceberg.

Paul had not only tired of Sheffield, his malaise was more serious – he was sick of the music business in general. To his credit he had always remained healthily cynical about the pop world. Whilst I marvelled at the whole scene and was increasingly starstruck by each and every potential pop star I met, he was rightly unimpressed and stoical, treating much of it as the hot air it so obviously was. I am sure it was Paul's particular brand of cynicism that had attracted Mal and Richard to him in the first place. Now his cynicism was such that he decided to give up pretensions of playing in a group and get himself a proper job. You couldn't really blame him. After years of scraping by and hoping for that big break, he had just had enough. Latterly both he and Roger had been supplementing their meagre musical earnings by working in the Sheffield Virgin shop. When the opportunity arose Paul took advantage of a transfer back to London while Roger went to Oxford.

Richard too had grown out of the gregarious nature that had dominated previous years. On each visit to Sheffield we noticed that he went out less and less. No longer was he to be seen holding court down The Washington, but sat in front of the TV at home. In short, he had started to prefer to venture out of the house to the off licence, rather than visit the pub. This routine involved calling a cab to take him the 2 minute journey down the road –

Richard wasn't exactly keen on exercise. The cab would then sit outside the off licence whilst he loaded up the booze and drive him the 500 yards up the hill to his house. On one occasion I was in Sheffield and bumped into someone in the pub and enquired as to whether Richard was coming out.

"No," was the reply, "he's taking a delivery of Mexican beer, I doubt he'll be out all weekend".

On visits to Sheffield, more often than not we would chew the fat in Richard's living room, watching the ever flickering telly, rather than in shadowy glow of the saloon bar. I was already beginning to long for the old days down the Beehive.

in the shadows – "going nowhere"

By the beginning of 1986, I could sense that a whole array of factors were combining to produce a general feeling of unease. For the first time ever, I started to try and take stock. My general conclusion was, "Things can't go on like this." My answer of, "Well, I'll have a drink and think about it," was not exactly the right one.

I did however reach a few decisions. I decided I wanted out of the flat. After three years of living there it was driving me mad. The people in the flat upstairs were Uruguayan or something and had taken to banging around at all hours of the night. God knows what they were doing. I had also still done nothing about installing central heating. It was so cold during the winter that the windows completely froze over. The one gas fire would more often than not fight a losing battle against the cold.

I was also concerned that the whole Cabaret Voltaire book episode was looking more and more like a one-book wonder. It was always next week and I would get down to doing something. Speed talking again. If I didn't start thinking about changing my job, I would be in danger of going crazy. In my mind I was back to the dumbstruck individual who on leaving University had spent the whole summer playing pitch and putt.

It was a cold February and I was off work with flu. I sat in my frozen flat and watched Roman Polanski's *Repulsion* and David Lynch's *Eraserhead* in one sitting. Agreed this was hardly guaranteed to cheer me up, but I was immersed in a kind of darkness that only too much drinking and drugging can bring on. My mind swam with unpleasant thoughts.

Things were made worse by the state of play at the Council. Privatisation was looming ever larger and there were all sorts of panicky reorganisations going on. To cap it all, one of my staff, the Indian woman I had employed, was trying to undermine my authority by telling all and sundry that I couldn't do my job. I might have been a bit worse for wear most mornings, but even I could do that fucking job with my eyes closed. None on this helped my already speed-racked paranoia. The reality of the situation was that I was actually being viewed in a fairly favourably light, as I had taken on some early computerisation of the department's admin systems.

However, during an audit of my office, the petty cash float was found to be £8.49 short. Ernie called me into his office.

"If I was going to rip the Council off for money, it would be for a fuck's sight more than £8.49," I explained to him. As I closed his office door behind me, I couldn't believe we'd just had a half-hour meeting about the whereabouts of £8.49. I knew I was going to have to get out of the place, no matter what.

Come the end of the week, I opted for the usual consolation prize. I would cycle back to the flat, have something to eat, do a line of speed, have a crap (most speed is cut with some form of laxative), another line of speed. Then, it was out drinking.

Certain friends were beginning to look at me with that disapproving look, "Oh, he's sniffing a lot again tonight."

I glared back with an amphetamine fuelled, "Get the fuck off my case."

The weekends flew past in a whiz. As I crawled out of bed on Saturday lunchtimes, my arms would ache and I would generally feel like dogshit until it was time to chop out a line ready for another night's drinking. Sundays you could just about forget about. They didn't happen.

In March of 1986, I decided that if I couldn't do anything about getting out of the Council, at least I would try and get rid of the flat. Having put it on the market, I soon realised that I had been badly advised on a price. At first I had delighted at the prospect of doubling my initial investment. As things wore on, I wish I hadn't done the predictable eighties thing and bowed to the great green-eyed God of greed. A silly season of house prices was beginning to rage and a general madness was taking over anyone who entered the maelstrom. It was soon clear that the whole business was not going to be a pleasant one, as little schmucks from estate agents began to constantly ring up and talk up their abilities to sell my property, always dangling that they had anxious buyers only minutes away. After six weeks, these eager buyers had yet to materialise and I lowered my price to somewhere near a realistic one.

In the meantime Dave and I had our eyes on a house even nearer to our favourite local pub. At least this would minimise the staggering distance home. I finally got two offers on the flat, only for them both to fall through. One guy even said he was so keen to buy it, that he would leave me his watch as a sign of good faith. Now I wish I had taken it – predictably I never heard from him again.

By now the Uruguayans upstairs were banging around so much that I worried that potential buyers would assume that I was living beneath an elephant reservation. Added to this, the new neighbours next door had two little snappy dogs that crapped all over the approach to my flat. Appeals to stop the monsters doing their business on my doorstep fell on deaf ears. Typical dog lovers who couldn't believe their little darlings could do any wrong. So, twice a day I had to go out and sweep away the dogshit. The whole thing was becoming a nightmare.

My real problems started when I noticed that it was increasingly difficult to sleep. The more I thought about it, the more difficult it was. Then that damn noise from upstairs. I relented and went to my doctor who prescribed some sleeping pills. Of course I didn't tell him about the amphetamines I was taking. Underneath it all, I knew that they were adding to my insomnia, but I wasn't ready to accept that yet. In any event, it was a disastrous move. Adding more chemicals into my system was hardly what was needed. Very soon, literally after a few days, I started noticing that I was going through startling mood swings that made the amphetamine paranoia seem like child's play. The pills were called Halcion and have subsequently been banned because of these dramatic side effects. But I just assumed that I was beginning to go crazy.

I drank so much at the weekends I hardly needed the sleeping pills because I collapsed into bed an incoherent and drunken mess. During the week my head swam with strange emotions as I battled to keep on an even keel. I would walk around at work like an automaton, trying hard not to fall asleep at my desk. Then at night, as soon as I climbed into bed, it felt like my heart was trying to beat its way out of my chest. I had no idea that it was the sleeping pills that were producing these side effects, I was convinced that it was due to the stressful combination of dealing with estate agents, noisy neighbours, and a member of my staff who was trying to get me sacked.

I started dipping into dark depressions for days on end. It felt like some thunderous cloud had engulfed my head and I could no longer see a way out. Irrational and sometimes suicidal thoughts started to enter my mind. To try and buoy myself up, I was still sniffing speed at the weekends, which of course was a major mistake. But my whole outlook on life had suddenly become nonsensical. It was almost like the last few years of drinking and drugging had come back to haunt me. I felt everywhere I turned I was being bullied into submission. It seemed like my boss was watching my every move, then an estate agent would ring and hassle me, then I would sit at home all evening waiting for prospective buyers who didn't show up. Then I would lie awake half the night wishing the world would basically go and fuck itself.

Every day seemed to present a new crisis of sorts. When I phoned my sister I surprised myself when I literally combusted in tears. Over the next few months it was to become a common occurrence. I was increasingly confused about my mental and physical condition. In an attempt to exorcise some of these demons I would pace about my flat like some caged zoo animal listening to loud aggressive music like The Birthday Party. My arms ached in the most peculiar way and my head felt like it was forever fogged up with cotton wool. I was severely worried I was about to have a nervous breakdown.

PART FIVE

get out of my face − "stopping the rot"

Sooner or later my lifestyle had to change. My first lucky break for a while came when my supplier phoned to say he was moving away. My first reaction was to panic. I breathed easy when he suggested a new outlet and I hurriedly jotted down the phone number. But something inside me clicked and I realised this was just the jolt I was looking for. As I tore up the piece of paper with the all-important phone number on it, I was convinced it was the wisest move I'd made all year. I guess I had reached the point where I had accepted that my insomnia was a problem mostly of my own making. It was just too easy to start blaming everyone else. For the real root of the problem I had to look closer to home.

My next step was to ration the sleeping pills, only taking one if I hadn't fallen asleep by two or three in the morning. Of course, there was still the ever-present problem of selling my flat. In the end I decided to sit it out. I again lowered the price and hoped for the best.

As a wretched summer neared its end, I moved into the new house, leaving the keys to my flat with a new estate agent. As they said they would show people round, at least I didn't have to keep going through the "this is the living room" routine. Not that the decor to the new house was much better − Mal on a visit likened it to an Indian restaurant − but I didn't care about that, it had central heating.

A hastily arranged holiday to Southern Spain was an ill-advised move. The weather in Andalucia was uncharacteristically awful, and my nerves were still raw and bleeding from the last six months. I positively scowled my way through the Alhambra in

Granada. Typical, the one good day of sunshine and we'd chosen to walk around some ancient Moorish monument. I buried myself in confidence boosting San Miguel with Tequila chasers. I had purposely left the sleeping pills at home. If needs be I would drink myself to sleep each night, which is just about what I did. As a result, I was unbearably bad tempered. I was still convinced that the whole world was conspiring to make my life a misery – even the friends I valued most.

Having returned from Spain with everyone pretty much hating me, I decided I didn't like myself much either. Looking as hard as I dare into my life without adding to my depression, I decided I wasn't facing the world head on. My final conclusion was that I was finally going to have to embrace the eighties and get aggressive. After all there was a limit to how much hiding behind drink and drugs I could do. Rather than taking it out on my friends, I got positively nasty with both solicitors and estate agents. "What the fuck were they going to do about selling this flat?"

As so often happens in life, just as I had decided to hold my ground, so the problems that were making my life a misery started to retreat before my eyes. Almost immediately a credible buyer for the flat appeared from the ether. This didn't stop the estate agents continuing to send people round to see the place. Another woman said she would meet my price. When the agents told her that the place was sold, she arrived back on my doorstep in tears. "Why had I done this to her?" A few months earlier, I might have had some sympathy with her, but I told her to go and sort it out with the agents. Of course, only fate could dictate that after a period of not being able to give the flat away, I now had people crying on my doorstep.

By Xmas 1986, my flat sold, off the speed, off the sleeping pills, but still drinking, I was even looking forward to 1987 and I was back to being relatively buoyant. I had even told the Indian woman at the Council to get off my case. I said I'd go to the Union and stir up merry hell if she didn't stop badmouthing me.

This was mostly a bluff, but to Ernie my manager, the very word Union still invoked the fear of God.

I was convinced that the only way not to slip backwards was to get involved with a new book project. A friend told us about this American guy working at Record and Tape Exchange who had collected a huge amount of interview material with most of the leading lights of the industrial world including the Cabs, PTV, Chris&Cosey and Coil. I was still interested enough in the fallout from the whole industrial scene to consider this to be worth a shot. In a large and inhospitable pub in Bayswater, Charles Neal handed over a huge pile of typed up A4 pages, complete with last minute scribbles. It turned out this whole collection of odds and sods had taken him about two years to get together.

Charles had the build of an American footballer, and a slow deliberate voice. I sensed he wasn't too sure about us and thought we hadn't a clue what we were talking about. He was right. But everyone else had turned the thing down, despite assurances from the likes of Stevo to the contrary.

Although the interviews featured some big names like New Order, Nick Cave, Mark E. Smith and Marc Almond, they were rambling and unedited. P-Orridge as usual had come up with a torrent of ideas and half-baked conspiracy theories. I now realised that the main problem with the man was that if anyone merely asked him what the weather was like, he was likely to give the poor questioner a two-hour lecture on the subject. He just couldn't shut up. Charles was obviously far too polite to interrupt him mid-stream, so a lot of his answers went to pages and pages of psychick babble.

Charles' response to our offer completely threw us. He wanted a contract. We had no idea what this meant in terms of publishing, or how to go about drawing one up. We were still in the frame of mind that dictated that you upped and did these things and worried about the consequences later. After all, if a band like Depeche Mode could get where they were without so much as a rudimentary contract with Mute, then surely a little book project didn't need one.

Now who was being naive? It was certainly hypocritical of me to be going on about the Cabs not addressing their big label status, whilst I was wilting at the mere thought of a contract. However, by December we had both signed on the dotted line and started to think of ways of collecting Charles' huge undertaking between the covers of a book.

shakedown (the whole thing) – "a breath of fresh air"

In March 1987, I was back in Madrid where the weather was sunny and warm, but the real heat was exuding from the people themselves. The city was so alive it was almost stifling. Everyone seemed to be living every day like it were their last. Perhaps they feared some son of Franco might suddenly proclaim that it had all been a dream and now things were returning to the bad old days. If I needed proof that I was back in the groove, this was it. I was on top form.

This brighter mood continued back in London as I set about pruning back the vast undergrowth of Charles Neal's manuscript by typing it into our newly acquired computer. This marathon experience gave me a chance to put my energies into a discipline other than drinking. I still went down the pub every night, but now at least I had something else to do beforehand.

Richard too was getting to grips with the advancing years. In 1987 he suffered from something approximating a mild case of gout in his foot which meant that he couldn't tie up one shoe. On doctor's orders he gave up drinking for a couple of months. He and Lynne also became vegetarians. On arriving in Sheffield we discovered that he had replaced alcohol with supposedly health-inducing mineral waters. He had also invested in a car that Lynne drove, but to our amazement he was also taking driving lessons.

During the same visit we went for a drive in the country in their newly acquired vintage Mercedes with Richard swigging away at the Aqua Libra, whilst Lynne fought to steer the large unwieldy car around the tight country bends.

"What a pleasant change, a bit of fresh air for once." I remember thinking.

"This car was originally owned by the South African military police," Richard informed me with relish.

This geographical origin meant it was remarkably rust free for its age, if rather politically incorrect. A couple of years in Sheffield's cold and wet climate would no doubt put pay to the bodywork, whilst it would take the release of Nelson Mandela before its origin was no longer a contentious issue.

As we wended our merry way out across the moors, Richard was adamant we went looking for magic mushrooms. He was obviously keen to find some natural stimulation, something that wasn't cut with god knows what. But I for one was glad that we didn't find any. My idea of getting "high" had now mostly reverted back to the warm glow of a few pints down the local. At our destination, Dave, Lynne and I went for a walk in a field. Richard stoically refused to move, sitting in the front seat in his rock star shades. He might have temporarily given up on the delights of drink, drugs or even meat, but doing any exercise was another matter altogether.

He was still confident that the group was about to make it in America. He even talked about upping and moving to Chicago. He had apparently spent a couple of wild weeks hanging out with Al Jourgenson from Ministry. He was also impressed that Americans were treating the name Cabaret Voltaire with the respect that he now felt it deserved. In Britain they were being looked upon as an oddity that had been tacked on to the end of punk. The general opinion seemed to be that they had outstayed their welcome.

However, with his tendency of viewing the world through paranoia-tinged spectacles, I couldn't really see Richard uprooting himself and living in the heart of one of America's cities. Anyway such a move was spoken about in the kind of abstract way. Underneath it all I knew that Richard and Sheffield was a love affair that would take some breaking.

Unfortunately, the upturn in Richard's attitude towards his health was not really matched by an improvement in the group's material. The previous year the Cabs had produced one more LP for Virgin with the rather unwieldy title of *The Covenenant, The Sword and the Arm of The Lord*.

"Well, doesn't that just trip off the tongue," Dave quipped. He was getting increasingly incredulous at the band's ability to make things difficult for themselves.

However, the title paled into insignificance when it came to the music. *Microphonies* had suffered from a haphazard feel, but was saved from obscurity when two tracks were remixed together with the help of M's Robin Scott. The result was the single "Sensoria", which by rights should have been a hit and was the pinnacle of their commercial dance-orientated period. Although it didn't trouble the charts, it sold well and put the Cabs up with New Order at the vanguard of the crossover between arty pop and the dancefloor.

What *The Covenant and the blah di dah*, proved was that "Sensoria" was more of a one-off rather than anything they could capitalise on. The trouble was that Mal and Richard weren't musicians in the conventional sense and thus couldn't really write tunes. They nonetheless became a little bit huffy about their lack of hits, and were still convinced they could command some clout in the music industry. This was seemingly proved right when their new management – Doublevision's Paul Smith and the journalist Amrik Rai – negotiated an even more favourable deal than that offered by Virgin, this time with EMI. Paul Smith was an obvious choice for a manager as he had worked on co-ordinating Doublevision. He was the sort of guy who could genuinely make things happen. His label Blast First was now releasing some great music.

Rai was something more of a surprise. He had become a regular contributor to the *NME* after he had shown Paul a live review he'd written of one of The Box's first gigs in Sheffield. Paul suggested he had nothing to lose by sending it to one of the music papers. The *NME* printed it and soon he became a feature writer. Rai had the sort of personality that was ideally suited to the rather cynical and bitchy world of the music weeklies. Once at the *NME*, he acquired a bit of a reputation for upsetting people, most notably The Birthday Party. He also went on to write a less-than-glowing live review of the Cabs. None of this seemed to deter Richard and Mal putting considerable trust in him. Rai's typical response to Richard would be a rather unsubtle, "Get the drugs out."

Rai seemed to treat the whole thing as a laugh, a rollercoaster ride that was good while it lasted. It was this devil-may-care attitude that presumably attracted the Cabs to him in the first place. Certainly, everyone in Sheffield had been impressed by the fact that he had persuaded MCA to part with something like £100,000 for a less than average local funk band called Chakk that he was also managing at the time. With his percentage he helped set up the Fon studios in Sheffield.

There was a general feeling of elation as the Cabs signed on the dotted line with EMI. Could this be big time recognition at last? Although it was giving them more and more money in advances, it was also divorcing them from the world that they knew and understood. EMI didn't give a fuck whether they were trendy or not, they wanted results in terms of sales. It wasn't an unreasonable expectation. They must have presumed they had signed up two guys who had got as far as they could in terms of indie chic. Surely it was time to shift some units.

The Cabs were putting their heads into the lion's mouth. The trick was not to get it bitten off. This meant holding one's nerve. Just as the Council was tempting fate by playing Maggie's game of privatisation, so the Cabs had been enticed into the maelstrom of the mainstream pop world.

Undeniably, this was a position that they had always craved. To their credit they never strived to be indie underachievers. But, conversely, it was no good continuing to act as if they were still dealing with Rough Trade, or even Virgin for that matter.

EMI had stumped up a considerable amount of money to ensure the group's signature. But this didn't stop them squandering it in grand style. Richard was a man who liked to travel everywhere first class, always staying in first class hotels, collecting as many receipts as possible along the way.

Neither of their new managers could do much about the group's lack of perspective towards getting their finances in order. While most groups were now tackling the issues of tax, VAT and working to budgets, they thought that all you had to do was wave a magic wand and the whole nasty business would go away. Reportedly any mail that arrived at Western Works in a brown envelope was immediately dispatched to the bin. This was typical of the "let's stick our heads in the sand" attitude I was so familiar with at the Council.

In any event, Paul Smith persuaded them that they must change to an accountant who knew more about the workings of the music business. Of course, this would cost more money – Richard baulked. In his eyes, although managers and accountants were necessary, he didn't want to pay them much money. I was beginning to appreciate these people might want to make a reasonable percentage for their trouble. Richard eventually came round and relented to Smith's wishes. The new accountant sat down and looked at the two band members' expenses. Meetings were called. The accountant's initial jokey aside accurately pinpointed the problem. After perusing Richard's list of expenses he looked up and said:

"Well, this guy has two options. He could either write a guide to the curry houses of Northern England, or become a snooker player."

The first referred to Richard's penchant for Indian food, the second option referred to the fact that the Canadian snooker player Bill Werbeniuk had managed to get the numerous pints of lager he drank a day to control a medical condition written off against tax.

Richard was typically old fashioned about it all. He made the music and he didn't want to get involved in the business side of it. It was not far different from the sixties way of thinking that had got so many of the early rock bands into financial trouble, or led the Council into financial disarray for that matter. But this was now the eighties and nobody could afford to do anything just for the love of it anymore.

Maybe things with their management and EMI would have gone swimmingly if finances were the only problem. But the artistic bank was also running short of funds. The new dance scene was fuelled by the same beats and noises that the Cabs had once made their own, but others were also coming up with melodic hooks and tunes.

So Mal tried to sing, but it was really more of a breathy whisper that sounded like a white man's rap. Later Richard rather cruelly compared it to Phil Collins. For his part, Richard could supply all the thunderous bass and drum programming, but was distinctly lacking when it came to that little memorable melody that could drive a record into the charts.

By 1987, many of the leading lights of the Sheffield scene were suffering a similar malaise to that of the Cabs – essentially a writer's block about how to get that "dance factor" into their music. The Human League, after a string of hit singles, were becoming increasingly sporadic in their musical outings. Their answer had been to team up with famous dance producers Jam and Lewis for an LP called *Crash*. Despite spawning a hit single on both sides of the Atlantic, it was a poor album. Clearly the album's only hit had more to do with their producers than the band themselves. Jam and Lewis had proved there was only so much you could do to make Northern white boys funky.

ABC also made an attempt to move back towards the dance-floor when they borrowed the beat from Shannon's disco favourite "Let The Music Play" and had a US hit with "How To Be A Zillionaire". They then returned to the UK charts with "When Smokey Sings" – a rather sickly pop confection.

Likewise, Heaven 17's answer to the problem had been to look toward black music as a way of progressing, mostly using a variety of guest singers. After all, as BEF they had virtually single-handedly revived the career of Tina Turner. But in terms of dance-floor action, Trevor Horn and Frankie Goes To Hollywood had set the pace with their highly produced epics like "Relax" and "Two Tribes". Then MARRS really upped the stakes when "Pump Up The Volume" brought Cabs-inspired electronic samples to the charts.

fool's game – "maggie 1 – rest of us 0"

Back at the Council, I was getting increasingly drawn into a similar kind of commercial battle to that of Cabaret Voltaire – our job was to try to fight privatisation. Having grasped the rudiments of a newly installed computer system – I had at least sussed out how to turn it on – this made me the resident "computer expert". My manager realised that this expertise could be useful in trying to drag the Depot's arcane practices out of the Victorian age and into some shape to fight off impending privatisation. The talk was now all about Direct Labour Organisations and how we could compete with the private sector.

Ernie stood up and made brave noises about his plans for money-making initiatives, but I got the feeling that this was all bleating in the dark. The last thing the Council was in a position to do was approve individual departments going out and becoming profit making satellites. Margaret Thatcher had local government just where she wanted it, on its inefficient knees with its lazy hands tied behind its good-for-nothing back. The deadline to put in our tender for running the Council's services was looming. Private companies were now looking at the Depot as having the potential for rich pickings and they too were preparing their own tenders.

I now spent a good proportion of my day analysing computer print-outs that broke down every item of expenditure virtually to each pencil being used. It was becoming obvious where money was leaking out, but still there was little we could do about it. The Union fought our every move and Ernie was becoming increasingly pessimistic about our chances of shoring up these leaks. I had to agree with him. On the face of it there was just no way we were going to be able to put in a competitive tender for running the Council's Transport requirements. The general feeling was the vehicle workshop stood an outside chance. The two new charge-hands, both called Mark, knew what they were doing and had instilled some sense of purpose into the guys on the shop floor.

The refuse drivers however were still living in the past. They were adamant they could hang onto their vastly inflated wages and restrictive working practices. We considered breaking up the drivers' pool by farming some of them out to places where they couldn't be threatened by competitive tendering – departments like Education and Social Services. The Catch 22 in doing this was that it would halve the workforce we had working for us and therefore begging the obvious question, "Why then did we need so many managers?"

"Are we saving their jobs, only to threaten our own?" someone rightly observed.

Internal arguments raged on about the wisdom of going down that road. When it came down to it, driving was a skill that nearly anyone had or could acquire. Come judgement day, surely any prospective contractor was not going to look too kindly on a workforce that was highly Unionised and skilled at drinking cups of tea.

The powers that be at the Civic Centre had set up a department called the Client Group. This essentially was to administer and monitor whoever won the tender, whether it be the Transport Section or an outside firm. This immediately built up an "us and them" type mentality. The smarter of those at the Depot realised that getting a job in the Client Group was a way of job protection. It was also amazing how many of the previously higher echelons of the Union were finding their way into this new department. Not for the first time, rumours of a senior management/Union carve-up were rife.

Tricia left for these greener pastures. Undeterred I replaced her with a likeable mother of two called Tania (incidentally Big Viv's elder sister). Another break for me came when the Indian woman who'd been giving me so much grief went off on maternity leave.

I was now fully in the swing of holding interviews, but still no-one remotely suitable came forward as a temporary replacement. In the end I settled for a Sri Lankan woman who was as mad as a hatter. She was a Tamil and hence I got to know a lot about the internal politics of Sri Lanka and the Tamils struggle against the Sinhalese. Such was her paranoia that I just could not persuade her that she wasn't about to be assassinated in the middle of town. But she made me laugh, and laughter had been in rather short supply at the Council. She said I looked like Sean Penn (no, no-one else could see the resemblance either). At least, office chatter was back to being more easygoing.

During her whole time at the Depot I don't think she understood an iota of what she was supposed to be doing. I didn't mind, at least she could answer the telephone, and she wasn't running off to my manager every two minutes complaining that I couldn't do my job. She also brought in some of the most delicious homemade cooking I had ever tasted.

chance versus causality – "a difference of opinion"

Charles settled on the title *Tape Delay* for his opus work. Despite misgivings about its anonymity, we just couldn't come up with anything that would adequately describe such differing personalities as New Order and David Tibet.

The book reflected a whole musical generation standing at a crossroads. The interviews portrayed a sense of diminishing optimism as to whether a band could produce something arty and challenging and still remain popular. One answer was to compromise in order to keep going – a road that Matt Johnson, Marc Almond, the Cabs and Nick Cave were already down. Likewise Swans had mutated from raw slabs of sound to more acoustic song-orientated music. Sonic Youth too had mellowed their feedback to a more grungey post punk pop. New Order had finally shaken off the Joy Division gloom and become just another pop group.

The other road was to hope there was enough of a dwindling audience for radical and abrasive music to keep financially viable. Diamanda Galas, Test Dept, Lydia Lunch and Foetus were typical of those who were still interested in playing less commercial games.

One of Charles' more successful ruses was to get each interviewee to present him with a small piece of writing or artwork to accompany the interview. This was a nice touch and added an air of authenticity to the whole project.

In terms of the original writing it was generally the Americans that were most generous with their prose. Michael Gira, Henry Rollins and Lydia Lunch all supplied efforts. Not really a new Hemmingway or Mailer amongst them, but at least they were trying.

Nick Cave donated the opening section to his forthcoming novel that only went to prove he was probably the only prose writer amongst them. Mal, for his part, had expressed a wish that his piece was withdrawn. I had no problem with that, at least he'd seen sense in realising that prose wasn't his forté.

As I managed to whittle the book down to 250 or so pages, I was becoming increasingly confident that this was a document about the end of an era. Just as the first wave of industrial bands had peaked with the Fetish Night Out in 1981, so the second wave's dilemmas were splayed over the pages of *Tape Delay*.

The Council too had all but lost its battle against commercial pressures. But we fought on regardless. At the Monday morning management meetings we were almost submerged in a bunker like Hitler waiting for the final assault on Berlin. We concentrated mainly on the workshop, trying to see it as a going concern. At least we would give it a go. My expertise, such as it was, was called into play as I had previously worked in the workshop. We tried to calculate budgets, work out vehicle service schedules that would in some way mimic the way a commercial operation worked. However, the more we tried, the more Council procedures conspired to get in our way. Dogmatic to the last, the Finance and Personnel Departments thwarted our every move.

The main trouble was that Council procedures actually forbade us from doing what was necessary to become competitive. We simply weren't allowed to operate like an outside company with its orientation toward profit. The Tories knew this all too well. It was the ace up their sleeve. They paid lip service to the idea of local government competing with the outside world but knew that the constraints being imposed on us would make it near impossible to achieve. In effect we were destroying ourselves from the inside and there was nothing we could do about it. Again it was like being in the middle of some Kafka-esque nightmare. Wherever we turned there was another corridor, but no doors out.

The Cabs too were beginning to press the self-destruct button. Worrying for those close to the group was that Richard and Mal were arguing amongst themselves about how the group should be progressing in the light of their signing to EMI. This wasn't helped by the fact that a new drug had arrived to accompany the burgeoning dance scene in England. Both Richard and Mal became obsessed by the new dance craze and its reliance on Ecstasy. However, it was a drug like any other, whose effects, if taken in quantities, promoted paranoia and cynicism. And paranoiac and cynical about each other is exactly what they became.

It was an age-old conundrum. Drugs can often provide the creative hiatus to launch a group, but equally they can also prove to be its demise. Perhaps it is simply naive to think that you can pump drugs in one end and not expect an equal and opposite reaction somewhere along the line. After all, wasn't that one of the basic laws of physics?

Personally, having tried to keep up with the peripheries of the Sheffield scene, eyeliner and all, I wasn't about to repeat the exercise with the new dance scene. Similarly, after cutting myself off from the amphetamines that had wracked my system for the last couple of years, I wasn't about to repeat the exercise with Ecstacy.

"Drugs are fine as long as you use them, and don't let them use you," Richard had said to me in one of the interviews for the book.

It was a fair point. But from bitter personal experience I realised that it wasn't that black and white. It is impossible for anyone to be objective enough to recognise when that line has been crossed. The shifts in personality are gradual, but the cumulative effect of taking enough drugs makes a person unreasonable and irrational. Sooner or later, it is too easy to forget the reasons why one started taking them in the first place, whether it be artistic, therapeutic or whatever. The end result is usually taking drugs just for the hell of it.

Where Richard was on safer ground was his assertion that drugs could be a useful artistic tool. I had to agree that Burroughs wouldn't have been such a great writer, or indeed one at all, without junk. Likewise, Kerouac's prose was undoubtedly oiled by drink, the Beatles and Stones music broadened by LSD, the list went on. Richard and I were both of a generation that saw drugs as a doorway to awareness, a different way of looking at the world. Unfortunately, there were now an increasing number of casualties around, particularly in the music business, to prove that with awareness came a price.

I would like to think it was my newly found self-control that enabled me to avoid further immersion into the world of drugs.

In truth, whilst the Cabs were becoming fully embroiled with rave culture, I was becoming removed from it. In London, the new dance scene, rather than revolving around venues and gigs, was initially all about driving round the M25 looking for raves. Whilst I was used to going to a gig loaded up with speed and drink, I simply couldn't get excited about these new events, where DJs were soon to become the stars, and where dancing like a demented zombie was the key to enjoyment.

As far as I could see, the further the Cabs dabbled in this new scene, the more they lost direction and momentum. Having gone this far down the road, I found it difficult not to believe that with a little bit of applied common sense most of these musical and personal difficulties could have been ironed out quite easily. But splitting up was exactly what they were on the verge of doing. Richard and Mal were hardly talking to each other and the general opinion was that it was only a matter of time before it ground to a halt altogether.

They had reached a point where they felt they deserved respect merely because they had been at it for so long. Most hurtful of all was the fact that in some quarters they were being viewed as has-beens. The music press was no longer so well disposed to the group. Many of the journalists that had battled so hard on their behalf were now doing other things. A new breed of writers generally saw the Cabs as those two blokes who had produced ground-breaking but unlistenable music, and who were now rather unsuccessfully trying to keep up with the times.

Instead of holding their ground, they panicked. Generally, they were unused to the idea that everyone went through bad times, had to do unpopular things, got criticised and generally shat on. For those of us out there in shitty day jobs it was something we had to deal with every day. But to them it was a whole new experience. Once under pressure, the two of them came up with different solutions. As a result their positions started to become entrenched.

Mal's idea was to fully go with the flow. If EMI wanted the works; promotion, tour, commercial album, that's what they would get. Richard was horrified. Suddenly all those principles that the group had stuck to so resolutely over the years were going down the plug hole. He carried on with the idea that they could subvert the norm and win over a larger audience by sticking defiantly out on a limb.

As it turned out they were both wrong. Clearly Mal's idea that they could compete with the Pet Shop Boys was nonsensical. They couldn't write songs for toffee. Just as evident was the fact that if Richard wanted to chip away as a radical outsider he should never have put his name on the EMI contract in the first place. It was a right old mess.

This was exacerbated by the release of their first EMI LP *Code*. Even though they were way down on EMI's priority list, a lot of money was spent on a lavish Las Vegas video shoot, remixes by trendy producers and a sleeve designed by Neville Brody. Bill Nelson was even brought in to add some guitar parts. Despite Richard and Mal claiming all this investment would pay off in terms of opening up the US market, it didn't produce the increase in sales that EMI was looking for.

But for all its faults, *Code* did have its moments and partially opened the door for the Cabs into club culture. Understandably they were thrilled when their music started to be played at the same clubs that they themselves liked to frequent. The real problem was that house music was mostly produced on indie labels and distributed through dance shops and underground networks. All these new house acts and DJs could experiment with sounds and cut-ups without worrying about record company politics. The Cabs on the other hand were washed up on a multi-national label that they shared with acts like Queen and Cliff Richard. Whilst all these house and rave records were being rushed out in a couple of weeks as white labels all around the clubs, it seemed to take the powers that be at EMI months to decide if and when a single might come out.

As we prepared to publish *Tape Delay* we found out that the book trade had no such indie network. Nobody seemed particularly bothered about an independent music publisher with pretensions about producing books on the arty end of the independent scene. It was difficult enough persuading bookshops to stock books about major acts like Dylan or The Beatles, yet alone Swans, Coil or The Fall.

Undeterred I personally financed the printing of *Tape Delay* with some money I had left over from the sale of the flat. The book finally came out in November 1987 to generally good reviews. Our problem was how to get it into shops. Exporters helped, but good book trade distribution evaded us. "What is this? A manual explaining how to use a tape recorder?" one book-buyer exclaimed when he espied the somewhat uncommercial cover. Nonetheless, sales were encouraging, especially through the specialist outlets. On Saturdays, Dave and I would personally check outlets like Compendium and the Rough Trade Shop were well stocked. The guy at Rough Trade raised an eyebrow when I told him we'd printed 5,000 copies.

"Are you sure you can sell that many?" he said.

I smiled knowingly as if it would be no problem.

"No, I'm not sure at all," I left the shop thinking to myself.

gut level – "keeping in step"

It was becoming clearer than ever to me that throughout the eighties I hadn't really been in step with the political, social and economic changes that were afoot. Basically, as a child of the sixties, the whole tide of Thatcherism, boom-time, stock markets, glossy style magazines and all, seemed hollow and directionless to me. Not to forget the distressing trend for people to start drinking Mexican beer that looked and tasted like bottled baboon's piss. Like many people of my generation I should have reacted more violently against the prevailing tide of greed. But instead I made the mistake of sticking my head in the sand, hoping that these attempts to undermine and eradicate what I believed in would somehow just go away.

Of course, by acting like a petrified ostrich I was also ignoring the fact that the Tories had achieved some positive results. Perhaps grudgingly I should have accepted that the money wasting antics down at the Depot were unsustainable. But what I couldn't accept was that in becoming obsessively money conscious, the Tories seemed hellbent on ruining the Health Service, Education and the public utilities. As I sat and watched one institution after another crumble, like many of my generation I had recoiled into a shell, generally believing that sooner or later things had to change for the better.

But it just didn't happen. In fact, by the late eighties, even to the likes of me, it was becoming evident that the days of the sixties and seventies weren't going to return. Maggie and her cronies had won and swept away much of what I held dear. There were only two ways to look at it. I could carry on reminiscing about old times, or I could make the best of it and join the race in some form or another. As a result we began to look at ways of making a go of an independent publishing house. I even started hassling exporters as to why *Tape Delay* wasn't selling quicker.

Like many of the people who had been involved with Mal and Richard, things were looking up for us. In an uncanny way, the Cabs had helped quite a few careers along the way. Neville Brody after designing some of the group's covers had become internationally renowned for his work with typefaces, even becoming the subject of an exhibition at the Victoria and Albert Museum. Paul Smith's Blast First label was going from strength to strength. Pete Care, who had directed many of the group's videos including "The Crackdown" and "Sensoria" had moved to America and had started working with the likes of Depeche Mode and REM. Likewise Flood, their engineer was now working with all sorts from U2 to New Order.

For the Cabs, however, the tunnel was getting darker and darker. Richard's dislike of touring was becoming terminal. Mal, a natural show-off, was furious. If they couldn't make it on record sales, surely they could still go out and play. Richard was adamant. Mal ended up doing interviews and promotion by himself. EMI were no doubt confused. They even tried to organise enticements like a brief promotional tour of Greece, a country where for some inexplicable reason the Cabs sold a healthy amount of records. Everything was done to try and couch this in a way that was acceptable to Richard. It would be all first class travel, the best hotels, a couple of TV appearances and then home. He declined.

Record companies like EMI were no doubt used to pandering to the foibles of even the most unpredictable of artists. They would put up with any old shit providing the units were still shifting. EMI's dilemma was obvious. Where was the next "Sensoria"? Why isn't this band touring? Virgin had understood something of The Cabs' position – after all it was a label with some kind of experimental pedigree, having started by releasing records by the likes of Henry Cow. EMI however didn't want experimental, they wanted sales. It was becoming a common eighties scenario as the record industry began to slip into recession. Eventually this distinction was lost completely when Virgin themselves were swallowed up by EMI.

In March of 1988, resigned to the fact that the Cabs appeared to be throwing away their career, and that there was little I could do to save the Council's fate, Dave and I headed off to China. Bruce was now based in Beijing and we didn't hesitate to take him up on his invitation to visit him.

I gave Bruce a copy of *Tape Delay* to read. Having been out of England for so long, I was not surprised when he found much of it nonsensical. After all, in 1978, whilst I'd been immersing myself in industrial music, he'd been to see the Grateful Dead at the Pyramids.

"So, rock music has became a University subject now?" He said as he put on another Neil Young record.

As I looked out over Beijing's smog-stained skyline, sipping something the Chinese had mis-spelt as "dried white wine", I mused that he might be right. In a way it had. Many of the music writers who had risen to prominence with punk had now acquired a stuffy scholarly tone. You got the feeling that it wouldn't be long before you could study punk rock as part of a Sociology degree.

I sat in Bruce's ex-pat flat looking at his life's collection of memorabilia. It was now fifteen years since we had merrily traipsed out of the school gates for the last time. Bruce had spent most of the intervening years immersed in EFL academia, moving from one country to the next. His nomadic lifestyle had completely missed out on Britain's grimey decline. Back at home Black Friday had already been and gone and everyone was now truly riding a roller coaster of the boom-bust cycle that was the late eighties. As a result I had now attained a certain harsh realism, whereas he retained a charming faded decadence. His life was all about gin and tonics at six, or going off to see a play put on by the British Embassy staff.

That summer, even the most conservative-minded members of the British public should have noticed that something was going very wrong with the so-called Capitalist dream espoused by Mrs Thatcher. But nonetheless the Tories won a landslide majority at the general election. It was really more to do with the lack of a credible alternative. The Labour Party was in as much disarray as those of us who were trying to keep pace with the changing times. Nothing was the same any more. Certainly the Council was a totally different place from that which I had entered nine years previously. All I now saw was gloomy faces, the days of sitting around drinking tea with Jock and Margie seemed like another era altogether. So too did the days of the Beehive and all the musical optimism of the early eighties.

However if anything I was bucking the trend. Having sunk myself into a terminal groove of pessimism through the previous few years, I decided it was time to lighten up. Of course I was continually horrified that the Tories were still in power and that people were still buying the line of greed and selfishness that they peddled. But nonetheless I was beginning to learn how to be at least partially optimistic. Even the drinking was now well under control and reserved for a couple of good sessions a week. Spirits like tequila and vodka were now saved for special occasions and I no longer felt the need to get blindingly drunk just to have a good time. As my head began to clear I started to think about how I could get a publishing company off the ground. I was no longer a starry-eyed teenager, I was 32 years old and it was time to put my money where my mouth was and take the plunge.

here to go – "a farewell to arms"

By mid-1988, other book offers started to come in, and we opted for a couple of largish projects that would generate some income. Neither happened to be about music, but we were desperate to get the ball rolling so we could fund some more books.

I walked into the Depot each morning singing that old Squeeze couplet "I'm up at nine, down the line, to watch the clock 'til half past five, I wish they'd sack me." As a job it was marginally more interesting and remunerative than it had been when I had first started, but it still wasn't what I wanted to spend the rest of my life doing. Of course we were still having our Monday morning meetings, going round and round in circles trying to devise ways of fighting privatisation.

Natural wastage had now seen the Depot staff shrink to almost skeletal proportions, and although we were truly fearing the worst by this stage, we could see that those remaining in management would probably be absorbed into other departments without being sacked. As a result we were close to holding our hands up and saying, "OK Margaret, get on with it, here it is, sell it off to the highest bidder and be done with it."

In November 1988, not quite ten years since I had first stumbled reluctantly through the Depot gates, I walked out for the last time. It was a scenario I had played out in my mind a hundred times over. But as is so often the case, the reality of it never lived up to the expectation. I had fully anticipated feeling a flood of relief, but in truth I felt very little at all. It was just like leaving the Depot on a normal Friday evening, the only difference was come Monday morning I would be struggling to run a publishing company.

As I looked back at the huddle of buildings cowering in a damp Autumnal mist, the spotlights picking out its muddy pathways, the Depot almost took on the appearance of a prisoner of war camp. In my own little way I suppose I had tunnelled out, and was now ready to be rehabilitated into society. As I turned around for the last time I couldn't even bring myself to make some kind of teenage gesture like sticking two fingers up.

I did spare a few thoughts for those I was leaving behind. I didn't give much of a thought to the management, they would probably find some job or other up the Civic Centre. But I genuinely felt sorry for those guys who were actually now putting in a hard day's work on the refuse rounds or repairing the Council's fleet. It was a strong possibility that they were about to be fucked over and out of a job – but this was the eighties and they would have to look after themselves. It was sink or swim, and presumaably some drowned. In truth, I don't know what happened to any of them. I vowed never to go back.

But some months after I resigned from the Council, a clue to the fate of my ex-collegues drew up to my doorstep – a shiny new dustcart, resplendent in its new livery and sporting a private company logo alongside the familiar Council crest. The crew – a driver and two "refuse operatives" – less than half the number previously deemed necessary, emptied my new wheelie bin in seconds in a blinding display of focussed efficiency. It was difficult not to watch in silent admiration.

So had ended my industrial years. I had looked at the bleak grey office walls for the last time. No more piles of rotting garbage, no more filthy canteen. Sadly too I waved goodbye to some kind hearts and losers. I had sat at my desk and dreamed of foreign places where I had snatched a week or two away. I too had spent time dreaming of the Sheffield crowd, all those people busying around, forming groups, playing gigs, making records, talking to journalists. I had sat and envied Paul for his gumption, Richard and Mal for having the nerve to do what they had done in the first place.

But a veil had been drawn over the musical industrial movement. Even though many people rightly quote punk as a turning point in late seventies music, important in its own way was the "Industrial Revolution" that came along in its wake. The Cabs and TG were forward-looking, creating a music that reflected the technological disassociation and dislocation of its age.

It was also a homegrown movement. Industrial music started out as essentially a British phenomenon. There wasn't a hint of anything American about it. No recycling of blues or R&B riffs. It saw the world as a mess of sound; a harsh, bleak landscape. In effect the reality that many people had to live with every day, particularly through the eighties. It wasn't escapist or full of the frills or trappings of rock 'n' roll. Bands like the Cabs, Clock DVA and TG held a mirror up to British life, and a lot of what was reflected wasn't very pretty.

With their noises, cut-ups, walls of sound, ethnic strains and synthesized bleeps, the early industrial groups were awash with the flotsam and jetsam of modern life. A snapshot in time. It wasn't that different from the dadaists and surrealists of the twenties who had jumbled up and reassembled their version of reality. Or, in the late fifties when Burroughs and Gysin had stumbled across cut-up writing as a way of peeking into the future. TG and the Cabs opened up a similar schism. The fact that many others have produced more musically adept and proficient ways of saying the same thing is to miss the point. It is probably better to learn from those who have kicked down the stable door, than from the horses that bolt out of it. Of course, it is just a fact of life that the horses will always earn more money and achieve greater acclaim.

It was somehow even sadder to think that by 1988 the Cabs were in the worst turmoil I had witnessed since I'd known them. They were simply rudderless. Naturally enough they were more than miffed that certain new industrial groups were touting around essentially the same ideas that they had championed ten years earlier. To me these copyists were pallid in comparison, but by now Joe Public was more than ready and willing to embrace industrial rhythms. Of course, many of these groups were also willing to do what the Cabs had never been prepared to do, and that was slog around every godforsaken venue in the world to build up a solid following.

Things were even worse for Genesis P-Orridge. Having moved Psychic TV's operations to Brighton, he became victim of a Channel 4 documentary claiming that he was running a dangerous cult. The programme even alleged child abuse. P-Orridge, who was on holiday in Thailand with his family when the story broke, was advised not to return to the UK. He resettled on the West Coast of America. The man who so craved notoriety had finally achieved it, but as so often happens in life, not quite in the way he'd have liked. As for the other members of TG, both Chris & Cosey and Coil continued to record and release music.

groovy, laidback and nasty – "or not, as the case may be"

For a while the Cabs ploughed onwards and wisely decided to defer the splitting up option. Not surprisingly they were both keen to associate themselves (as were Psychic TV, Chris & Cosey Coil and Clock DVA) with the burgeoning dance scene with its endless remixes, and never ending sub-divisions like house, garage, techno, hard core and rave. Just as punk had driven a wedge between new and old wave music, so rave culture drove a similar wedge between those who still liked guitar music and those who didn't. Those who believed bands should still play live, and those who thought the whole music business had progressed beyond that.

My association with the Cabs lasted a couple more years. In 1989 we republished *The Art of the Sixth Sense* – which contained two new interviews with Richard and Mal (see appendix). In terms of group unity these interviews weren't conducted at the best time. The two were hardly talking to each other let alone in the mood to talk up their career. But in a way, it made for an equally interesting book. I met up with Mal in a pub in Great Portland Street and from what he was saying it looked like the group was to all intents and purposes finished. He had even taken to going on promotional visits alone, on one preposterous occasion dressing up as Santa Claus in Milan. It seemed a far cry from the cool potential pop star I had first met nine years earlier. He seemed genuinely disillusioned with Richard's inability to relent to some of the realities of being in the pop business.

Mal's main concern at the time of my second interview was that he had just completed a 12" version of War's "Galaxy" with a loose co-operative called Love Street. In truth, it wasn't the greatest of cover versions, but I had no doubt that had it for some reason hit the charts he would have had no hesitation in waving goodbye to Cabaret Voltaire.

On visiting Sheffield, Richard played his cards much closer to his chest. I tried to prise out some of his feelings about it all, but he remained adamant that it was business as usual. He even claimed that their Doublevision label might still have some life left in it. But with Paul Smith now running Blast First, I doubted his words. Most of his answers were slow and deliberate as usual.

I thought long and hard about whether I should paper over the cracks. In the end I decided to go for the warts and all approach and risk Richard's wrath in the process. I was beginning to realise that I could be bloody-minded too. It just seemed ridiculous to give an impression that everything was hunky dory when it so obviously wasn't. What was the point in lying?

The Cabs brought out one more LP on EMI called *Groovy, Laid Back and Nasty* – which if nothing else proved they had still lost the plot when it came to picking titles. One friend cruelly suggested that it should have been retitled "Paunchy, Middle-aged and Drunk". Many a release has recovered from a dodgy title, very few recover from dodgy music as well. It was their last ditch attempt to serve up something commercially dance-orientated and was in recording terms their nadir. I had to wonder at Amrik Rai's assertion that it was the best LP they had made in years. I guess he had to say that being their co-manager, or perhaps he was just plain deaf.

I had long argued that they were capable of making music with a wider appeal, but with this blatant and flaccid stab at commerciality I had to relent and say that I was wrong. I, like many others, had been urging them to become more mainstream, mainly out of the desire to see them make a success of it all. But even I had to admit that I was mistaken, it just wasn't in them. The more people attempted to guide them down the road toward the hit parade, the more fans they lost, and the less commercially viable they actually became.

In 1990, Dave, Paul and myself accompanied the Cabs on a brief tour. Our job was selling T-shirts and books. We hired a transit and slogged up the motorway to the group's first gig at Sheffield Polytechnic. Even in their home town the audience wasn't so much a rush as a trickle. I had to wonder about my sanity in persuading Paul, now safely settled in a Civil Service job, to take a week's holiday in order to help us out. It was obvious it was going to be an uphill struggle to break even. Attendances in Coventry and Nottingham were no better, but counterbalanced by healthier crowds in Edinburgh, Manchester and London.

How the group ever made any financial sense from these brief promotional outings amazed me. In Edinburgh they were staying in one of the most expensive hotels in town, where the tour manager helped himself to room service at 12 quid for a glass of Scotch. For our part we drove back to Glasgow and kipped on our mate Geoff's floor. These sorts of cost cutting measures ensured that in the end we made a bit of cash out of the enterprise, but I was left with a bad cold and some sympathy with Richard's dislike of touring. In just a week I had become fed up to the back teeth with the hanging around, bad tempered punters, bossy security guards and the continuous, loud thumping music. Or put another way, I was getting old.

Musically the Cabs' hearts weren't in it either. They were promoting an LP that I got the impression they knew was a pile of shite. The backing tapes were bass heavy and boomy. Not even the best sound engineer in the world could make it sound halfway decent. They even failed to make a personal appearance at the Nottingham Virgin, despite the fact that some hardcore fans had bothered to turn up. Maybe it's my upbringing, but I thought it was bad form to kick your most ardent supporters in the teeth. They also bickered endlessly with their two managers. I hasten to add that these still weren't full time managers, Paul Smith's main job continued to be running Blast First (and later the Disobey Club and various other enterprises), whilst Amrik Rai was still involved with Fon Studios in Sheffield.

On the tour, I chatted on amicably enough with both Richard and Mal, but none of us were the same people that we had been ten years earlier. Richard was increasingly reclusive and guarded. Mal who had recently had a baby daughter with his new Australian girlfriend, was more interested in fatherly concerns. You would have easily been forgiven for thinking that the whole Cabaret Voltaire chapter was drawing to a close.

The last gig I attended was in 1991 at London's Subterrannea where they were supported by an upcoming duo called Orbital, who only proved how stiff the competition was becoming. The crowd was a mix of Ecstacy-taking clubbers and a few old fans (like myself) that had stayed the distance. But it was hardly a gig to me, more like a club where the Cabs happened to be standing on stage. Earlier in the evening, Richard nodded in my direction, but it was clear that he didn't have the time or inclination for a conversation. As for the music itself, it was full of the confusions and contradictions of two middle-aged guys trying to keep up with the times. The voice of some drunken guy shouting out for "Nag Nag Nag" only highlighted how difficult it was to escape the past. Most artists just say the same thing over and over again. Burroughs essentially wrote the same book time and time again, the Stones have recycled the same old riffs. Perhaps it's best to stick to what you're good at. Maybe if over the years the Cabs had obliged a few more people with that version of "Nag, Nag, Nag", who knows?

As I left Subterrannea, their backing tape was still pumping out muffled and confused dance beats. On wandering into Ladbroke Grove station to catch the last tube home I felt a mixture of sadness and relief. On the platform a cool summer breeze helped blow some of the stale smell of smoke from my nostrils. As I climbed aboard the train, I knew it was not only carrying me home to a welcome bed, but away from the last decade.

PART SIX

keep on pushin' – "just keep on pushin'"

Just as I waved the Cabs a fond farewell, so they partially dug themselves out of the hole they had buried themselves in. They disentangled themselves (OK they were dropped) from EMI. Their complete Rough Trade back catalogue was picked up by Mute (as was TG's) and people began to realise what pioneers they had been. Groups like Ultramarine, Future Sound Of London and Orbital started namechecking them as important in the development of electronic and ambient music. They got back to being on a small label producing largely uncommercial music – always what they were best at. And as the whole ambient music scene began to take off they were once again at home working within their own limitations.

Richard in particular was still convinced that he could continue to make a contribution to the scene he had done so much to inspire. The name Cabaret Voltaire did make a couple of reappearances throughout the nineties, most notably on *The Conversation*. But with Mal having moved to Australia, these musical outings were few and far between.

As a result Richard turned his attentions elsewhere. His first move was to team up with a local DJ Parrott as Sweet Exorcist. It was a bit of a second wind for him. He once again proved that he could come up with genuinely innovative and different ideas. He then launched himself on an exhaustive set of releases under his own name and various other pseudonyms like Electronic Eye and Sandoz. Unshackled from the cynical eyebrows that were being raised every time that old workhorse Cabaret Voltaire came to be mentioned, he began to claw back some of the ground that had been lost in their commercial foray.

That is not to say that whole explosion of bedroom technology and the faceless cult of the DJ that Richard joined in with wasn't without its drawbacks. As the nineties progressed, a lot of musicians, Richard included, became convinced that personality didn't count. After all, it was the music that mattered, not what you looked like or said. Richard was even approached by the dance section of the *NME* with a view to writing a feature on him. The idea was dropped when he refused to supply a photo of himself. But in removing the personalities from behind the music, most ambient music became a like an endless film soundtrack, only without the film.

As time wore on, I tended to hear of Richard and Mal's activities through mutual friends. In the end, I guess we never quite breached that gulf between good time acquaintance and genuine long lasting friendship.

Certainly, the days of sitting in the Beehive waiting for the speed to kick in, drinking endless beer, exchanging quips with Mal or Richard, talking on and on about the scene in Sheffield, seem like memories from another time altogether. I wouldn't pretend that I was anything other than an occasional outsider to this scene. But perhaps this meant I was in a better position to be more objective about the Sheffield music scene's strengths and limitations.

Slowly I began to realise that the music business was just a business like any other. In the seventies I had become so obsessed with all things musical that I was really blinkered to its realities. During the eighties I had clung on to bands like Cabaret Voltaire as a way of keeping in touch with a mythological idea of the rock 'n' roll ethic. Now I can see that all I was doing was falling foul of that old cliché that the other man's grass is always greener. Because I was so keen to become involved with something to do with music, I was naturally assuming that there was something inherently better or of a higher quality about the whole world that surrounded it.

Of course, now I can see the shallowness of this thinking. Once one has jumped over the fence, on closer inspection the neighbours lawn is as full of weeds as one's own. This is not to say that I have lost any of my enthusiasm for music of all sorts, it's just now that I can see beyond the branches of its incestuous forest.

I can now even appreciate the qualities that were inherent in working for the Council, not to mention all my fellow workers that I had mostly dismissed as losers. I had been so wrapped up with thinking that there was some pot of gold at the end of the rainbow, that I had ignored much of what was right beside me. Only when I came to put this down on paper, did I realise that I probably missed certain elements of the Depot as much as the excitement of something like the early eighties Sheffield scene. Having a job at the Council wasn't really that different from being in a band. Everything has its petty jealousies, its ups and downs. In a way, being part of trying to prepare the Council for the rigours of privatisation taught me as much as sitting around drinking with the Cabs.

However, as I took the first tentative steps toward publishing and immersing myself in producing books, I found that I could constantly draw strength from the way the Cabs, and Richard in particular, had set their stall out. The Cabs had always allowed their instincts and obsessions to lead them into uncharted waters, often upsetting people or experimenting beyond their musical bounds. It was this whole vision, a vista of possibilities, that took hold of me and forced my life into some kind of direction.

In looking back over the events for this book, it has sometimes been like spying on the life of another person altogether. But I have attempted to describe events as much as I can from how they appeared to me at the time. Now, in a much more sober and reflective period of my life, it would be all too easy to start to re-evaluate my actions from the benefit of hindsight. In retrospect it would be all too easy to see other subplots and motivations.

Looking back on the eighties, most people were fighting a battle of pitching acquired idealism against the new tide of expediency. The Cabs, the Council, or even my own outlook were little microcosms of this war. How well off anyone was (financially or ideologically) depended on which side you were fighting at any particular time. But like any war, there are never any real winners or losers. It is all a matter of balance, or finding some kind of equilibrium.

afterglow – "jump back 1981"

I am looking at my reflection in the bus window. Somehow I am ghostly transparent. The speed is half way between mirror and bloodstream. My journey is half-way complete, Sheffield's grey towers are looming ever nearer.

The Depot now seems a million miles away. I think about what I did at work today as I stare out of the coach window. Never quite finished the crossword. Unusual, Friday's tends to be the easiest of the week. This morning one of the dustmen cut his head open and the blood dripped all over the carpet to my office. Had to dial 999.

"He'll be alright," the ambulance driver said.

Tried to wash the blood from the carpet. It's so dirty already, I don't know why I bothered. Had a laugh with Bill in the canteen. Can I really believe what he says. Everyone's so full of shit, why shouldn't Bill be the same. Still at least he's a laugh.

Got some crap circular from the Civic Centre. The new Director of Engineering wants to know everyone's comments on the department. We all had a laugh. "Who the fuck's he trying to kid?" The cunt doesn't even know where the fucking Depot is. I wonder what the Cabs are up to. Looks like we might see Richard tomorrow. Probably go up the studio and listen to some of their new stuff, watch a few videos. Looking forward to getting drunk as a fucking skunk. What's the time now? Should be in Sheffield by nine. Could make The Beehive by ten. God I need a beer!

afterglow – "jump forward 2000"

Wandering into the Queen Elizabeth Hall on London's South Bank, I purchase a ticket for the evening's performance. It is a new millenium. On stage Richard H. Kirk ambles on and activates the necessary switches on his bank of equipment. Behind him three screens flicker random images at me. I am completely sober. Not one beer. The American guy in the seat next to me explains that he is on a visit to London. Eventually he asks me, "Who is this guy?"

"It's Richard Kirk and he used to be in a group called Cabaret Voltaire." Years ago I would probably have bored him to death on the subject. I choose to leave it at that.

He looks blankly back at me. "I just thought I would pop in and see what was going on," he explains. "I am really only passing through."

Aren't we all, I think, as I close my eyes and let the music thud through my body.

PART SEVEN - APPENDICES

cabaret voltaire - the art of the sixth sense

cabaret voltaire: the art of the sixth sense

Cabaret Voltaire: The Art Of The Sixth Sense was originally published by SAF in 1984. It was subsequently updated in 1989. In the appendices that follow, the complete interviews for both editions of the book are reproduced.

introduction

The following was written during an-amphetamine addled night in 1984. Abandoned as the introduction to the first edition of Cabaret Voltaire: The Art of the Sixth Sense, it gives some idea as to where my head was at.

The Orson Welles camera angle is long and low, at about knee-height, and is tilted. It looks down a road where Burroughs' discarded syringes roll and smash against the kerbside. The road is straight and gives the appearance of calm carnage. At the end, unattended video cameras project the humiliation of animal and human experiments. These are currently constantly interrupted by random items of news.

The soundtrack has the heavy scent of religion, the claustrophobic incense of persistent repetition, but is somehow Godless. There is no storyline. The lighting is by Strobe Enterprises who guarantee that "nothing is like *it* really is". Nonetheless, sycophants continue to hang on Huxley's last drug-crazed words to find out what *it* actually is.

The road is a natural avenue for its creators – there is the revelry of promise, but no ultimate expectation. Hesse or Hess, where the camera stops, it is illuminating, degrading, or just plain everyday. Our two directors move steadily forward. Hitchcock's ghost has already bowed out, "I'm not sure about this," he says. De Sade's books lie discarded in nearby flowerbeds. Flags and symbols flash out of the screen; the rallying call is bugle, sitar, tabla, drum machine, good and evil.

The side streets are filled with tribes in full ceremonial regalia, dancing with their highly coloured death masks. Their feathers are blown down alleys where neon rape and pillage is advertised via bill boards for Degradation Pictures – their promise is to bring you "pornography and violence beyond your wildest dreams".

These images and music, out of context, mean what? Our presenters point you down these roads, but don't push you. Whatever is there, is there. They gather under no guiding star, refusing to squander opportunity by explanation. Our curse is theirs. We are them. And they are Cabaret Voltaire.

Ladies and Gentleman, please take your seats. The next presentation begins in a few minutes.

appendix 1

These interviews were conducted in 1983/4 from two main interviews conducted with Richard and Mal and two with Chris Watson and pasted together and formed the basis of the first edition of Cabaret Voltaire – The Art of the Sixth Sense published in November 1984.

1. FROM NAKED MEALS TO RECORD DEALS

Was the initial idea to be a music group?

Richard: I suppose that depends on how you define 'music'. No, the initial idea was to be more of a sound group, just putting sounds together like jigsaw pieces. If the end result did sound like music then it was purely coincidental.

Mal: It started off purely as an area of interest – in the sense that it was something we all felt we wanted to do. We had always been interested in literature, art and music, but sound was the way we developed – not as music specifically, but using sound in general.

Why do you think you chose to develop in sound and not other areas – film or photography for example?

Mal: Well, photography is very much an individual activity, there's nothing corporate about it. Film-making is similar perhaps – but as far as we were concerned at that stage, they both lacked the advantage of immediate feedback. With sound you can get an immediate idea of what you are doing by listening to the interrelation of the ideas you are trying. With photography or film you have to wait – just literally having to wait until they are developed. With sound we had the automatic feedback from the use of the tape recorder. The only other thing that might have been available in the visual media was video – but the immediacy of that was not available to us at that time.

Also, a lot of it was tied up with the fact that we didn't want to involve ourselves in the snobbery associated with many of these other artistic areas. We didn't see ourselves as actors – we didn't want to go on stage in that sense. Music in general has a lack of snobbery. Popular music specifically, is very much a working class culture. No matter how much it has been manipulated by big business, it is still a working class culture.

Richard: Although we concentrated on sound, I had always been interested in film. I bought a standard 8 projector a long time ago, and while I was at Art School I used to make collages.

Was the initial idea spontaneous, or did you have a definite idea of what you wanted to do with the sound you were generating?

Mal: No, we didn't have a definite idea – initially it was just audio masturbation, it was just having fun with tape recorders.

Richard: It was just three friends with common interests – we didn't take it that seriously. For instance, before we even played live, we would drive around playing tape loops out the back of a van, or just turn up in pubs and just turn on the tape recorder for the hell of it.

Mal: We literally went up to Chris's loft two days a week and just messed around. It was still just the idea of tackling boredom and of actually feeling that you were doing something rather than just going out and getting pissed. We felt we needed to exorcise some sort of spirit, some sort of devil that was there.

I know Chris Watson was a telephone engineer, what were you and Richard doing at that time?

Mal: When we first started I was between school and college. I had just taken a year off and was labouring at the time.

Richard: I was at school.

Did you first become friends at school?

Richard: No, we met literally on the streets, just hanging around the city centre. Mal and I were skinheads.

Could you name any people in particular that directly influenced what you were producing at that time?

Mal: There were certain points and influences I can see with hindsight that triggered it off. I think Eno in a lot of ways was quite an influence, in the way that he used a tape recorder on the first Roxy Music LP. It was the things that he was doing with tape – and as we had access to tape recorders – the whole idea of messing around with a tape loop became interesting.

Richard: I wouldn't say it was the way that Eno approached sound that influenced me so much, it was more the fact that here was someone who was making music but actually making the point that he was not a musician. At that time most people thought that if you were going to make music you had to learn to play an instrument. Here was someone who was saying that anyone could do it – just give it ago!

There were no other influences I could name specifically, other than the odd thing we might have picked up on in an interview for instance, Eno might have mentioned the name of a German band that sounded interesting, so we would try and find out more about them.

Mal: I think we grew into it, rather then having a reservoir of influences behind us. We didn't start off with that sort of reservoir of ideas filtering through from people like Can, John Cage, Stockhausen or whoever. It started off in very purist terms – it was just a very simple thing, the idea of messing about with a tape recorder. It was only as we developed that we picked up on people like Can, Velvet Underground, Burroughs, or Kraftwerk, and seeing how they related to what we were doing.

What instrumentation did you have at that time?

Richard: When we first started we didn't have a synthesiser, Chris and I both had tape recorders and we had an oscillator that Chris had built, along with some odd percussion.

Mal: I think that Chris approached it from a technical as well as an artistic standpoint. Because he was a telephone engineer, he was interested in sound as a technical source as well as an artistic one. Richard and I provided more of the artistic link to it in some ways, but the whole germ of it was very spontaneous. When I think about it now I still don't know why we started to do it. I think it was out of pure boredom more than anything else.

The next step in terms of instrumentation was when we went up to the Music Department of Sheffield University where we had access to a VCS 3 synthesiser and a Revox. Obviously that appealed to us because Eno used a VCS 3 – however, the idea of using a very technical synthesiser rather than a keyboard based one was also very appealing to us. Those were the only instruments we had access to.

So, when did you first start to acquire instruments?

Mal: As I've said we started working in Chris's loft with only tape recorders and a few things to bang as percussion. However, the first instrument we bought was an AKS, which was a suitcase synthesiser – again it was a non-musician type of synthesiser, more of a sound generator. I suppose the next thing that was an indicator as to the way we would develop, was that Richard bought a clarinet for about £15. The a few months later, it was Richard's birthday and Chris bought him a guitar for £5.

Richard: Looking back, I think the conscious decision to include electric guitar was quite significant. It didn't matter so much whether you played it or hit it with sticks, it was the fact that we could draw on a whole new sound source, and that gave us more scope.

Mal: At the time we bought these instruments, we saw them as just a way of generating a noise to relate to the things we could generate using tape recorders and Chris's oscillator.

How did you achieve a rhythm, or was it simply a case of using anything that made a noise?

Mal: The whole rhythmic side of things came about from banging anything that was around the loft at that time – pure percussion. Whatever sounded good, you hit it. Also we used a lot of tape loops, and although not percussive in themselves, the whole notion of the tape loop is based on repetition, and it therefore becomes a percussive pulse.

Leading on from that, as another way of generating rhythm we bought a drum machine. What appealed to us was the idea of providing a faultless beat, a pulse behind what we were doing to link things together. We didn't really want to use a drummer at that time because we didn't want to be part of the 'rock music' tradition. In a lot of ways we wanted to parody that whole 'rock' tradition and integrate it into the basic idea of sound collage. We wanted to juxtapose different forms of music, such as the avant garde experimental tradition, with a parody of rock music. However, it is only really now in retrospect I can see that those were important formative things in the way we developed.

You mentioned your early recordings were purely for your own benefit but obviously your attitude must have changed at some stage. Why was that?

Mal: Well, after a while we realised we had hours and hours of stuff and we thought it was pointless just doing it, it must be to some end. The first thing we did was to start compiling a tape of some of the things, sifting through to find the best stuff. When we had the master tape, we prepared a cassette of which we did a limited edition of 25, which we duplicated one to one. We packaged it with a Xeroxed sleeve, a track listing and some photos – then basically we just started sending them to people. Eno was one of the first people to get one of the tapes, because at the time he seemed to be a kindred spirit. He was more interesting to us than any of the avant garde musicians we could have been associated with, because he was doing something interesting whilst still within a 'rock' field.

I think we realised that, although we still had an independent mind, by compiling a cassette we were starting to make ourselves accessible in more traditional ways – although we did not want to let this change what we did, or the way in which we presented it.

Around that time you put together a package for the Edinburgh Arts Festival. How did that come about?

Richard: It was through some people who were involved with the Department of Music at Sheffield University, but I can't remember how they got in touch with us. They used to put on performances, and they must have heard of us and asked us to do something as part of some things that they were taking up to the Arts Festival. We put a 50-minute package together for them. Unfortunately, at that time I was going to Europe, so we never actually went up to Edinburgh to appear. We never got it back either!

What did the package contain?

Mal: We did a 50-minute piece of tape that was cut-up and linked with a drum machine and sporadic pieces of sequencer. There was also a film to go with it, as well as an inflammatory type of hand out. The hand out was also a cut-up, the idea of which came from Duchamp more than anyone else – we weren't Burroughs influenced people at that time. We did it literally in the Dadaist way, we took the pieces out of a hat and Xeroxed them off.

You say that the hand out was inflammatory. Was the idea of it to shock?

Mal: Yes, it was literally to shock people. One of the lines was, "Murder the Angolan bastards that killed Colonel Callan", which was quite provocative at the time.

Would you say that this constituted a political input to your material?

Mal: Yes, but we felt divorced from it. Although it was inflammatory we also felt we were taking the piss out of artists in some ways, as well as being artists ourselves. That gave us the right to be inflammatory. We believed in our naive way, then and now, that the artist can be inflammatory and remain divorced from his actions.

Did you think the package might change people's opinions?

Mal: Yes we were naive enough to believe that. We never thought we would become famous, but we thought for one brief moment we might become notorious.

You were obviously becoming increasingly confident about presenting your music and material.

Mal: Yes, I think we were coming out of our shell. We didn't have much respect for most of the people we associated with – like the Music Society of Sheffield University. We began to feel the need to express ourselves beyond the confines of Chris's loft.

Richard: I think it was because there were very few people doing anything like what we were doing outside of the very avant garde scene. There was nothing else going on, everything else seemed very safe to us – there was nothing that interested us, except for a few German bands and a few odd things we had heard. We were trying to work within a 'rock' framework because there was more of a potential audience. We obviously couldn't continue to play to people at the Department of Music at the University, otherwise nobody would hear us!

So you had the idea that you might expand from just experimenting in Chris's loft. How did that actually come about?

Richard: The first gig we ever played, some bloke said to Chris, "You've got a band, what sort of stuff do you play?" Chris told him that we played a bit of rock, a bit of everything, which of course was a total lie but at least we got our foot in the doorway.

Mal: This was around the time when the band was expected to play two sets in between the disco. We also played a school in Bury which was arranged through the Music Society. We were beginning to realise the potential, it was far more anarchic playing live, seeing those germs of ideas that had gone onto tape coming to fruition live.

What was the audience's reaction?

Mal: People really hated us. However, a lot of friends of ours would come along just for the laugh, and a lot of them were nutters, so nobody really dared do anything. Often the people who were our friends were a lot heavier than any potential troublemakers.

So, initially was playing live more just for a laugh, or did it add to what you'd put on tape?

Mal: On the one hand it was literally for a laugh. We did it for fun, however perverse that fun might have been. On the other hand it was done within a serious mode of wanting to create. However, we weren't serious about it in the sense of wanting to make it into a career, it was done with the idea of, "Let's go out and shock people". It wouldn't shock people now, but it did then. What we did then was like what a lot of other groups are doing now – only in 1975 people's outlooks and links with music were very different.

So, what were the next steps after those initial concerts and the tape?

Mal: By the end of 1976 the punk explosion had started and there was a very early fanzine in Sheffield called *Gunrubber*, it appeared about the same time as London's *Sniffing Glue*. *Gunrubber* was run by Adi Newton (later to form Clock DVA) but it was mainly his sidekick Paul Bower who picked up on us, he thought the whole idea of us was hilarious. He knew of us from years back – because for some time we had become fairly notorious figures in Sheffield.

Why was that?

Mal: Because as well as being into music we were also into fashion. We used to buy all our clothes in London, wear all the Teddy Boy gear etc. I think the whole idea of us intrigued people. We had looked rather peculiar stemming back to the early Roxy period and I think people thought that we must be doing something interesting because we looked so odd.

Were you ever physically intimidated because you looked so odd?

Mal: No, not really, because there were loads of us and we all used to be drunk half the time. It was mock bravado similar to the old adage, "If you can't fight then wear a big hat". So, we didn't get intimidated that much, but people were wary of us. Also, we knew our limits, we wouldn't go down the East end of Sheffield and go into the pubs dressed like we were, but we would go to the University and some of the clubs. In those places we were looked on as weird characters – it was safe but it was also funny to intimidate people – not physically, but by our looks.

I think that was what was interesting to people like Paul Bower. We had brought out this weird tape that more people had talked about than actually heard. At that stage our mystique was larger than ourselves – rather like the early Residents. It was that whole mystique that *Gunrubber* picked up on – and so they did an article about us. We played a couple of times with this reputation built up around us, so even though people thought we were absolutely crap, there was still this air of mystique.

So you were fairly notorious around Sheffield. What led to that notoriety spreading further afield?

Richard: There were two things that led to us getting our name around outside of Sheffield. Firstly, I sent a cassette to Jon Savage, who was then working for *Sounds*, and two days later I got a letter saying that he wanted to come up and do an interview with us which led to the first article about us in the music papers.

Secondly, I also sent a cassette to New Hormones, who had released the first Buzzcocks EP, and Richard Boone (The Buzzcocks' manager) was really into it. Word got around with a few people in Manchester, and that led to us being asked to play the first Factory club. In those days we never asked to play dates – we never pushed ourselves, people always came and asked us to do it. We've never really had to sell ourselves.

I think also, that the things we cited as influences helped, maybe you could call it namedropping. I think there were a lot of people in England who were into The Velvet Underground, Kraftwerk, Can and other German groups, but there was no other group in England putting that sort of thing together at that time. I think the word got round that someone in England was working along those lines.

How did this increase in interest in the group culminate in the recording deal with Rough Trade?

Mal: Jon Savage was really the person who got us the Rough Trade deal, because he was the person who persuaded Geoff Travis to come and see us supporting The Buzzcocks at the Lyceum.

Richard: I think also Genesis P-Orridge had a lot to do with it. We wrote to them at Industrial and sent them a tape. Originally they wanted to bring it out on the Industrial label but they didn't have enough money. In the end it took a year for the Rough Trade deal to happen, before we actually went down to London to meet them.

What was it like playing The Lyceum at the height of the punk era?

Richard: It was really quite scary, because in the past we had only played infront of about 100 people, apart from the time where we had played for about 400 people at the school in Bury. At The Lyceum it was also the first time we'd played infront of an audience who hadn't come specifically to see us – and there we were playing infront of a load of thrashing punks.

Mal: The gig itself was horrendous. The only good thing about it was that we went on first and people weren't as drunk as they were later on. At first, we thought we had got it bad, we got spat on and had glasses and bottles thrown at us, but later when The Buzzcocks came on, they had an iron bar thrown at them as well – and it was them everyone had come to see! So we reckoned we hadn't come out of it too badly. Needless to say, the sound was abysmal – it was quite funny looking back on it.

What were your personal reactions to punk? All of a sudden a whole load of groups appeared who were trying to be provocative.

Mal: Yes, shock became a wholesale industry.

Did that make you want to do something different?

Mal: Well, it did and it didn't. The whole spirit of punk was fine and some of the music was too. In the initial stages at least, you were getting people saying that it was really different and breaking down barriers, and to some extent it did. It was only later that it collapsed in on itself and became a stereotype like any other – like rock 'n' roll, for example.

Richard: Although I liked a lot of the punk music, I always felt that a lot of it was not looking forward. To me a lot of it sounded like The Rolling Stones, who I had always been into anyway. I thought we were saying similar things to the punk bands, but hoping to do something a little different in terms of what we actually produced.

Do you think that it actually changed what you were doing?

Richard: Yes, obviously there were influences. I think our music became a little bit more guitar-based. However, that kind of influence had been there anyway from The Velvet Underground with that kind of scratching wall of guitars.

How much do you think that you were a part of punk?

Mal: We were swept up with the momentum of the whole thing but it was very much a movement of the moment – so we utilised it for the time being. We played gigs because we were asked to play just carrying on because we fitted in somewhere. We were left to our own devices, but we still fitted in. We didn't think about where we would progress to from there, because the whole climate was totally different then. Now, we have a climate where people tend to think in the long term. Maybe, it's media pressure, but we tend to be in this situation of not thinking about the moment because the future is upon us.

So, what were your attitudes at the time of getting the Rough Trade deal. How committed were you?

Mal: Very committed, because we had taken so much time getting to that situation. We thought, no matter how subconsciously, that someone was going to latch on to what we were doing and at some stage we would be in a position where we could spend more time doing it. I don't think I ever thought that I would be doing this for the rest of my life, but I thought at some stage we would be able to concentrate on it full time – whether it would be for one or two years or whatever.

When did you first start recording at Western Works?

Mal: I think it was just after the Lyceum gig as I can remember rehearsing for that gig in Chris's loft. But we recorded the first EP at Western Works on a Revox we had bought about that time, having toyed with the idea of hiring one. We thought that Revox was the ultimate thing to have at that time.

With all the independent labels just starting up then, I suppose it was an ideal time for you to get a record deal.

Richard: Yes. Mind you, we had tried all the major record companies by sending cassettes to them.

Did you get any response at all?

Richard: Well, we always got letters back, I've still got them all. I've actually got one from Simon Draper who was then just an A&R man for Virgin records – ironic in view of what has happened since.

If at any time a major record company had come along and offered you a deal, do you think you would have signed?

Mal: If the situation had arisen, I think to be honest we would have done. Although we were thought of as one of the pioneer independent groups, we were still not entirely at home on Rough Trade – so if a major had come along we would have seriously considered it.

So, what was the set-up with Rough Trade?

Mal: Initially when they approached us they said that they weren't a label but a licensing agency. They had already licensed 'Mister Basie' by Augustus Pablo, and they were just about to licence the Metal Urbain single. So, initially they were just a distribution set-up that dealt with weirder sorts of records. By the time they approached us, they suggested that they would like to release a record, but that we would have to wait 6 months until they had enough money. Later that summer they got in touch with us and said it was financially OK. So we recorded the tape, went down and cut it, did the artwork ourselves, and Rough Trade released it – and that was it. In fact we were their first British release.

At what stage during your relationship with Rough Trade did you become self-financing?

Richard: It wasn't until 1979, just after the first LP *Mix Up* came out. We got our first royalty cheque for £4,000. I had been kicked off the dole anyway, so it was quite fortunate for me that the album came out at that time. The money we got from the first single was negligible really, only a couple of hundred pounds.

Were there any other labels interested in you at that time?

Mal: We had done a couple of tracks for the Factory sampler, and at that time we weren't too sure what was going to happen next. We wanted to do an album and both Factory and Rough Trade were interested in bringing it out. Basically, Rough Trade came up with the money first. I think that was probably a good thing – in a lot of ways we would probably have been too much the ideal Factory band.

Factory work very much on a corporate identity whilst Rough Trade tend to have the identity of championing the independent group. Do you think that was a weakness?

Mal: That was Rough Trade's weakness in the sense that they wanted to be all things to all people. They tended towards being an enormous amorphous blob, drawing too much in, rather than concentrating on a few things that they actually wanted to do. I think they were scared in case anything escaped the net. Factory, on the other hand, were more selective working on the Bauhaus principle of the same producer, same type of artwork for all their bands.

In some respects Rough Trade was the ideal label for you, because they let you get on with your own thing and all you had to do was supply them with the tapes and they would release them?

Richard: Yes, it was an ideal situation in some ways – and that is probably the reason why we decided to change it – because it was too safe. The whole process of making an album at Western Works, sending Rough Trade the tapes, the album selling X amount but never any more, became unsatisfactory.

Were you disappointed with Rough Trade?

Mal: Well, we never really fitted in with Rough Trade – it got to the stage where the only contact we had with them was sending them the tapes, and them bringing the albums out. We had never wanted to be part of that Rough Trade scene – that whole Bohemian 'Ladbroke Grove scene' – pseudo-intellectual and pseudo-ethnic.

Richard: Rough Trade at that time seemed to be going downhill. I think one day we just realised that we hated most of the groups on the label – and we began to question why we were on the label at all. They did have their ups and downs, mind you, and they did try and get a bit more organised later on.

Mal: I think they hated us because we remained in Sheffield, and they were very much into this commune type thing. A part of that was their idea of seeing other parts of the record business – i.e. "You're on Rough Trade, we bring out your records and you work behind the counter selling records in the shop." We didn't give a fuck about that. We said, "We're not selling fucking records". We were also the ones who wanted better sleeves – we wanted things done classily, we have never gone for the sloppy hippyish extreme.

As well as sleeves and presentation, do you think Rough Trade short-changed you in terms of advertising and promotion?

Richard: Yes, they never really went for that, and they still don't. It got to the stage where we were in Sheffield, and they were in London with the whole clique that was The Raincoats and Scritti Politti. We began to find out that these bands were being supported by Rough Trade, but they weren't actually selling any records. We were making two albums a year and they were making one every two years and still getting the money for it. That really pissed us off when we found out about that.

A lot of people internally at Rough Trade fought against that I'm not going to mention any names, but it resulted in the sacking of some people. At this time there was also an attempt to reorganise the whole set-up and become more business-like.

Were you playing a lot of gigs at that point in time?

Mal: We were doing them sporadically. We were starting to play abroad – we did a week at the Gibus club in Paris. The main turning point in terms of performance was when we were supposed to do the Rough Trade tour with The Raincoats and Kleenex. The day before the tour Chris suddenly said that he didn't want to do it. I was quite pissed off at the time because I thought it would be a good way of learning, despite the fact that it was a very traditional way of selling ourselves. In retrospect, I'm really glad we didn't. The prospect of going out on the road with a bunch like that didn't appeal to me.

I think pulling out of the tour was one of the best things we did, because it stated our independence. Of course, it really annoyed Rough Trade – to the point where apart from Peter Walmsley, everyone hated us. However, it did prove to them that we weren't going to toe the line.

Richard: Apart from that, we didn't particularly like what any of the groups involved in the tour were saying – particularly the feminist thing, we felt rather out of place amongst all that.

So, you didn't particularly identify with the Rough Trade image. What about Cabaret Voltaire's image? It seems to me that there were times during your early career when you could have been described as the New Wave's answer to Hawkwind. Were you worried about comparisons like that?

Mal: No, because with us there was always a certain amount of personality coming through. People related Cabaret Voltaire to me, Chris and Richard. With Hawkwind the stage show was a lot of fuzz guitars and a load of hair, whereas we had our personalities coming through. I think the Hawkwind reference is valid – but I don't think we were ever as cosmic as that!

2. CHRIS WATSON

If we could start by talking about your decision to leave Cabaret Voltaire and go and work for Tyne Tees Television. How did the offer of the job come about?

Chris: I came up to Newcastle for an exhibition of recording equipment and I met up with a few people who I had made acquaintance with previously. I was aware of some of the things that Tyne Tees were doing and someone at the exhibition suggested that I ought to get in touch with them – so I did. From there I went up for an interview and they offered me a job virtually immediately – the following day I think it was.

Were you thinking of leaving the group at that time or did the offer of a job prompt you to leave?

Chris: It wasn't a deliberate decision of mine to say that I must leave the group and find another job. The job offer came up and I thought about it for some considerable time. I decided, after talking to Richard, Mal and Margaret (Chris's girlfriend, now his wife), that I would like to do it.

Richard said that it appeared to him that you weren't enjoying being in the group as much as you had in the early days.

Chris: Yes, the job seemed to come at a time when it appealed to me more than being in Cabaret Voltaire. I don't look at it as a right or wrong decision – I still think about it a lot.

At the time you left the group they were becoming more musical, were you becoming more distant from that?

Chris: No, not necessarily. It was a mutual interest in the way that the group was going. We were all interested in the non-musical side initially – but that was my main contribution throughout my time with the group. My contribution was not through a particular instrument as it was with the other two -Richard with the guitar and wind instruments, and Mal with the bass, percussion and voice. I was more concerned with sounds generally and in the production of the records. I worked more as an engineer of the sounds rather than actually playing an instrument to produce them.

So, were you the one who provided most of the 'found' material?

Chris: We all did it, but as I say, I tended to do more of it than the others because I have never had any interest in actually playing an instrument.

But you were credited as playing organ on a lot of the tracks?

Chris: Oh yes, I was. That was really through force of circumstance. I played organ in order to go out and actually reproduce some of the stuff that we did live – which we had made a conscious decision to do early on. The fact that I had used a keyboard with one of the synthesisers I used to have, meant that I said I would work the keyboards, so I ended up playing them.

However, I very quickly lost interest in keyboard synthesisers so I bought a very old Vox Continental organ which was quite superb – I fell in love with the sound and the look of it. It was red with reversed black on white keys, it just looked superb. I got interested in actually trying to create a rhythm with that. The only keyboard player I've ever had any respect for or been interested in the technique of, is Irmin Schmidt of Can. He seemed to use the keyboard in an interesting way that hadn't been explored by anyone else.

What about Eno?

Chris: Oh certainly. Early Roxy Music for us was probably one of the sparks for the group. I remember seeing them in early 1972 at a college in Sheffield. I was completely knocked out, it actually changed my aspect on virtually everything I did regarding music both listening and production. I was interested in Brian Eno's technique and some of the sounds he produced. I learnt a lot about contemporary music through that, whereas my interest before that had come more from the classic avant-garde such as Stockhausen, Schaeffer, Satie, and people like that.

Any other influences you could mention?

Chris: The greatest influence of all was learning, reading about and reliving the period of Dada. Seeing various films, exhibitions, shows, listening to old recordings. That was my initial inspiration to actually do something.

You mention film, what was your input to the visual side of Cabaret Voltaire?

Chris: My practical part in the construction of the films was very small, as was Mal's. It was mainly Richard, although the decisions of what to use and what not to use were fairly democratic. As jobs in the group became allocated that became one of Richard's roles. He had experience of film at Art College and he was interested in the application of it – he also had a certain amount of equipment initially. He has gone on from there with his interest in video.

Talking of roles, it appears to me that Richard has absorbed more of your role in Cabaret Voltaire more than Mal has.

Chris: I always worked very closely with Richard, because a lot of our interests outside the group were very similar. It goes back again to the connection with Dada – the films, publications and literature.

Would you say that Mal's interests were slightly different?

Chris: No, not really. I would just say that Richard's and my interests seemed to be closer because we had a closer working experience. Richard and I worked on a few basic things together before Mal actually joined the group, although we knew him then. I don't know if you went that far back with them, but there were times when there were six or seven people in the group that became Cabaret Voltaire. This goes back to going around to people's houses in the evening and going into pubs and playing tape loops – there was quite a crowd of us at that time.

Anyone you could mention that has moved on to anything of note?

Chris: No, not anyone that was connected with the group – but around at the time were people like the Human League who we were in close contact with. They weren't actually connected with us but a lot of the interests were similar and we would talk about things in pubs etc.

Would you go as far as to say there was a Sheffield scene at the time?

Chris: No, I wouldn't say that at all. It was just people getting together and talking about things that they were interested in. I'm sure it's happening now in every major town or city in the country. There was no way you could call it anything more than that. It was just people going out and enjoying themselves, getting in touch through parties – a lot of contacts were made through parties, just good fun.

What was your attitude toward playing live, was that a side of the group you liked less?

Chris: No, I thoroughly enjoyed it as a physical experience. It was incredible, it was like nothing else I have ever done. It was enjoyable providing you didn't do too much of it. We were never a touring band, that wasn't something we were interested in.

However, I did find when we travelled as Cabaret Voltaire that there was a feeling of empathy when we did gigs. We always met people whose views and opinions were so close to our own without ever having made prior contact with them. Abroad in particular, where people have been brought up in different ways yet arrived at a similar point. There was definitely a feeling of international comradeship if you like – various links of communication between groups of people who didn't know they could communicate. It was a certain feeling that was utterly incredible – to talk to these people and realise that you are of a similar opinion. It gave us great heart at the time and a stronger belief in what we were doing. We felt generally we were on the right lines.

Returning to the records, have you got a favourite track by Cabaret Voltaire?

Chris: I haven't really, no.

Have you a least favourite track?

Chris: No, not really, there is nothing that sticks out because you are so closely involved when you are recording. I still play some of the things, they sound very raw, that is one of the things that I am still very pleased about.

Was that rawness purely down to the lack of technology and equipment?

Chris: Yes, but also because of the spontaneity, we weren't actually going for quality or clarity.

Certainly Cabaret Voltaire have moved towards both clarity and quality since your departure. What is your opinion of their material now?

Chris: I like it, I think it sounds great.

Could you envisage yourself fitting in with the more dance-orientated material if you had still been in the group?

Chris: I don't know. They are doing so many different things. The dance material is only a part of what they do. On that basis I would say yes to the question, but obviously if I had still been in the group I would have had some influence on the output, otherwise there would have been no point in me being in the group in the first place.

Could you envisage any future collaboration with Richard and Mal?

Chris: Yes, I would love to. I still keep in touch with them quite regularly, fortunately we still seem to have kept reasonably good friends, as we were primarily before the group. I would love to work with them again, I could never establish a similar working attitude with anyone else.

Are you worried about being forever labelled 'ex Cabaret Voltaire?

Chris: I think it is inevitable to a certain extent, what with people's attitudes. There is no point in being worried about it, it is bound to happen. I don't regard it as detrimental, I'm proud of some of the stuff I did.

You haven't totally given up recording. Could you outline how your project under the name of The Hafler Trio came about?

Chris: Since leaving both Sheffield and Richard and Mal, and moving to Newcastle, I became aware of what I was missing. After the initial period of coming to live in a different city and working for someone else again, I realised I was missing both Richard and Mal as friends who I had known for years, but I was also missing them as working partners. As I said before I don't think I could ever establish the relationship we had between the three of us with anyone else. I could never work with a group of people as closely as I worked with Richard and Mal. I also missed working in the field of record-ing and producing something, and working toward future projects – be they records or whatever.

I became aware of someone who supported us at a concert Cabaret Voltaire did in Newcastle years ago. They got in touch with me through the seeds of information process. We talked and we found we had similar interests in a few areas – quite a few areas in fact – and that he had been interested in cer-tain things that I had been thinking about. Anyway, the upshot of it was that we actually got together and started recording material for no other purpose than to satisfy our own desire to do it – which was remarkably close to the initial intention of Cabaret Voltaire. The result of which is the LP, *"Bang"* – *An Open Letter*. The content was collected over a number of years, using some old material and some which was recorded specifically for the record. It embodies a lot of what I wanted to do while I was with Cabaret Voltaire, and also things I have thought about since I left Richard and Mal – and now have actually been able to put down on tape. It has ultimately been quite satisfying in a selfish way.

Are there any other activities that you have been involved in, or anything that you particularly want to do in the future?

Chris: I have also done one or two things for radio – a 45 minute documen-tary and one or two other pieces – which have been fascinating to produce and great fun to make. I see them all in a way as a continuation of my work with Cabaret Voltaire, because I still have the same feelings about it as I had then. A passion for certain subjects that have carried through. It is something that I have found I have got to do, because I believe very strongly in it, and I enjoy doing it basically.

So, I hope to produce a number of things ranging from general natural history subjects right through to various sound processes. I am trying to avoid the use of the word 'music', because that is something that has gone down and down hill as far as I am concerned. I am losing interest in it all the time, which is very sad. It is not a conscious decision to do so, but I am more and more appalled by what I hear. I am feeling more and more drawn toward natural sounds of every description. I have been listening to one or two live concerts on Radio 3 which are mainly classical music, but some are what they call avant-garde as well. I'm more and more drawn to a live sound produced by a single pair of microphones to record specific subjects.

I have had some contact with, and use of, the Carl Reich Sound Field Microphone and I am interested in that field, in the use of ambiosonics and peripheral sound sources, and live recordings of things in general. Recently I have been interested in ritual music, the use of chanting, again attached to my old interest in rhythms and repetition which was very strong in Cabaret Voltaire. Again, not as music but in pure sound and dynamics, ambience and timbre.

I know some of the pure sounds that interest you most are those made by birds. How long have you been interested in ornithology?

Chris: I am not actually interested in ornithology, that impression has come about because of my initial interest a few years ago in the recording of natural history sounds. Some of the most accessible and easy from a recording point of view come from birds, as well as being the most interesting natural sounds. So, it was necessary to acquire some working knowledge of ornithology in order to record these sounds and achieve some level of success. The good terrorist ethic of 'knowing your subject'. So, in that respect ornithology was a secondary interest brought about by my interests in natural history recording, something I have continued to do. In fact, something I have continued to do a lot more of, as I find it more and more an abiding passion. It is something I enjoy tremendously, actually being in the middle of a wood at midnight, or four o'clock in the morning, with a pair of gun microphones – sat underneath a bush or secreted away somewhere, listening over a pair of headphones to sounds that are so different that they really defy description in the proper sense. It is almost like you are listening in to another world completely, a world which has an atmosphere and mystery about it which I find completely fascinating. The physical sounds themselves I find quite stimulating because they are like nothing else I have ever heard. Particularly as over the last couple of years I have become less and less interested in music.

What about video. What is your opinion of it?

Chris: Video is a huge question – obviously tied up with broadcasting, television and the media in general – unless you look at it purely as a technical instrument or tool. It will continue to develop technically, but I don't know if it will become more available to people. Certainly the price of it has probably bottomed out I would guess. It is quite a latecomer into, for want of a better phrase, 'the music industry'. Video production is one of the major sources of material for TV broadcasting – but what I'm particularly involved with is post-production regarding the sound. The facilities for that are increasing rapidly at the moment, and have done over the past year, which only serves to increase the power of the medium. A medium which can be used or abused depending on whose hands it is in. I also believe that video has rather limiting problems and dimensions that are not constrictions when using film. I believe film is generally a more powerful instrument and something I am more interested in at the moment. Having had experience with video I quickly got saturated with it. As with anything else, as soon as the music industry got hold of it as a promotional tool, a lot of the techniques were bastardised and therefore a lot of the power has gone out of it.

Finally, have The Hafler Trio got any plans for live presentation?

Chris: Not in a conventional stage presentation – I'm not interested in that side of it anymore at all. We have got some ideas about short films that might go along to exhibitions or shows of some description.

3. GENERATION OF THE BEAT

How would you describe your method and approach to the construction of your music. Has it always been a case of putting a percussion track down and then constructing all the sounds over that?

Richard: Yes, I would say that is probably true 75% of the time – at least these days anyway. Come to think about it, it always has been. Sometimes we might start with a voice tape or a tape loop and we would construct something around that. For instance, on the LP *Microphonies* I used a tape that I found which had me, Mal and Chris talking to this American bloke three or four years ago. So I cut it up, stuck it onto tape and put it on one of the tracks. Doing things like that appeals to me, it goes back to the Duchamp principle of a 'found object'.

Mal: A lot of the times we would try not to consciously use rhythm but try to be aware of it in a non-percussive way. We would nearly always start off with a basic track that would run all the way through to give a whitewash or a background. In a lot of ways it was like a soundscape. I think as we've progressed we tended to concentrate more and more on rhythm.

Richard: I see it rather like building up a painting, sticking the background down and then adding stuff on top of that. There is no difference really, that is exactly the way I would approach doing a painting.

Mal: As we build it up we tend to know what clicks and then we embellish those ideas. Sometimes we have a set idea and sometimes we just mess about and see what happens. Often it's a case of building things up to lose them later because they have become superfluous.

Does the lyric always come last?

Mal: No, that is not strictly true – particularly of late. Often the vocal will go down two thirds of the way through. Sometimes I find it hard to work purely to a rhythm, so I may wait until there is a simple musical thing for me to feed off. Often once the vocals are on we put more stuff on top – but as soon as the track has some bare bones I start working on the vocals.

How has the way that you fit the vocals within the lack of a conventional song structure changed since the early days?

Mal: Initially I was more of a traditionalist, I saw lyrics fitting in with musical structures, whereas Richard saw them as cut-up prose which would be totally juxtaposed to the music, a sort of poetry on top of sound. In the early days I didn't write many of the lyrics, Richard wrote more and I played more. Nowadays the roles have become more clearly defined and polarised. I took on more of the lyrics as I became increasingly conscious of the way the words fitted into the way our music developed.

So, initially you used the voice more like another instrument?

Mal: Yes, exactly. We were interested in the voice as a rhythm, using it as just another instrument rather than straight singing. Certainly, using a song structure of verse/chorus/verse wouldn't work for us because we would lose a bit of the feel and the spontaneity.

The lyrical subject matter is sometimes very obtuse and indirect – not the same as the sort of insular lyric a rock group might produce.

Richard: I don't see anything particularly bad in rock lyrics because the people who write those sort of lyrics produce a lot of good music. That is because they think of themselves as producing rock music, whereas I see what we are doing as something other than that. I suppose you could say that we were jacks-of-all-trades and masters of none.

Is provocation still an important side to your music, or is the accent on dance-orientated material more important to you now ?

Mal: We are still a bit of a paradox because people tend to class us as some sort of new dance group now – but no one at our performances ever seems to dance much. We are the dance group that no one ever dances to.

I think the provocative element has diminished over the years, mainly because people's idea of what is provocative has been eaten away. There was that whole period during the punk explosion of 1977 to 1979 where shock value was being sold wholesale. Today you would have to make a really determined effort to go out and shock people, and we don't particularly want to do that now because it would dismiss the other ninety percent of what we do.

Do you think that there are a lot of people who are disappointed that you are not as provocative as you were in the beginning?

Mal: Yes, there probably are. It is easy for them to say that, they don't have to do it themselves. It is like you have been given this role in life – you are the provocateur and you have got to do that. They don't take into account that at some time you might want to do something more subtle.

If we provoked at the time, it was because we hit a nerve, maybe we don't hit a nerve anymore. The Sex Pistols wouldn't be the slightest bit provocative if you put them in the context of today. The point is that they were provocative at the time. Now, you just get John Lydon still playing 'Anarchy in the UK', acting like a real wanker, thinking he's still being provocative.

Richard: I don't see much point in being controversial just for the sake of it. I just don't like the idea of retreading old ground, and that is why we try to keep moving on all the time.

What do you think of your old material now?

Richard: Every now and then I dig out some of the old tracks and give them a listen. I think it is a good idea to do that. I would stand by everything we have ever done personally. With all the stuff, there must have been a good reason for doing it at the time and that is good enough for me. I don't know whether Mal would agree with that.

Mal: I don't listen to our old stuff very often, in fact I rarely listen to our music at all. When I do listen, it is with a mixture of pleasure and embarrass-ment – embarrassed in the sense of growing up in public.

In general, as regards listening to music, I can home in on things that have a certain amount of spirit, but are also listenable to. What we were doing with some of the early stuff was producing something that was interesting, but in a lot of ways totally unlistenable to. In those days the ideas were more important than the end result, but we always believed that the end result would catch up with the ideas. In particular, a lot of people say that they think *Three Mantras* is unlistenable to.

Would you say that it was your least favourite Cabaret Voltaire record?

Mal: No, it is not my least favourite. In fact, I loved it because it was a record that stuck out in people's minds. It was the record that people couldn't work out why the fuck we did it. For that reason it is probably the most valid record we have ever done.

The fact that there were only two tracks on the record was obviously a joke (this was lost on one reviewer who reviewed it as three tracks) – also the length of the tracks seemed rather extreme for what they were.

Mal: It was a joke in that sense as well. It was attempt to push things to their extremities. I don't think we would do it again.

Do you think you are inflexible about the length of your tracks. There almost seems to be a standard length to a lot of them these days?

Mal: I think that is a valid point. I think some of our tracks are too long – then again some of them are too short! We still work on feel more than anything else as regards the length of our tracks.

Do you think that because the newer material is more music-orientated that it might become dated a lot quicker than your older material?

Mal: That's true, but it is not so much the way we have developed, but more the way the link between music and technology has developed – which has tended to stereotype certain sounds. Before the mass availability of sequencers and drum machines it was very polarised – you had guitar and drum based music, and you had electronic music. This situation still exists now to a degree, but there are people like us and New Order who are making the crossover. However, a lot of records now have drum machine and bass sequencer on them, so the technology tends to become the common link.

Your use of drum machine and bass sequencer has inevitably meant that your material has tended towards a dance sound. Do you think that an LP like 'The Crackdown', for example, was successful at being a dance album with a difference?

Mal: Yes I think it was. My only qualms with that album was that it came out a bit late. It lost something to me because it took so long in coming out. I never thought it was going to be an album that would last forever, but I still stand by it.

Richard: I think that album was successful because it got us across to more people than we normally would have done. We virtually doubled the record sales and therefore doubled the number of people we could communicate with. It meant that our music got played a lot more in clubs, and it got in the bottom end of the charts which certainly helps in terms of getting noticed.

You obviously try quite hard to keep up with the ever-advancing technology in recording techniques and instruments. How do you choose the instruments you use?

Mal: We haven't got that many new instruments, actually. Most of the equipment we have bought has been studio recording equipment. We still only have two synthesisers and one of those is six years old. Other than that we tend to hire them in when we need them, use them on a couple of tracks and then send them back. If we had bought them we would feel obliged to use them on all of the tracks, but by hiring you don't have that obligation. We soon get to know which ones are good for certain sounds.

Do you not have a problem trying to work with some of the more complicated drum machines and sequencers that are available to you?

Mal: Yes, with something like a Fairlight, for instance, you have to rely on the expertise of an engineer. They are so expensive to hire that you couldn't contemplate doing it all yourself because it would take three times as long.

What would you say to people that say that Cabaret Voltaire was based on one idea and you are only using increased technology to say the same thing?

Richard: I would go along with that. Mind you, I think the one idea was a very good one! I think it is the same with most bands – they generally have one slow piece and one fast piece and just do variations on those two themes. As long as you can keep people interested enough to want to buy it, I don't see anything wrong with that. I think the same is true of most film-makers.

How do you see your music developing?

Richard: In the format that the music is in at the moment, I don't see us as doing it for years and years, although I think we have got a few more albums worth yet. However, in the future I still think we shall continue with music, but it will probably tie in more and more with the film aspect. This will mean it will probably be more abstract and atmospheric in nature. Soundtrack work is something we would like to push for. When we sign a new publishing deal we would like it put in the contract that they look for soundtrack work for us. It is one of the functions that a publisher should serve.

On the whole I think our music will become more schizophrenic. I think the music on our records will become more accessible, but on the other side of the coin, we will retain the facility for producing soundtrack music. I think it is a more effective for us to work that way. That is what I like about the way we operate, we always try to keep it open-ended so we can go off into any area without it being too contrived.

When you say the music will become more accessible, do you think that could stretch to a top ten hit?

Richard: Yes, I think that would be really good.

Mal: But we wouldn't lose any sleep if we didn't get one.

Richard: The main advantage of one would be that it would put us in a more powerful position. You tend to command more respect out of the whole industry, and if we were to do a film we would be able to go and ask for £50,000 and get away with it.

'Just Fascination' was probably the closest you've had to a hit single to date. Did the fact that you used a producer on the remix of that make the difference. Will you continue to use producers?

Mal: Yes, we will for the singles – but with an album it is hard for us to work with a producer because we are so used to working on our own. With a single it is a bit different because you are drafting in someone else's expertise on the subtleties of what a single is. It is quite nice to learn from someone else in that context, in the way that we did from John Luongo on the 'Just Fascination' single, for example.

Richard: It is quite nice to let someone else loose on your material, but it is not something I would like to see happen all the time. I'm too personally involved with it to allow someone else's grubby fingers all over it. I feel too close to what I do. It is sometimes difficult for us working in a studio in London, because we have to work through an engineer, as opposed to when we engineer it ourselves.

But a good producer is necessary for a single though?

Richard: I think a single is an artform unto itself. There is nothing better than a good single, is there? Although I'm not sure about what people like Trevor Horn get up to. It seems so contrived. I don't know how contrived the pop singles of the past were, but it does seem that the innocence, naivety and freshness are missing a lot of the time these days.

But even in the past there was a heavy reliance on the producer. George Martin, Andrew Loog Oldham for instance.

Richard: Obviously these people are important and have a role to play.

Do you think there are any advantages to not ever having had a hit single?

Mal: Yes there are. A disadvantage with a hit single is that you gain a millstone around your neck. However, it would be good to have a top seller because it might get the record company off our backs.

Would you say that you were moving further and further into the 'music business'?

Mal: Yes, but the further we move into it the more we find ourselves going off at tangents. It is alright as long as you accept it as a mechanism that you want to use rather then become a part of.

Richard: I think in our case, the more successful we get, the more freedom it is going to allow us. We'll be able to turn round and tell people to piss off!

Mal: Maybe I have just become more cynical about the whole business since we started. It would be nice to remain fresh and naive, but to get out of it what you want, you have to be realistic.

I think we reached a crossroads a few years ago and we had to make a decision. We had achieved a certain amount but we felt we had reached a plateau. Although in some respects it would have been nice to retain a level of obscurity, after a while that was beginning to lose its appeal. We could quite easily have found ourselves washed up. As with The Residents, the obscurity principle reaches a certain stage, and after that people turn round and say, "Well, who gives a fuck anyway". You can only remain mysterious for so long, eventually you can just end up on the side sad-faced.

Would you say that in the independent ethic is becoming more and more redundant, and you might as well go straight for the widest possible coverage?

Richard: Yes, provided that you can retain control of everything that you do – which is still the case with us up to now. Nobody can force us to do anything we don't want to, like taking loads of singles off one album, for example. They cannot market any of our product, in any way, without our consent – we have to be consulted about everything. That would be the only way that we would enter into anything of that nature now, especially dealing with a major record label.

Do you think that you would have held out for those principles if a major label had been interested in the early days?

Richard: Probably, who can say? We were a lot more naive in those days. We have learnt a lot more now about the pros and cons which gives you a standpoint with which to fight against them.

However, you think you are in a good position now in terms of controlling what you do?

Richard: Yes, I think even now we can do exactly what we want. Although I'm only just starting to realise what makes half this business tick, and what things you need to do to reach a wider audience. For instance, in retrospect it was a mistake to make 'Just Fascination' a double A side, because as 'Just Fascination' was the A side of the 7", 'Crackdown' was ignored. We learnt through experience that if you release what you think is a good value record with two A sides, one of them will get ignored. Now I would say release them separately, even though that has gone against what we have said in the past.

Do you think that Chris Watson leaving the group influenced your decision to take a further step into the limelight?

Mal: I don't know really. To Chris' credit I don't think he was interested in that side of it much. It is difficult to analyse anything like that in hindsight.

But could you see yourselves as doing the same sort of music as you are doing now if Chris were still in the group?

Richard: Well, yes and no. I don't think the question is particularly relevant because it seemed to me that he just wasn't enjoying it anymore. He always said that if he wasn't enjoying it he would stop. He never saw himself as doing it for the rest of his life. Mind you, neither do I!

What do you see yourself as doing then?

Richard: Living a life of luxury!

Financed by?

Richard: Ah, there is the rub!

So, you don't see yourself like Jagger – still on stage at 45?

Richard: No I don't. Mind you, he's probably a lot fitter at 45 than I am now! I still respect them because they are a fairly controversial bunch, even now.

So, have you never really thought about what you do in terms of a career but very much taken things as they come?

Mal: I think it is all wrapped up in the way that we like to approach what we do. Some people working in our area have very specific goals, which they either achieve or fall short of. We have never put ourselves in that situation, because we have never actually defined what we want to achieve. Therefore, we never have to worry about falling short of goals because we don't know what they are. We try not to blinker ourselves. We fell into music, we fell into films and video, so I suppose in a lot of ways you could say we were complete upstarts.

Although you say that you have a lack of direct goals, there is still a general impression that you know what you are doing.

Mal: Yes, I think that goes back to us working by instinct rather than having a direct message. I think we live in a world where instincts are very important because of the pressures of situations around you. I think the whole idea of being totally in control of your destiny, or even feeling that you are, is totally false. This maybe an existentialist point of view, but I do think there is a danger in being disappointed with not achieving something.

When I say that we don't set ourselves goals, it doesn't mean that there aren't certain standards that we try to achieve. I think the amount you learn on the way is a hell of a lot more useful than achieving goals. Christ, I'm making it sound like the Olympic Games – competing is greater than winning!

Would you say that you would extend that philosophy of not setting goals to your personal life?

Mal: Yes, I think I do really, although I do have aspirations. It is difficult not to sound hypocritical about this, because on the one hand I am saying that I don't have any specific goals, while on the other hand I have to have aspirations. It is a paradox, but I think as long as those aspirations are not too clearly defined, then they are OK.

Similarly, would you say that your amoral attitude to your material extends into your personal philosophy, or do you have a set of morals which dictates things that are acceptable to you?

Mal: Yes, I do think I have a set of morals. There is an amorality about our material, but there is morality in our personalities which possibly tempers the whole thing. Obviously I have got morals – but then again my morals must be quite flexible because I'm not exactly sure what they are!

There must be some morality. I think it is all a case of dignity, the whole idea of not shitting on somebody. For instance, I thought Jock Macdonald making a record with the bloke who broke into The Queen's bedroom was totally immoral. It's not that I give a shit about The Queen, but it is unfortunate that we are at a time when people can do that sort of thing and make money out of it. This might seem an old fashioned viewpoint, but I couldn't be totally Machiavellian or opportunist like that. So, although I'm in it for myself, it's not to the extent of downgrading other people or stooping below certain standards or levels. It is all about dignity even if what I've done really sucks, at least I will have done it in a way I would be proud of.

Richard: I suppose I must be moral somewhere. I mean, I disagree with violence and exploitation, but I am a firm believer in individualism and doing things for yourself. Maybe it is a crude attitude to take, but I think if you have got something to say, and you are determined enough, then there is a way to get through and do it.

But there is a thin line between encouraging individualism and arriving at the position of allowing an 'anything goes' policy which can lead to exploitation.

Richard: Well, what do you do? It's a bit of a horrible world we live in – so do you just say, "Fuck it", and just look out for yourself, or do you try and change it. I still don't know which is the best attitude to adopt. I probably use a mixture of both.

A lot of musicians, Paul Weller or Elvis Costello for example, take the change the world attitude and get involved in promoting their politics and political parties.

Richard: I don't like that kind of sloganeering. Mind you, I think we are more political than any of those people, purely because what we are advocating is individualism. This might sound like a sort of anarchy – it is very difficult to explain – I think we are political but not overtly so.

Mal: Personally I think the whole thing of political preaching really sucks. There again I can't really knock anyone for doing it if they do feel motivated in that way, and do feel that personal responsibility. Personally, I can't see myself using whatever position I am in to toe any party line because I don't believe in any party line. However, I am sure that a person like Paul Weller, much of a tit I think he is, sincerely believes that he is helping by taking that personal responsibility to push people along a certain line. I find that whole aspect a bit frightening in the fact that people do take notice of his position and what he says, and that people are stupid enough to change their politics by what pop group they like.

One area that a lot of musicians traditionally get involved with is that of nuclear disarmament and CND. What are your opinions on nuclear issues?

Richard: That is one thing I'm not too sure about. Obviously there are lots of different arguments you can put forward, but nuclear arms are a reality and they are not going to go away overnight. The superpowers are not going to destroy all their nuclear weapons because there is no trust between them.

Mal: The thing that frightens me most about nuclear weapons isn't America or Russia, it's the Third World. God help us when the Arabs or the African states start lobbing nuclear warheads at each other, because they are getting the technology.

I find it interesting because in a lot of respects the threat of nuclear weapons is just playing on people's obsession with death which we are all subject to. However, it doesn't affect my day-to-day living particularly. Basically, again it is almost an existentialist thing. Whatever I might think or however much I hate them it isn't going to change the situation. I think CND sells crap to people just as much as the government does.

Richard: Yes, I have never supported CND, I don't think that is a way to go about getting things done. No one takes the slightest bit of notice of peaceful protest, it has been proved many times before. People only take notice of violent protest. That is why I admire some of the European peace movements more. In Germany, for instance they get really heavy – which is a contradiction in some ways for a peace movement – but at least they stand a chance of getting things done.

Are you saying that some violence is justifiable?

Richard: It is never justifiable, but it is something that is there, and it often works.

So, are you a pacifist then?

Richard: I hate the word pacifist, I don't like what it smacks of. I prefer the word humanitarian.

By using some political material do you think that people are going to inevitably label you one way or the other?

Richard: Yes, I suppose so. For instance, I remember when the first EP was released with 'Do the Mussolini Headkick' on it, a lot of people thought we were a bunch of fascists, while a lot of others thought we were punks. I remember getting collared around that time by some National Front people in Leeds.

So you don't think artists should get directly involved in politics, what about when politics gets involved with art?

Mal: That is where we in Britain are starting to play a very dangerous game – where standards are going to fall because the politics are coming first. This is why you are getting all these Channel 4 programmes made by people who haven't got a clue about making a TV programme or a film. However, because their intentions or attitudes are such, then they get it shown. Conversely, you have a whole generation who have something to contribute, but because it doesn't toe the line they never get a opportunity to present it – which is really sad. It ends up where you get the situation of a load of left wing Oxford graduates making programmes about steel workers when they don't know the first thing about it.

Richard: Obviously everyone's taste is different in terms of what is good and what is not – but I think generally I would agree with that. I remember going to a meeting about Cable TV and Cable stations and ending up walking out. The whole thing was a pile of shit, programmes about the community, the oppressed, all that sort of stuff. People don't want to see that, they should be talking about making things that are worthwhile and interesting to watch, Also, they are very suspicious of you if you don't belong to an organisation, 'somebody against the something or another'. It's the same with these government bodies that give out arts grants – if you go along as an individual they think you are an out-and-out fascist.

You have already stressed that you don't want to preach at people, but how important is it for you to influence what other people think?

Mal: It is important for us to make people think, and thus I suppose influence them. However, I also find it quite sad that people take influences quite literally, in some respects all we have done is clone a number of Cabaret Voltaire type bands and people. It's just part of human nature.

Richard: It was much the same with punk and The Sex Pistols, although I'm not saying it was on such a wide scale with us. It's a case of seeing something and latching onto it. I'd say we take the basic underlying point of an influence and use it to do something, but not doing a carbon copy. It's OK to be influenced by something, but that doesn't mean you have to do something that sounds or looks exactly the same.

You could take the attitude that people get what they deserve. It is down to way that people are educated, I think the people are educated in the wrong way. I don't think that people are encouraged enough to think along their own lines and act in a way that they think is right. I think there is something radically wrong with the whole education system – it just isn't working, from the day you start school to the day you leave.

So, what would you say your influence on people was?

Richard: I don't know, it's difficult for me to say. I mean, you tell me what our influence is. I think the one thing that people do miss about us is our sense of humour. I mean, everything we do is definitely not deadly serious.

At times you have encouraged others by helping to record and produce their material.

Mal: Yes we have done, but I'm drawing back a little bit from that now. It was becoming very easy to slip into a village-minded attitude, collecting like-minded people around you and helping them. I'm probably not doing that as much as before, because I was tending to lose perspective, and I felt I was becoming a bit of a parody of myself. I was beginning to think that it was the way that Cabaret Voltaire should act, and I was doing it because of that. So, I felt the need to back off a little bit, not in an aloof or elitist way, but just keeping my distance.

Richard: In terms of people using Western Works, it got a bit ridiculous. It wasn't a commercial studio and we had our own things to do. We couldn't play engineers to every local band that came along because we wouldn't have had a chance to develop ourselves.

Also, it is difficult to work in a production capacity for another group – in some respects if you are asked to do so, you should be given a free rein, otherwise what is the point of having you there at all? I'm very wary about working with other people in that capacity, because some people are never satisfied and are always wanting to change things. I just haven't got the time to go along with something like that.

Do you see yourselves, along with people like The Human League, ABC, Clock DVA and Heaven 17, as having promoted a music scene in Sheffield?

Richard: No, not particularly. I can see that people might look at us and think that here were a few people from Sheffield who have gone out and done something – made a few records. We have never gone around preaching to people, telling them to form a group and then we would give them a hand.

I think the 'Sheffield music scene' is a bit of a myth anyway – there has never been that many venues or platforms for expression here.

Particularly in the early days, Cabaret Voltaire tended to be portrayed as having a rather gloomy image. Are people disappointed when they meet you and find that you aren't gloomy introspective types?

Mal: A lot of people are disappointed, I don't know why. Mind you the ones who are, tend to be boring depressing people themselves. Groups like New Order and The Fall would seem to suffer from the same thing.

You once told me that they were two groups that you most felt an affinity with?

Richard: I was lying! No, it probably was true at the time, but I'm not so sure now.

Mal: I still see parallels between us and New Order, because they are also regarded as long mac, philosophical, almost Kafka types. We both still have that stigma.

New Order seem to play up to that image, especially in interviews, whereas you approach them with a more straight forward attitude.

Mal: Well, that is because they don't like doing interviews and they would rather let the music speak for itself. As a group they don't like coming out with blanket statements. The fact is that some groups look good in the press and others don't. For instance, Echo and the Bunnymen talk in phrases that look good in the press – they are a media group. New Order don't talk in those phrases and I don't see why they should. The point is that they are interesting people but they can't pin-point what they do in a few sentences.

You on the other hand, always seem to be very honest in all your interviews, you never play those coy games.

Mal: Yes, we are. Maybe that is why we have lost our appeal to some people. Perhaps a lot of people who originally liked us, went off us, because there was a mystique built up around us which disappeared when they realised we were real human beings. I think maybe we shouldn't have been real human beings!

Maybe a few temperamental tantrums in the press would have helped?

Mal: Yes, I suppose that's it. We are just ordinary working class Northern people and perhaps we should have hidden it better.

So, do you think you are typical Yorkshiremen?

Richard: I should bloody well hope not!

4. A CONTEMPLATION OF DANGEROUS GAMES

If we could talk for a while about some of the things that are censored or banned for public consumption in this country. It must raise a problem of how far you can go with the images you choose for your videos and subject matter for your music. For instance, you have used clips of pornography in your visuals, why?

Mal: Actually, pornography doesn't matter that much to me. The way I see our use of it, is as a way of spitting back at censorship as much as anything else. Richard is a better person to ask, maybe it's my Catholic upbringing!

Richard: I think pornography is very powerful imagery in much the same way as Nazi symbolism. Also, it is something that society has ruled as being taboo. For that reason it is something that I go for straight away – even now it gets people's backs up.

What do you think would happen if there was no censorship?

Richard: In terms of pornography, I think people would lose interest in it. The whole taboo stems from when you are a kid and you are told that nudity is not the done thing – people are not supposed to see you naked. It's just another example of society's tricks to keep you in your place.

Mal: I don't think the situation would change much from what it is at present. However, there is so much money made out of pornography, I don't think it is in a lot of people's interest to stop censorship. If it did stop, I think it would be like water finding its own level, it would be the same with drugs and licensing laws. I can't envisage a whole society motivated by pornography.

Richard: In the case of drugs, a lot of people equate them directly with crime, but the reason why they go hand in hand is the fact that they are illegal, and therefore a lot of people who get involved are really nasty pieces of work. Most of the crime comes from the buying and selling of drugs, and not the effect that the drug itself has on people.

So, what is your attitude toward the use of drugs?

Mal: I think a lot of people still believe in the old hippy ethic of searching for something, which is quite interesting in some ways, but doesn't mean anything to me personally. Basically I would rather read about that sort of thing in books like Aldous Huxley's *Doors Of Perception*, because it is a lot safer, and a whole lot cheaper!

I think people take drugs for three main reasons. The first I have already mentioned – those people who are looking for something, whereby it is another form of religion, just another crutch to lean on. The second are those people who are totally screwed up, in which case they are the wrong people to be taking drugs. Thirdly there are those who take them for purely hedonistic reasons, which would be the reason I would take them. I think it one of those stages you go through in life.

Richard: I think it very much depends on the type of drug you are talking about. A lot of people do take them purely for pleasure, whilst others take them for the way it alters the state of mind. In terms of LSD, and to a lesser extent marijuana, it is seen as a means of achieving a trance-like state, and as a means to a vision.

This trance-like state, or vision, is what Huxley defined as 'suchness' – or seeing objects in a different light. Do you think there is anything in that concept, or would you tend toward the view of the people who say that drugs are a limiter to perception?

Richard: Well, I think there is something to be said for both schools of thought. Personally, I would tend toward Huxley's viewpoint. For example, anyone who has ever taken acid is unlikely to see the world in the same light as they did before. To a lesser extent the same is true of marijuana. I think there is definitely something in seeing things out of context like Huxley did.

So, do you think that within that context drugs can be a useful artistic tool?

Richard: Yes, I think there is more to it than pure hedonism. Obviously it is down to personal interpretation. Even down to the use of alcohol – would Kerouac have been such a good writer if he hadn't been a drunk?

People have used stimulants of one sort or another for a very long time. They have been used in religious ceremonies for centuries. The old Shamans and healers would always get wrecked before a ceremony. I see little difference between that and a load of musicians doing the same thing! It's just another ritual procedure.

I think the important point to stress is that drugs are fine as long as you use them, and you don't let them use you. The most dangerous of all in that respect is heroin. I have never taken it myself, but I have seen enough people who have, and read enough about it to know that it is something I wouldn't want to get involved in.

Mal: I think you have to be specific about certain drugs, in that certain people can use them to the right ends, but they are very few – most people would tend to get side-tracked.

Do you think that censorship is over-excessive in Britain, for instance in the case of licensing laws?

Richard: In the case of licensing laws you only have to look at Europe as a whole, where you can buy a drink any time of the day or night and there doesn't seem to be any more people drunk. In England, because you have only three hours to get blotto you go at it full pace, whereas in Europe you can take your time.

Do you think that censorship restrictions have anything to do with the fact that Britain seemingly produces a larger share of musicians working in a similar vein to you?

Mal: I don't know whether Britain does, or whether it is just that we have the channels for it to come out. I think it would be to easy to say it was due to the way censorship confines people.

However, it is still the case that you could count the number of notable French rock groups on one hand, for instance.

Mal: More like one finger! I think you have to look back and see the way the particular cultures and societies have developed. The French are a very leisure-based people in a lot of ways, whereas in Britain we still have this 19th Century work ethic which carries through society. I mean you can't name many British philosophers, whereas philosophy is a very strong French thing. Those sorts of traditions are steeped a long way back, but I don't know why it manifests itself in Britain in terms of contemporary music.

There are more outlets for contemporary music in Britain, perhaps?

Mal: Yes, people do tend to tailor their expression to the way they can get their material the best exposure.

In tackling taboos and censored subjects, do you think there is a danger in becoming obsessed with the darker side of life?

Richard: I suppose concentrating on those areas is a kind of obsession. It's something that I find very interesting, constantly delving and researching more and more about it. I suppose that you could say that it was obsessive to be interested in taboos rather than gardening or something like that!

Mal: I think it is a criticism that could be laid at a lot of people's doors – many people concentrate on the obsessive chic of certain things. Personally I am very wary of that sort of thing. I think it is to our benefit that we are a lot more rational than some. I mean, no criticism of Psychic TV, but Gen has always run that thin line where there is a possibility of opening up something where he would have no control of the end result.

Might people then argue that Cabaret Voltaire is just a watered down version of a group like Psychic TV?

Mal: Yes, to a degree that might be true – we have the same general interest areas as Psychic – so people are bound to see parallel trends. I think the big difference between us is the language we use. We use the language of music and film without particularly knowing what we are trying to say, whereas with Psychic TV the most important thing is what they are trying to say, a message.

One of the largest general interest areas would appear to be the notion of control.

Richard: I think it was Burroughs who said that the machine had gone out of control. I think that is true to a certain extent in that the people who are in so-called control don't know what they are in control of anymore.

Mal: Yes, control is sometimes manifest and sometimes subliminal and sub-conscious. I think when you analyse it, the whole notion of control is actu-ally an internal thing – it is within you, you are the one who is conscious of the control. Control is a thing of your own mind and the only way to liberate yourself from it is to liberate your own mind.

But how can you liberate yourself from those aspects of control that work on a subconscious level?

Mal: I don't think you can. I think the only way is to try and become more aware of it, to become more knowledgeable although in some respects the more you know the worse it becomes. I don't think you can shut yourself off from it. I think you are a participant whatever happens, whether you are part of a police state or part of a bureaucracy, and whether you have access to the media or not.

So, do you think that by the method of research and knowledge we can negate some of those areas of control? Come out on the other side with some greater understanding?

Mal: I don't think there is another side actually. I don't think there is some black hole that you can come out of the end and say, "Great, we've washed the streets clean, now we'll start again."

In the light of that, what is your opinion of the media?

Mal: I think the media is a strengthening of those control bonds that exist already. The media just embellishes them.

Richard: I think that most newspapers are a joke, they are rubbish and it is sad that people believe them. People actually believe what they read in *The Sun*. You hear people talking, repeating things that they read in the newspa-pers, believing that they are the absolute truth. I used to read the *Morning Star*, the communist newspaper, and if you compared what they said about an event, and what *The Sun* said about it, it was as if you were reading about two different events.

I remember when Tony Benn was standing for the Chesterfield by-election, the Tory gutter press went out to do a smear campaign on him. I can't understand the mentality of these people who write these articles. They are either really clever or really stupid, I can't make up my mind which it is. They write in such away that is really simple but it is pitting their opinion against public opinion in order to influence people. I find it really sick and sinister as well.

What about TV? Do you agree with the opinion that ours is the best in the world?

Richard: I think it probably is. I've watched TV in quite a lot of other countries and certainly in terms of documentaries Britain seems to be the best.

What about comedy on TV? What sort of things make you laugh?

Richard: Bilko, Russ Abbott. I think one of my all time favourite comedy films is *The Rebel* with Tony Hancock. It is so well done, you can see people just like the character he plays in the film, wandering about all the time. I'm probably one of them!

In terms of what we do – anybody who can bring out 'Do the Mussolini Headkick' can't be totally serious. That was black humour inspired by a piece of film footage of all those people laying the boot in on old Musso's corpse. I'd draw a comparison with a lot of Bunuel's films – there is something subversive about it, but it is also really funny.

So would you describe your humour as pretty black?

Mal: Yes, I'd love to have seen Tommy Cooper die on TV!

A lot of people wouldn't admit to that. It is a bit taboo to say that there is something funny about someone dying on stage.

Mal: Yes, it is a slightly morbid thing to want to see, but he died happy doing what he wanted. I'd love to see someone die in their moment of glory. Tommy Cooper dying on stage – live on TV – it's like someone dying in battle!

It was a powerful piece of television. I suppose there is a detachment watching that sort of thing on TV – whereas if you went out of your way to go and see it live you would be considered a ghoul.

Mal: It is the sort of detachment that journalists have to have in order to report or film certain things – so as to leave the viewer open to see it. The viewer also has that detachment – because it is on TV the viewer can remain anonymous – rather than actually physically having to go and see it.

Do you think that people flocking to the scene of a disaster is just an extension of that, or is it something more? I couldn't see myself doing that.

Mal: No, I couldn't join in that sort of thing – that goes back to that real '*Sun* mentality' .

There is a fine line between journalistic interest and morbid fascination. Most people are happy to watch it on TV and let the cameraman do the dirty work for them.

Mal: Yes, because it gives the viewer a moral detachment from it. It is the same with a lot of the material that we use, the viewer has that anonymity and they can see the things that they want to see.

It is undeniable that people enjoy watching violent images? Is that inevitable? Are people always going to be obsessed with violence?

Mal: People always have been. It has always been the same, it is just the tools and wording have changed over the years. The hypocrisy of it is -that what society rejects are the things that society loves the most. As you say, people do like to watch violent images – so the things we knock the most are the things we want to watch. It is what gets the adrenalin going, it is basic human instinct. It is a fascination, we all love to watch horror films, we all love to hear ghost stories. It makes you more aware of mortality. The actual emotions and issues, and the points raised are the same. The way people are sold violence has never changed. People were sold Hitler in the same way that we are sold nuclear weapons.

Your lists of reading matter and visuals often include a lot of material on Hitler and the Nazis. Why do you think that the Nazis represent a fascination to a lot of people?

Mal: Ironically, although a lot of people wouldn't admit it, much of the fascination stems from the fact that they could perpetrate such atrocities which had such repercussions, but still have this very cosmetic point of style. It is a very cosmetic point about the Nazis, but it is still true, that however much you hate the Nazis, they still had style.

Do you think that the power of Nazi symbolism is what people still find interesting?

Mal: Yes, I think people are very interested in the way that they worked psychologically, which has probably made the Nazis the largest public relations exercise the world has ever seen.

Richard: Oh yeah, they had the best designers working for them of any army I have ever seen. I think it is very powerful imagery, and even today people are saying that the subject is taboo and should be swept under the carpet. There is definitely something to be said for that phrase, "Those who forget the past are condemned to repeat it". I don't think Nazism is something you can forget about and just sweep it away.

5. SLUGGIN' FER JESUS

You have used religion as a theme fairly extensively, both in your music ('Sluggin' Fer Jesus', 'Red Mecca', 'Three Mantras' etc.) and your visuals. What are your reasons for doing so?

Richard: Our use of religious material is a mischievous thing. I see religion as a totally ridiculous entity, so why not take the piss out of it? That's what is really good about Bunuel's films, I mean he built a whole career around that.

Would you say then that you had no religious beliefs?

Richard: I don't know. No, I don't think I do have any. I tend to believe in a combination of science and mysticism – and that somewhere between the two lies the key. There are so many things that can't be explained purely scientifically at the moment. However, the whole of religion is such a farce, it's just another form of control and repression. It dates back to the inquisition – and before that – when it was used as a tool to create fear in people and keep them in their place, and I think it is still like that.

You always wear a cross around your neck though?

Richard: It's just jewellery as far as I'm concerned. I used to tell people that I wore it to keep the vampires away.

What about your religious beliefs, Mal. Would you describe yourself as a religious person?

Mal: It sounds a bit paradoxical, but I am quite a religious person in that I am aware of it all the time, and I think that is because I was brought up a Catholic. I am not a Catholic now, but I think being brought up as one has really helped me. The whole idea of Catholicism sucks, but nothing has benefited me more than being brought up in that sort of atmosphere, because it gives you some sense of value. It was only after realising that sense of value I could discard it.

So would you say you were an atheist now?

Mal: No I wouldn't because I do believe in something but I'm not sure what it is. I'm a bit of traditional agnostic in that sense – a bit of a liberal. I think the ultimate truth is in yourself. In some respects the religion I believe in is myself, by developing knowledge through experience. First hand knowledge is the main point for me, reaching into yourself, and as a consequence of that, yourself is the only thing that you can ever really find out more about.

Did you both have a religious upbringing?

Richard: Well, I went to a church school, and on Christian religious days we'd have to go to church in the morning and then we'd have the afternoon off. So, in that respect religion was a good thing!

Mal: I was given a very traditional religious upbringing, being brought up by monks and having to go to church every Sunday. It was good in the sense that it really made me realise how much shit there is. Whereas, if you don't have that sort of background there is a tendency not to realise how religious other people are, and more basically what religion actually is.

A lot of the motivation for religion appears to born out of fear – usually the fear of death.

Mal: Both religion and the occult are motivated toward sex and the fear of death. Christianity in a very passive way, and I think the occult is something that negates that.

Richard: It' s the fear of damnation or hell-fire or whatever. Like in Islam, where if they don't bury you facing Mecca then you don't go to wherever it is you are supposed to go.

Are you afraid of death. Does it worry you?

Richard: You've caught me on a bad day actually – I'm not feeling too well today! Every now and then I wake up and there's a little nag in the back of my head which says, "I'm going to snuff it one of these days". I suppose everybody gets those, you just push it to the back of your mind and get on with it.

Mal: Yes, we are all subject to an obsession with death, but it doesn't affect my day-to-day living particularly.

When you say obsession with death, do you think it is an obsession that artists are more prone to?

Mal: No, I think we are all much the same. Maybe that little bit of soul searching that artists tend to do elevates it by trying to put death in perspective. Whereas, with other people it is just more subconscious. Everyone is obsessed with sex and death, artists just question it a little bit more, where other people might accept it.

A lot of people, particularly artists and writers, get drawn to religion later in life – Salvador Dali, for example.

Richard: Yes, and Burroughs talking about space travel is just sublimating it into another area. I think as you get older you become more resigned to your fate. It is pretty inescapable! That is unless you are a great believer in reincarnation.

Could you ever see yourself turning to a belief in reincarnation?

Mal: Yes, I suppose so, because I am open to anything. I don't know whether I would go as far as religious conversion though. I think that is why religions are so strong, because a little bit of them exists in everybody. I think it is a bit foolhardy to just dismiss it by saying, "Oh God, that's a load of shit". I don't think you can be too rational, too black and white, about deeply emotive areas. I think the whole notion of religions and mortality is fascinating.

You both also seem to be interested in the occult?

Mal: Yes, I do find it interesting. I think in general there is a resurgence in interest in it – because modern life, and Western society in particular, has eroded people's values to the point where they feel the need to latch onto something or find some sense of being. I don't think that Christian religion has been able to keep up with that need. I find the occult intriguing because of the gradual destruction of the old knowledge of what happened before Christianity – so from a specific and objective point of view I find it interesting to try and find out a little bit more about this old knowledge and the old cultures. I have come to realise how much Christian values have eroded what has gone before.

Richard: My interest in the occult stems from the fact that it is something that you are supposed to shy away from. To a person like myself, if I'm told it is taboo, that just makes it all the more interesting to me and I have got to find out what it is all about. I'm not saying that I'm interested in conjuring up demons, but I don't think you can dismiss the whole thing.

You look at it as tackling one of society's taboos?

Richard: Yes, for example, if you go to the library and look through the index under Aleister Crowley, you will find a long list of titles but you might only find one of them on the shelves, the others are out the back. That makes me wonder why all those other books are not on the shelves?

Is your interest totally academic or have you had any direct experiences?

Richard: I think deja vu and coincidences are all experiences of that sort. The whole idea of psychic phenomena really interests me. I recently read a book about psychic discoveries behind the Iron Curtain, it is obviously an area which interests them greatly although a lot of people are bound to say that they are looking to use it as a weapon against America. I would imagine it is done purely for research, like the people who research into it in England and America, but there are enough people around who will just say, "It's those nasty Russians at it again".

If you start to dig around and look at things from an occult viewpoint, there are a lot of strange coincidences. A friend of a friend did a lot of research into this and he found things leading to addresses in the UN building tying in with UFOs and the men in black. I think there is a hell of a lot to it. I couldn't begin to explain it but there is obviously something strange going on behind the scenes.

It would seem to me that it is easy to draw conclusions from these sorts of coincidences. Do you think the sort of people who do this sort of research are too susceptible to connecting everything they find?

Richard: Yes, in some cases, but I do think it is healthy to always be on the look out. However, it is easy to start reading things into it that aren't there in the first place. You have to watch out for that.

Isn't the occult merely the other side of the coin to religion – just an alternative way of controlling people?

Richard: Like anything else there is bound to be a hierarchy in an occult society, but from what I have read, it is to be used for your own ends rather than someone else telling you what to do, and therefore controlling you.

6. MAKES THE WORLD ROUND

How do you approach your finances and is financial control very important to you?

Mal: Yes, it is important to us, and we are still aware of what is going on, although not to the extent of doing the bookwork.

So, the Cabaret Voltaire financial set-up is basically two people and an accountant?

Mal: Yes.

Exactly how important is it for someone in your position to remain aware of the finances available to you?

Mal: I think it is very important because it is one of the yardsticks by which you can judge how you are able to develop, and how to continue working. I think there is a real danger of people jumping in and not realising what their true potential is. If you can keep control of the financial side of things – not to the extent of knowing where every penny goes, but at least keeping a clear picture of what's happening – then you are less likely to overstretch yourselves, or take the wrong decisions at the wrong time.

What is your attitude to making money? How do think it would affect you if you made a lot of it?

Mal: It's bound to affect you. There is always the case where you might say that having money would be great because I could put the money to a use – you know, "I am the one who knows how to use it". Howard Hughes, for instance, didn't have a clue how to use the money he made.

Have you any qualms about making money?

Richard: No, not me. If anyone asks me about money and earning it, my answer is always that there is nothing wrong with earning money, it's what you do with it when you have got it that's important. I mean, if you make a lot of money and choose to waste it on indulgence and trash, then I suppose that is fair enough. If I had a lot of money I would put it to some creative use, but I see nothing wrong with making money – I've never said the opposite.

Mal: I think it is a sad state of affairs when people slag you off if you earn a lot of money from what you do – particularly in an artistic way. It's not the money itself, it's the fact that you've made it in that way. Nobody has ever knocked Kraftwerk or Yello for having really rich parents and not having to work at all.

Would you say that your philosophy was basically capitalist – in terms of making the best of what's available to you, and using it to affect people?

Richard: Well, you could say that I was a capitalist, but I see capitalism as a concept based on exploitation, and I don't see that I am exploiting anyone in particular. As far as I can see, we make good music and people pay money to hear it. Fair enough.

Mal: Yes, I agree. I have no qualms about it. I mean, years ago I was anti-capitalist, but I was an idiot. Now I have no qualms about it or about making money. I think if you are in that sort of system you have to utilise it – you have to use those channels and those formulae, meaning that you have to be basically capitalist in your outlook.

So, you believe in the market economy?

Richard: Yes, that's why I would never vote for communism. I suppose you could say that I was a capitalist, but not in the exploitation sense.

It is difficult to ascertain the levels of unemployment under communism, but do you think that in Capitalist countries in the future we will have to accept it as inevitable?

Richard: I think the whole thing relates to the way that society is geared to the work ethic. That is what is drummed into you at school – at least it was when I was brought up. Perhaps now there is mass unemployment people aren't told the same things anymore.

Possibly people need some sort of work ethic to hold on to. For instance, you work pretty hard at what you are doing, but you are in the lucky position of doing the thing you enjoy most for a living.

Richard: Yes, I can see that point of view. Myself it is always a struggle between pleasure and getting on with creative outlets. I don't like getting too lazy. There is only so much time you can spend sitting on your arse drinking beer, or whatever. There is always something nagging me in the back of my head to get on with something useful!

However, the way things are going with the increase in technology and computerisation, the work ethic has become less relevant. Technology is making people redundant, so what are you going to tell people who leave school in five years time?

Have you ever been tempted to spend any of your money on the more typical material things such as cars?

Richard: Well, I have a mortgage and Mal has had one. I have never been motivated to drive, and now I can afford a car I am not that bothered. I quite often take taxis, which is a bit extravagant, but unlike owning a car you only have to pay for taxis when you use them.

However, I am really fond of 1958 American Chevrolets. I do love those big old cars, and if I did ever own a car it would definitely be one of those. I think they are palaces of kitsch on wheels.

The fifties and sixties produced such wonderful examples of kitsch style because of the relative prosperity. Is it a whole period that fascinates you?

Richard: Yes, I have a soft spot for it even though I wasn't old enough to experience it, but I have read a lot about it in books. It might just have been crap at the time, but on the other hand, a lot of people who did experience the sixties did reckon it was as good as it was made out to be. Some of the things I read in that Warhol book on the sixties (*Popism*) just made me green with envy.

What about some of the Beat writers like Kerouac, were you influenced by that 'On The Road' mentality?

Richard: Well, I thought *On The Road* was a bit over-romanticised – the whole bit about being a tramp. However, I did get quite a lot of motivation from those books I must admit. I think they changed my attitude toward a lot of things including money, and opened up a lot of avenues. After all, why should you follow others? Why shouldn't you choose your own path, regardless of whether you make money out of it or not?

'On The Road' could only have been written about America and that period in the US holds a fascination for a lot of people. To a lot of people America still appears

as the ultimate in affluence – what are your impressions of the country when you visit there?

Mal: Well, a lot of our visits are for pure pleasure – we treat it like a holiday, so we tended only to see the good side. However, although we are never there long enough to see the bad side, you still get an impression of it. We have spent quite a bit of time in San Francisco and that is more like a European city. I thought Los Angeles was really the most disgusting place I've ever been to in my life.

Richard: I enjoy America while I'm there – I think it opens your eyes a lot. People might speak the same language as us, but it is still very different.

What is the reaction like when you play out there?

Mal: Really good, For instance, in Los Angeles the people are just totally psychotic – the whole place is on the brink, on a knife-edge and the people just reflect that.

People always say that we are just ten years behind America. Do you think we have got that coming?

Mal: Yes, I mean I can see it happening already. A lot of it is linked to how linked they are to the consumer society – a society with a built in obsolescence, which is what we in Britain are becoming.

Richard: As regards them being ten years ahead I think they are in some ways. Certainly in terms of technology, but I don't think they're ahead culturally speaking. I don't see the same parallel with crime either, because basically there are so many firearms in America – especially with the police being armed. I think violence breeds violence.

You're not exactly renowned as a prolific touring band, so how did you come to play in America in the first place?

Mal: Rough Trade were setting themselves up in America by opening an office on the West Coast. Peter Walmsley, who was the person we worked most closely with at Rough Trade, was the person who went to set it up. He was a friend and a fan, who was continuously working for us while we were at Rough Trade especially after the incident where we pulled out of the Kleenex and Raincoats tour. He and his girlfriend went to San Francisco, and we went with them almost as a public relations exercise, helping to establish Rough Trade in America. In fact, a lot of the places we have played have been linked to what Peter Walmsley was doing at the time. It was the same with Japan, because Peter was the one who dealt with the licensing.

What were your impressions of Japan?

Richard: One thing I found very interesting about Japan is its split personality – on the one hand they have got all this incredibly high technology, whilst on the other hand you have got people walking around in Kimonos and all the traditional gear. I think I also liked it because everyone was really polite – I don't think I met anyone who was obnoxious the whole time I was there. Generally, I admire the way things are done out there. Particularly the efficiency is something I admire. I can't stand inefficiency. For instance, I always try and be on time – little things like that.

Did you find it a culture shock going to Japan?

Mal: It was a tremendous culture shock, especially the way that their traditional way of life carries on in their psychology. As people, they still retain a very medieval self-respect and caste system. It is odd, because they also have this consumer society while still retaining the ideas of self-respect.

They have very much absorbed American culture, the fast food etc. The kids have also absorbed American teen culture like Happy Days and rockabilly – they seem to look toward that trash American culture. Ironically, the Americans have totally shit on them. America still uses Japan as an area to dump nuclear waste and the Japanese just sit there and accept it. I do like them for their self-respect, that is something that has totally fallen here in Britain. However, the bad side of it is that they are very happy to accept their role and bow to whoever.

I think there is going to be a tremendous backlash in Japan. The right wing element is really growing, not in a fascist political way, although that might develop as well, but there is this segment of society that the older generation really resents and this has filtered through to the younger generation. They resent the way that they have been Americanised and lost some of their traditional ways of life. This is more than just a 'back to the land' sort of thing. It is more ethical, where you are getting this type of reversal to the Samurai way in a lot of their thinking.

They seem to have an extraordinarily high set of personal standards and morals.

Richard: Yes, I think that is mainly to do with the difference between Eastern and Western ideals. Their minds seem to work in a totally different way.

Why do you think they like your music?

Richard: I haven't got a clue. I think some of our music may have Eastern leanings.

Could you see yourself living in Japan or America. In fact is there anywhere other than Sheffield that you would consider living?

Richard: Yes, but it probably wouldn't be in England. I would mention Tokyo and San Francisco because they are two of the places out of those I have visited that I have been taken with. I like the idea of living in Tokyo because of the technology that is racing along all the time. I probably couldn't handle living there all year, but maybe for three months or so.

Amsterdam also, I would put that on my list. I like Amsterdam because the people there are really pleasant all the time. There's something abnormal about people who are really pleasant all the time! In terms of living abroad, I quite admire what Bowie has done. He's lived in a lot of different places and obviously if you can afford to do it I think that is a good thing to do. It makes you so much more broad-minded, it opens you eyes to see how different societies and cultures live.

A lot of touring inevitably means a lot of flying. Are you nervous of flying?

Richard: It's not natural is it! It's not the actual sensation that bothers me. Once I've got over the shock that the thing has actually got off the ground, I start to think that there is a lot of distance between me – in this metal cylinder 30,000 feet up – and the ground. I just take some tranquillisers, down loads of booze and put my Walkman headphones on.

Do you think that you will be under increasing pressure to play more abroad?

Mal: I don't think our touring will increase to the extent that it could do. We are still a very British band – we still look to Britain as the main litmus test for what we do. We certainly wouldn't want to fall into the trap of touring more instead of developing what we do. I certainly have no interest in flogging the same fucking thing to everyone else.

7. TOWARD NEW VISIONS

As a group you have always put a heavy emphasis on the visual side of your presentation. This culminated in you setting up your own video label Doublevision. You obviously considered that there was scope for an independent video label at that time?

Mal: Yes, as we progressed we realised that we were in the position to achieve some of the things that other people had talked about. In particular, the link between the music and the use of visuals, film and video. In our own quiet way we found that we were able to fill a gap in a practical way.

When you set up Doublevision you presumably had a lot of footage accumulated that you had used in live performance over the years. Your first video release, like a lot of the films you use live, contained a great variety of footage including the violent and political as well as fairly anonymous imagery. Was it just a case of throwing in everything but the kitchen sink?

Mal: With the visuals it is very much like that. I don't think we can discard the chance element, the whole idea of the cut-up principle. I think that if we threw that out of either our films or our music, we would probably make everything we have done in the past redundant. I think if we tried to synchronise the visual side with the music, we would be doing nothing more than the early Human League did. With us it is more of a case of chance juxtaposition, but remaining selective about the material we choose to use.

So, it is more of a blanket presentation rather than trying to make a point at any stage?

Richard: That's true to a certain extent. I think it goes back to the Dadaist notion of being mischievous, just playing around juxtaposing different images and sounds and seeing what the end product is.

There would appear to be an amoral attitude in the presentation of a whole range of visual material which leaves people to make of it what they will. Is it important to you not to be making a particular point?

Richard: Yes, because if you do take a moral standpoint it becomes something you are known for, a millstone around your neck that you may get stuck with.

Couldn't you then be criticised for sitting on the fence and hedging your bets?

Richard: Yes, sure.

Also relying heavily on chance elements, aren't you laying yourselves open to the criticism, "Anyone could do that", or are you saying that you have a special instinct for it?

Mal: Definitely an instinct. Only an idiot could believe that it was totally random. It all depends on what you choose to include. That is where you stamp your identity on it. The point is, we choose the source material, we choose what to cut up, we choose what to juxtapose.

Is your success at this selection process because you have a clearer idea of the images you want to portray, or because your instinct for imagery is better then others?

Mal: I would go for the latter, because we still feel instinctively what will look or sound right – or on the other hand what is not visually right for us.

Richard: I can't really explain a lot of what we do, I don't know why we are doing it half the time. It is only afterwards when I sit down to think about it that it makes any sense. It is a very instinctive thing.

So, it is not actually knowing what you are trying to do, but instinctively feeling it?

Mal: Yes, exactly. I think if we knew exactly what we were trying to do it would be too conceptual, and we are not those sort of people. That is where we differed from Throbbing Gristle, who we were often compared with in the early days. They had a conceptual idea of what they were doing and what they wanted to get across. It's the same with Psychic TV, it is very much a game to them in the sense that they know what they are saying, and if you rumble that you are in. That is all very well, but I don't think we play that sort of game.

From watching some of your videos, it would appear to me that you have been fairly successful in throwing images back at people, especially news footage, that are familiar to them and highlighting those images in a different context.

Mal: I think what we do in a very primitive way is to throw back some of those images. I don't know whether the way we use media footage actually works in terms of people recognising some of the biased and hypocritical aspects of the media – or whether it is just that the pictures look nice and they fit in with the music.

You mean pure flirtation with imagery?

Mal: Yes, exactly. You can talk with hindsight about a lot of these things but I'm sure for a lot of people our use of imagery just looks nice. Maybe that is a lot of the appeal for us as well.

One of Doublevision's releases was the 'TV Wipeout' video which was a sort of disposable video magazine compilation. It contained a fairly wide variety of contributors, from people like The Fall and Test Dept to some more mainstream groups like Bill Nelson and Japan.

Mal: The point was that Virgin Films were quite happy to work with us – they even gave us money in terms of advertising revenue for using some of the clips from the Virgin catalogue. We were then able to camouflage them into the whole set up and make them look as if they were part of the whole nature of the video compilation.

One of the clips was a particularly inane interview with David Bowie. Was its inclusion merely a selling point?

Mal: Yes, it was purely that. There are a lot of people who will buy anything with David Bowie on it. So we said, "Fuck it, why not use that as a pure selling point". Actually the interview is appalling, it's terrible. Our including was almost like a piss take. We were saying, "You really will buy anything with David Bowie on it if you buy this".

I particularly enjoyed the Renaldo and the Loaf piece of film.

Richard: Yes, apparently they are a couple of really normal blokes who live in Portsmouth who happened to meet The Residents when they visited America.

Did you see The Residents when they finally got to play over here?

Richard: Yes, I was a bit disappointed. It was a bit too much like a sixth form drama class with all those tacky drops that kept moving around the stage. Parts of it I quite enjoyed, but it was a bit too much of the concept album scenario. That whole business of 'The Mole Trilogy'. I mean, why bother to try and explain that out?

Doublevision also released the Derek Jarman film 'In the Place of the Sun' on video. How did that come about?

Richard: Derek Jarman had his own film company called Dark Pictures which he set up in conjunction with 2 or 3 other people. I think they got in touch with us with regard to releasing the video.

It seems to me that Derek Jarman as an independent film-maker has the balance about right between the avant-garde and the realistic.

Richard: Yes, I watched *Jubilee* again recently, and I think it watches a lot better now than it did when it came out. I don't know whether my attitude has changed or whether I've become a bit more educated about certain things, but it seemed to make a lot more sense now.

In terms of film makers Bunuel is someone who seems to interest you particularly. Have you read his autobiography, 'My Last Breath'?

Richard: Yes, I have. I was impressed with the way that he described how they made *Un Chien Andalou* – they just got their finger out and went and did it. It is reading that sort of thing that makes me think that it is about time that we got up and did something like that. Also, he describes how, when they were making *Un Chien Andalou*, they put in a lot of pieces that had no meaning, reason or logic. That has always appealed to me.

Generally up to now you have always stressed that you put your ideas across in a very unstructured way. Can you envisage that method of working ever changing?

Mal: Yes, with video I can envisage us taking a more structured approach, because it is a more controlled medium. I think with the use of editing techniques you can emphasise certain things and still keep it stimulating, whilst still retaining some chance elements. When we finished editing the Doublevision Cabaret Voltaire video we decided that it was the last time we would do that sort of grainy video. The texture of the video was nice, it worked well, but we would never want to do that again.

However, I can't envisage us taking a more structured approach in terms of live performance. Live performance has got to be spontaneous – it has got to have that chance element. If you take that element out, you take out all the fun for us.

So, if you were to make a film, for instance, would you take a more structured approach?

Richard: It is a case of making some kind of structure and fitting that in context. I think that is what we would want to do with a film, actually take it one step further and put it to some use, make it do something.

Could you imagine producing something that was scripted?

Richard: I don't know whether we would stretch to a narrative running through it or whether it would be scripted. Whether a narrative would make any point or a script any sense is another matter. In some respects a script and dialogue would force us to be more structured. It would be a case of learning where we would need to take a more calculated approach as we went along. What we hope to do with the visuals would be similar to what we have done with the recent music, and that is to produce a more disciplined order of things, but within that use the cut-up technique. So, the cut-up principle would be used more to some effect, and less as an end in itself.

However, you will be concentrating mostly on the music for the moment?

Richard: Obviously, as it provides our main source of income. If we didn't make records we couldn't do the visuals because we couldn't afford the resources.

Are there any other areas in which you are interested in getting involved? For instance, in an old interview I remember reading once that you were interested in opening a club.

Richard: The more you go on, the more you realise the impracticalities of a thing like that. You begin to realise why other people haven't done it.

Factory's Hacienda club, for instance, very soon turned into just another rock venue.

Richard: That is how it ended up – all the prices went up. You can't really do it, even if you take over an established club one night a week. The only thing that comes close to what I would want to do are the Jamaican Blues Clubs where the police won't touch them. Just somewhere to go.

Is there not a potential for some sort of video club where videos could be shown on a more ambient level, rather than having to sit and watch them?

Richard: Well, we did a video performance at the Hacienda that nobody came to, and it went along its own little way. The videos got shown and people wandered around, some of them watched some of them didn't. There was only a couple of hundred people there, which was little bit daunting in a place as big as the Hacienda. I think we learned how not to do it. The next time we do something like that it will be better.

One thing that has struck me as surprising about your live presentations is that you have nearly always stuck solidly to playing and performing at established rock venues.

Mal: The reason why we play established rock venues is because we tread a thin line between being the arty band and the ordinary band.

Richard: It was a conscious decision to play those places because we hated the performance art side of it. Doing the sort of music we did, it would have been really obvious to do gigs in performance art places. We felt that to achieve anything we had to take it to rock places. I think it goes back to the provocation, putting on things like we did infront of people who were used to rock 'n' roll. That was where the appeal lay. Perhaps we should do the reverse now!

You have occasionally played less rock-orientated sets. You did a sort of video presentation in Belgium.

Richard: The Belgian show was more fun than the video evening at the Hacienda. I was really into the idea of intimidating the Belgians, because it was advertised that we were supposed to be playing someone fucked us over somewhere there. It was great, we appeared in total darkness and people complained that we weren't even on stage! Blaine, who used to be in Tuxedo Moon, would go on stage before the shows and start winding the audience up and insulting them. He would make up all these ridiculous names for bands. At one point there were three different groups on stage just churning out some kind of noise!

The Belgian shows were directly after you played the third night of The Final Academy. The whole event was an attempt to mix readings by Burroughs and Gysin with some of the contemporary groups who have been influenced by them. What was your opinion on the success of that?

Mal: I was quite disappointed with it. I found it very establishment, very arty, very strict. Very gallery-ish.

Richard: I spoke to Gen quite a few times about a year before it was organised and I don't think it was his intention to make it cosy and cliquey. I don't think he viewed it like that at all. I think it was successful insomuch as it brought a lot of people together with similar aims and a similar outlook on things.

The whole thing did seem to be very strict. People being forced into seats and no bar etc.!

Richard: Just because the Final Academy was a literary thing, why shouldn't there be a bar? Why shouldn't people be able to wander round. The idea of seated venues is horrible.

Mal: It didn't appeal to the people it was meant to. It was too strait-laced. What was on show was supposed to be contemporary poetry, music and literature but it seemed to have no spirit or spontaneity. I think the organisation of the event was so difficult that it had to be done like that, but half the time I felt like I was watching an auction.

Richard: The whole thing failed in the same way as the Kodo drummers did when I went to see them recently. It was like seeing them in a church, you couldn't speak in case someone turned round and told you to shut up. I didn't like that whole atmosphere.

Do you think the Final Academy was over-ambitious? Do you think that an event like that could ever work?

Mal: I think it could, but not in England, and certainly not at the Brixton Ritzy! In retrospect it seemed very clinical, it didn't seem to have an awful lot of life of its own. However, we were only there on one night. I thought Burroughs was good though.

Richard: I thought he was hilarious. He's a great stand up comic that bloke.

Is it true you met him in Belgium once?

Richard: Yes, it was a few years ago now. It was more a case of just sitting around a table drinking champagne and listening to him. There was some French geek asking him what he thought of Suicide. Burroughs started talking on about people killing themselves – obviously he had never heard of the group. I gave Burroughs a Cabaret Voltaire badge.

That was in 1979, when you were on the bill with Joy Division amongst others at Le Plank.

Richard: Yes, and in some respects that whole thing was a lot more successful than the Final Academy. It was held in this sort of arts centre, which had a bar for one thing! There were a whole load of things going on. They had a bloke playing improvised saxophone at one end of the building and Burroughs was on a different floor doing his readings. There were TV monitors everywhere so you could see what was going on. They were showing all Burroughs' films in another room.

Somehow you could never imagine that sort of event happening in Britain.

Richard: We can't get our shit together here. I think in Europe there is so much more money available for that sort of thing. For instance, that whole Le Plank event was sponsored by the government. The same is true in America where there seems to be the facilities to get things done. Certainly with regard to something like big budget films, the money always seems to be there somewhere. For instance, John Carpenter made *Dark Star* while he was still at college. You certainly couldn't do that here. The money must be available in England – it is just that the Arts Council grants go to the biggest wankers imaginable.

I think a lot of it boils down to the fact that we seem to be really embarrassed by the arts in this country.

Richard: Yes, they always seem to be discredited. At school there were kids who were shit hot artists, but they never seemed to be encouraged. People in this country don't consider the arts to be a genuine way to earn your living, unlike a plumber or a decorator. Art tends to only be thought of as OK as a hobby.

Returning to the visual side of your performance, you nearly always play infront of a video backdrop. However, at one of your shows in Sheffield 1983 you played in front of a bank of televisions. Do you think that was the most successful visual presentation you have attempted?

Richard: Well, it would have been if most of them had worked! I was quite impressed with the way it looked. It was a one-off thing though.

Mal: I thought it was pretty good, the whole thing worked really well on that one night – it might not work on another night.

Do you consider yourselves as entertainers when you play live, or are the films the entertainment?

Richard: I don't know, it's a bit of a grey area to me.

Mal: I don't know really – it is almost like the whole meaning of the word entertainment has changed since we started. I don't see ourselves as strictly entertainers – if people find it entertaining then that's OK. People dance more at some of the gigs. I don't know what we are live, we just perform and enjoy what we are doing.

Would you think of expanding into more sophisticated live shows?

Richard: No, in terms of the music, that was one of the bad things about the tour we did in 1983 as far as I was concerned. We kind of rushed into it and went for the easy option of putting things down on tape. That was fair enough, but 1 don't think I would want to do that again. I'd rather make it a lot more improvised, because I get a lot more out of it when it is like that. However, playing to backing tapes was an interesting exercise in discipline, actually having to restrict yourself to a certain format.

In terms of the visuals, that is another thing we are re-thinking. The whole thing with the films and slides is getting a bit boring. People expect us to have films, so maybe it is about time to change them. At one stage we did go through a phase when we didn't always use films, it all depended on the suitability of the venue. Some days we just didn't bother with it. It would be quite nice to do a few shows again without back projections. I mean if you go to any gig in Sheffield these days, the chances are you're going to see a back projection. I'm not saying we invented it or anything.

Mal: I also think that we have got to be careful in the way we use the visuals – we don't want to turn into a Pink Floyd! It works on a crude level but we've got to avoid over-sophistication and avoid creating a white elephant.

I suppose it must be difficult in some respects because you never get to see the full effect of it at the time.

Richard: I quite often just turn round and watch the films. I can remember particularly enjoying them when we played in Berlin once. Mind you part of that was due to other reasons!

Do you always have a drink or something before you play live?

Richard: No, I have done loads of gigs straight, but I don't know which is best. It's like when we're mixing an album – part of it is done straight and part of it isn't. It is an interesting way of working. For instance, we might start setting up mixing completely stone cold sober, and then when you get down to the actual mix it is like voodoo time – you've got to get some magic going.

The only area of the visual side to your work we haven't touched upon is the promotional video. I thought the video to 'Just Fascination', and in some respects the one to 'Crackdown', were a dilution of your ideas – a compromise.

Mal: I think it was a psychological thing. It's horrible being signed to a major label when it affects you psychologically. I think because it was our first video for Virgin, we thought we would play the game, and we played it too safe and watered it down. It was mostly our fault and not Pete Care's. I think in his own way Pete made a very good, subtle video and the more I see it the more I see the subtleties. It was Pete's video really and we gave him full rein, and therefore it was his interpretation. Whereas with 'The Crackdown' it was more of a conscious effort between us and Pete.

Richard: I think the 'Just Fascination' video was made purely with the intention of getting it shown on TV.

So you think that if you had done something more like the Doublevision cassette it wouldn't have got shown on TV?

Richard: It would have been pretty pointless because we had already done that. We did get part of the Doublevision cassette shown on TV, I don't know how mind you!

Out of those two promotional videos that we did, 'Just Fascination' looked very slick and professional but of the two everyone prefers 'Crackdown'. It was much more interesting since it was done as an extra and the pressure was off.

In some ways, slickness doesn't seem to fit in with your image.

Richard: I think with the 'Just Fascination' video, not very much happens in it. I'm not knocking it certainly when you compare it against some of the crap that passes itself off as promos. It is far better than most of those which I have seen – but it was pretty minimal.

Are there any promotional videos you have seen that have impressed you ?

Mal: I think most of them are crap. I can't think of any particular one. I don't think anyone has broken the format.

Do you think that it is inevitable that most promos are crap?

Richard: Yes. I think it is especially a shame as there is so much bloody money available to do them. Obviously the director of the video, unless it is someone particularly famous, has got to please the record company who is paying him or he is not going to get any more work. After all, a promo that can't get shown on TV is not really worth much to a record company however good it is.

It still remains that you are one of the most under-televised groups considering the position you have reached.

Richard: We are hoping that is going to change. We are not going to do any live dates for the moment, so we are trying to get more TV so we can get across more in that way.

Anything you would like to say before the tape runs out?

Richard: Well, something that I've thought a lot about is the concept of amassing money. I'm really into the idea – and I'm waiting my turn to play the ultimate Dadaist joke. It could take any form – it could be in a film. But you have got to have a lot of money to do anything that would have a lot of repercussions – apart from an act of terrorism like shooting the president or something!

Appendix 2

The following interviews with Richard and Mal were conducted in 1988, and were published in an updated version of Cabaret Voltaire – The Art of the Sixth Sense in 1989. At the time, the group was in a certain amount of turmoil about their future. As the two individuals were now very much polarised, I made no attempt to mix the two's answers and presented them separately.

RICHARD H KIRK

How has your attitude towards making music and the music business changed over the last few years?

Richard: A lot more cynical more than anything else, but it is still basically the same. I think you just get more cynical as the time goes on.

What has been the difference between Virgin and EMI, have you found it more constricting being on a larger label?

Richard: No, we have complete freedom. The only time we've run into a problem is when we made a video – but in terms of the music, the choice of producers, the choice of studio, we've had no interference at all. I mean I'm not saying that it might not change in the future.

What about your attitudes towards playing live?

Richard: I mean, it has been talked about, it has become a bit of a bone of contention. It's something that we've held back on because of not wanting to just present the same thing. If you upgrade the music it makes sense to upgrade the way it is played live. It's a difficult decision – we don't want to get in loads of musicians and that, but at the same time the idea of performing with two people doesn't seem right somehow.

So, if you were to use other musicians, presumably you wouldn't be putting such a heavy emphasis on backing tapes?

Richard: Well, basically backing tapes are just a way of storing information – and that can be upgraded by doing it with computers. I think maybe using live percussion again would be quite a good thing. So even if we are using backing tapes it makes it more live. The last time we played live in 1986, a lot of what we actually did was live, half of it was on backing tapes and half of it was using sequencers and live drums – it seemed to work quite well. The other problem is the material we have recorded for EMI is a lot more ordered, so we're faced with the problem of having to present that live or making it much looser as it has been in the past. Basically it is the difficulty of not trying to repeat ourselves.

Would I be right in saying that you are less keen on the live work than Mal is?

Richard: Mmmmmm. (pause)

What about the promotional aspects of the work?

Richard: I've never particularly seen that as my role anyway. I've never been a great one for doing lots of interviews and stuff like that. A lot of that is down to the fact that a lot of the people who we seemed to get interviewed by harp on about Rough Trade and why we left and things like that. The questions don't seem to be as interesting. It doesn't stimulate me as much as it used to, but I mean, a lot of the interviews have been confined more specifically to the 'pop press'.

Is it that the questions have become less interesting or have you become more cynical about the kinds of questions you get asked?

Richard: I mean obviously, that's there. A lot of it seems to be people asking why we moved to EMI. I thought that would have been particularly obvious.

For the money?

Richard: Well, it's a bigger machinery. Also the other thing is America – we never had an American release with Virgin. That's changed and it has worked quite well in terms of getting records pushed and everything.

A lot of the music in the charts at the moment uses heavy rhythm tracks with bits of found voices, things that you have traditionally been associated with. Basically, they are getting the records in the charts and you as yet have not. Are they presenting it in a different way that makes it more commercial?

Richard: I don't know, as you say, it amazes me. We have had a really bad response from the people who take the records into Radio One. I think it's just to do with the name and the history, it almost seems to work against us.

Will you carry on using the clips of found voices in the future in the light of that?

Richard: I think we've tended to use that less and less. On the last record, I think that side of it is played down. When it's there, it's really pushed to the front like on 'Don't Argue'. But that sort of use of it we decided not to do too much of. We mainly used tapes of things – not spoken pieces – but just for sounds.

The last time we spoke you were talking of the music developing in a schizophrenic way – with the dance music but also some atmospheric stuff as well.

Richard: I can't really see EMI going for 20 minute a side ambient records – but where that would work well is with film sound tracks like the one we did for 'Salvation'.

Wasn't one of Doublevision's initial intentions to provide a release for that sort of material, but you haven't used it much of late. Is the label dead or just dormant?

Richard: It's dormant – it's not dead by any means. A lot of the actual day to day work has been delegated to Factory's video label, Icon. They handle the distribution, the manufacturing and everything.

Have there been any recent Doublevision releases?

Richard: No. Not to my knowledge anyway! (laughs)

Are there going to be any in the near future?

Richard: There was a compilation album that was being put together but it ground to a halt. I think that a lot of it has to do with the fact that everybody has been too involved doing other things. Paul Smith who is the main driving force behind Doublevision in terms of getting things done, is now running his own label as well, he's involved with a lot of people.

A lot of people involved with the group are involved with other things, for instance Paul Smith with Blast First, and Amrik Rai with Fon. Do you think that in some ways detracts from what you do? Would it be better if you had someone that was concentrating on your promotion 100% of the time?

Richard: That's a situation I would prefer, but unfortunately it's difficult to find someone. The way a lot of people seem to organise things these days is by setting up management organisations and they tend to deal with several different groups.

Some sources have indicated that the finances of the group aren't as healthy as they were. Have you run into some tax problems?

Richard: We spent a lot of money on equipment – and bad accounting from the past has caught up with us. We are beginning to get that sorted out.

What happened? Were you relying too heavily on an accountant?

Richard: We had an accountant in Sheffield, who was OK up to a point – it was OK but it got a bit out of hand. He was unable to deal with it – I don't want to go into too much detail about it.

Is it irreparable?

Richard: No, I wouldn't have thought so. There is the possibility of selling the studio, which is coming more and more of a reality as time goes on. But with the circumstances we are in at the moment that would make very little difference because EMI pay for all the recording, so they're quite happy to put us in a studio. We were the exception to the rule, I don't think there is any other group that uses their own set up.

You're used to taking a fairly long time building up your material in your own studio. Do you think that the material would change if you started recording LPs in 2 weeks?

Richard: I'm against the idea of getting rid of our own studio, but I'm for the idea of going into another studio with a blank sheet of paper so to speak. I think it would be interesting. *The Crackdown* album was done in that way. We went into the studio with half an idea and recorded an album in four days. I think the next recording that is done might include a third party – a producer or someone to bounce ideas off. I think there needs to be someone else there. When you work with someone for so long it can get a bit jaded. A fresh input from people is welcome.

The roles do seem to have become extremely polarised. Do you think there is a danger of becoming too insular?

Richard: Yeah. Also working with the same equipment. I would like the idea of maybe going into a Fairlight studio and actually just working from scratch there – actually building things up in a computer to see what can be done that way. I like the idea of a new paintbox of sound, so to speak, it appeals to me.

What about the development of the video side. The 'Don't Argue' video must have been very expensive I would imagine. Do you think you can carry on being funded to make those sorts of videos without chart success?

Richard: Well, when we first went to EMI there was talk of doing a long form of video, but I think that's just been shoved to one side. I don't know whether it will happen or not.

The last time we spoke we discussed the possible making of a film. The footage that you started for that eventually ended up on the 'Gasoline In Your Eye' video. Do you think that a film or long video is unworkable in the pop format?

Richard: Yeah. If you're highly successful then I think you can talk to people on your own terms, because the people that fund those sorts of things know, that because of a certain name person being involved, then people are going to be interested in it even if it is not a string of promos. But I think in our position at the moment it is difficult. It would be quite easy to turn out another *Gasoline In Your Eye* but what's the point? Without quite a lot of financial backing I couldn't really see anything good coming out of a thing like that.

Godley and Creme have just started a project that is attempting to take video out of the promo mould and into an artform in itself. Do you think that could be successful?

Richard: We were actually involved in that when it first got going. We thought we were going to be funded along with Pete Care to do a 25 minute piece, which we wrote and went ahead and approached J.G. Ballard with a view to him writing 3 or 4 minutes of some kind of scenario. To take maybe 10 themes and intercut the whole thing together but in the end they just backed out and the whole thing fell apart. But as regards the question, it depends on what people they approach I suppose.

The later videos like 'Sensoria' and 'Don't Argue' have used a director and taken more of a 'plot' format and featured less of the cut-up imagery. Have you moved on from that?

Richard: You might think that it is more of a plot format but try telling that to someone at a TV station! Their concept of a pop video is some flashing lights and a few people dancing, you know. I don't know whether it's our name or our reputation or what, but no one in England would show those videos – the recent ones.

Why was that?

Richard: Well, no one would be specific. Maybe they just think they're crap videos. Maybe it's the ideas and the imagery.

Didn't EMI exert quite a lot of pressure to get them shown?

Richard: I mean, I'm not really sure as to what goes on to get things done – who pays who or what. As far as I know they tried to get the things shown. They've not been a problem out of England. In Europe they've been shown and in the States.

There does seem to be a very moral tone around at the moment in England – probably partly as a backlash to AIDS. A lot of people are beginning to feel they are being hampered in expressing themselves artistically.

Richard: A lot of people in the TV companies seem to set themselves up as some kind of moral guardian for the Nation's youth if you like. While things like that are going on it doesn't leave much hope. Even chart groups get problems with stuff – get asked to take bits of things out. I mean it's quite a dilemma with what to do, and say, "Right, we're not going to take anything out", and then no one gets to see it apart from a few of your mates.

With the resurgence of a moral tone, some people argue that it has proved that the sixties permissive society has turned in on itself. Or is there still some mileage to be made out of it?

Richard: It is really difficult to know where things are going in that respect.

However, I think it would be difficult to imagine someone like Warhol, even with his ability to attract attention, starting out and making the films he did now.

Richard: Yeah, there are always going to be things like that in existence but it is going to be stuff that is kind of underground – it's going to be privately shown and done really cheaply. But Warhol had very little to do with his later films anyway. He put his name to it which was enough for him by that time – he'd put his name to anything.

Now that he's died what are your opinions about the man?

Richard: I still have admiration for him and respect for his work. I always did – it's always inspired me. In the end Andy Warhol just became the work. He was invited to the parties, he had his own TV show which is what he always wanted to do.

The success of Warhol always seemed to typify America to me. What are your opinions about the place now that you have been there more often?

Richard: I like the place. I could get to like New York but I don't think I could live there because it's too difficult to get some peace and quiet. I mean if you're stuck in the middle of Manhattan, there is so much going on – when do you stop? (laughs)

If your success grew out there you would consider living out there part of the time?

Richard: Yes, I would welcome something like that, I'd be quite happy for a change of environment basically. I'd like the idea of actually going and working there, whether it would be recording or anything else – just getting a different sort of stimulus and different surroundings.

What is your favourite type of music at the moment? What have you been listening to?

Richard: I've started listening to Can again quite a lot. A lot of dance music – but not the kind of soul stuff. But the sort of stuff that I believe to be where the forefront of experimental music is at this point in time.

Do you think that white English people can produce that kind of music or is it primarily a black American phenomenon?

Richard: No, I don't think it is. I think basically there's a lot of snobbery involved. It is interesting that you find that groups from England or Europe can actually become part of the nightclub thing in New York. They seem to like it over there, whereas over here it has got to be American. The MARRS record proved that to be exactly what it is – it's snobbery. That record's initial success came because people assumed it was an American import.

Quite a lot of your contemporaries, like New Order, have moved towards the dance vein with considerable success, do you think that is because they structure their material more as songs rather than pieces of music?

Richard: I think a lot of New Order's work has always been fairly song-structured to me. With them you're dealing with a band. The comparisons between us and them aren't that large, apart from the fact that we started working around the same time. We probably don't work in any remotely similar way.

You've always stressed two things – firstly that you don't write songs and secondly that you don't class yourselves as musicians. Have either of those views changed?

Richard: I wouldn't know how to go about writing a song as such, but having said that, using technology it is possible to create structures which people would identify with as being songs.

What about your view of not being a musician. A lot of people might take that with a bit of cynicism seeing the type of material you have been producing and the length of time you have been producing it?

Richard: I still don't consider myself to be a musician. I can't write music as such. Still one of the main compositional tools that I favour is the multitrack tape. Given the technology available anyone can be a musician these days anyway. It's no problem anymore.

Everything in terms of music in the eighties has become very mainstream. Might there be a turn around to the more independent scene, or do you think that is well and truly redundant now?

Richard: It's by no means redundant because there's still a lot of people out there who have got this notion that they'll only go out and buy things if it's on an independent label. I'm sure there's a lot of people around who are still of that view. That's probably affected us after we've been seen to go to the 10th major corporation in the world or whatever. It might upset a few of our die-hards!

I can understand all too well why it would appeal to a lot of people to go from an independent label to a major. If you've been making music for two or three years and you're still signing on the dole or penniless all the time, then I can understand people getting pissed off with that situation, looking elsewhere and doing something about it. As it happens that didn't particularly affect us with us only being two or three in the group we managed ably financially when we were with an independent label – you had to wait maybe a little bit longer to get royalty payments. I can see that side of it. The frightening side of it is that you get so many people now that are willing to run forward and be exploited and not even question the whole thing. That disturbs me.

Looking to the future, how long do you think you will continue doing what you are doing now without having a hit or major success?

Richard: I don't know, it's difficult to say. I wouldn't have thought for that much longer. I think at some point in time you have to say, "Right, let's put this thing to rest and move on to something different", or on the other hand try and become even more cynical and go for even more mainstream success. We have done everything else, you know what I mean? (laughs)

Critics might say that the Cabaret Voltaire bandwagon has run its course.

Richard: Yeah, I'm sure they would. A lot of them have said so in print as well! (laughs) I mean, I think a lot of people are cynical – I think they take what we do for granted because we've been around for so long and they think, "Oh, yeah it's another Cabaret Voltaire record". I think in terms of the music press, the people who review our records are from a different generation to us. It's bound to happen where it's the thing to do to have ago at people who have been in existence for a long time – but personally I think they've picked on the wrong people, because as far as I'm concerned we're still as credible as we ever were. I don't think they are justified in having a go at us.

Who do you think comprises your audience now?

Richard: I don't know, there again I've never known anyway. I mean it's difficult to judge – that is one thing about not playing live for a couple of years – at least you did have some contact with people at concerts.

Do you think you've finally managed to lay the 'long mac' image to rest?

Richard: No, that's still there. As I've said before, when you do interviews people still see us as the indie group that went to a major label. I mean there's that magazine called *Underground* that deals just with independent music and we're still in that – I mean I'm not knocking the magazine, I think it's quite good – it's just a bit strange.

Do you think you will ever shake off that tag?

Richard: Yeah, by having a mega hit single. Maybe then it might hit home.

Do you think that is any closer than it was three years ago?

Richard: Yeah, maybe – maybe not. If it happens it might not be here – more feasibly it might happen in America or Europe or somewhere. I would like that anyway because it would mean that the radio over here couldn't ignore it which would be quite a good situation to be in.

If that were to happen the pressure to promote and play live would be more prominent. Would you respond to that pressure?

Richard: The pressure to do that is there now, but I'm not actually sure whether playing live sells records.

It must be a good way of making money though?

Richard: It always has done in the past. But I remember reading that it was only really the stadium bands that made the real money – and they were all established bands. It is a way of making money and it's separate from any income from the record company. A lot of bands do go out for a cynical reason – you find out that a lot of tours are just set up because someone has just got a tax bill. You find out things like that as you go along.

With Mal living in London, increasingly more and more so, have you found that it is more difficult to work on things now?

Richard: Not really, I've a lot of the time been left to my own devices, which I don't mind – I'm quite happy to get on with that. But as I say it is a good time to actually try a different approach I'm all for that. That would probably involve me travelling to London more – working in a studio.

Basically, Western Works had to close, was that the scenario?

Richard: Yeah, the building was falling apart and someone broke a big hole through the roof and tried to take all the equipment away with them. At the moment we've moved to a new studio which is a lot bigger – and a lot more expensive. (laughs) It actually resembles a studio more than Western Works did.

So, you have carried on buying more and more equipment.

Richard: Yeah, the other problem with that is that is not allowable as it used to be for tax purposes. You only get a very small proportion of it – whilst 5 or 6 years ago you'd see an accountant and he'd say, "Yeah, go ahead spend all your money on equipment", which is what we did. But 5 years later you find that isn't the case. The other thing to bear in mind these days is that 8 track or 16 track equipment is far better than it ever used to be. There's one 16 track available now that's better than the 24 track we've got. If we sell the studio I'll get a smaller set up just for composing things at home. Which I don't mind.

Lynne: But I do!

What about your interests outside music are they still much the same? Do you still enjoy the same type of literature, same type of movies?

Richard: Yeah, the same old rubbish. (laughs)

You haven't discovered any new obsessions apart from the old tried and tested? Would you still say that your obsessions were firearms, kitsch and pornography?

Richard: Yeah, still of interest – obsession might be too strong a word.

Might you end up like Burroughs with his collection of firearms?

Richard: I don't know, I don't know whether I'll live that long. (laughs) It's funny because it's only now that he's getting the recognition – a few years back you couldn't have imagined someone like that getting on the front cover of the *Sunday Times* magazine. Now he's been claimed as America's greatest writer.

Although the TV media never seems to accept things like that. For instance it seems ironic to me that someone like Genet can die with little or no coverage whilst 5 hours or whatever gets allotted to an appreciation of Eammon Andrews merely because he was a TV personality. Do you think that to be respected in this day and age you have to be a TV personality?

Richard: I mean TV is where the majority of people seem to get their information from these days. Although cinema is making a big comeback over the last few years – a lot of people seem to be actually going out and seeing more films.

Lynne: Yeah, but they're all going to see *Top Gun*.

So is the media still crap?

Richard: Yeah, it's still crap but I'm still fascinated by it for all its crapness. It will be quite interesting when the thing opens up with cable TV – you know, who'll they'll let have a programme. They'll probably keep it really controlled.

Not like in Amsterdam where the cable TV is either pornography or religious broadcasts.

Richard: I can't see religious TV being that big over here like it is in America, somehow I just can't see it.

What are some of the films and books you have enjoyed recently?

Richard: *Blue Velvet* like everyone else. *Robocop*. There's a couple of Ballard books I've read recently, the Kray Twins' *A Profession of Violence* is a good little read.

The whole notion of violence still fascinates you. You still like watching all the gory films.

Richard: Yeah, splatter. I mean it's just ridiculous the extent to which some of the videos now go.

Lynne: It doesn't affect you anymore – it's like eating chips or something.

Do you not get bored with them? It's like with porno movies, people say after you've seen the umpteenth one you get to the point of saying, "So what".

Richard: I must admit I tend to check out a lot of Hollywood films as well now. I don't bother to go to the cinema to see them, I'm not that interested, but just to get to see *Top Gun* and things like that stuff that is really successful – I watch them because I want to know why people go to see them.

Do you still think most of them are crap though?

Richard: Yeah, if at least you take the time to see these things at least you can justify saying that. It interests me what appeals to the masses.

Personally, I am more interested in European films, they seem to take a totally different approach to that of Hollywood.

Lynne: People don't want to know what you think. (laughs)

Richard: Neither do they want to know what you think. (laughs)

Do you still keep in touch with Chris Watson?

Richard: Yes, he's sometimes a difficult man to track down. He was in the South of England for quite a while working for the RSPB and I posted him some records and there was a delay of some two months until I heard from him – the letter came from Newcastle and apparently he'd got sick of it down there and decided to move back to Newcastle.

The Hafler Trio in some respects have carried on the idea of sound experimentation in a purer form. Do you think in still doing that they are barking up the wrong tree?

Richard: No, I don't – I still respect Chris tremendously for what he's doing. I'm not saying that I would want to that myself but I think what he does is extremely valid.

However, those types of groups who were doing that sort of sound experimentation were very much a thing of the late seventies and early eighties what became to be known as the 'industrial tag'.

Richard: That 'industrial tag' was never something we particularly encouraged. It was the tag people used.

So, your connections with some of those groups, Psychic TV for example, have become less over the years.

Richard: I think, of the people that were working at that time – you can't expect everyone to be working in each other's pockets and remain the same. Everyone diversifies. But that is not to say that we've severed contact with these people – I'm still quite happy to speak to all those people. It's just I very rarely bump into them these days. A lot of that is probably to do with my geographical location more than anything else.

Do you often think that maybe you're the last of your contemporaries who are still going, that haven't had major chart success. People like The Cure, Echo and the Bunnymen

Richard: Yeah, but I wouldn't associate myself with those types of groups. What they were doing was completely different -I mean that was purely a musical thing.

What about New Order and The Fall?

Richard: I can't speak for The Fall – but just looking back at what we've left behind if you like, it's not just a bunch of records. There's a lot of other things as well.

Say the records didn't sell or the group split up completely, would it be the visual media you would move into do you think?

Richard: I think I will always be interested in that and I always want to do something. But it is just a case of not wanting to repeat oneself given a limited budget.

Do you get many offers to do anything of that nature, or production?

Richard: Visually I don't think there's been anything – that's more difficult because our main collaborator Pete Care lives in Los Angeles so it is a bit difficult to discuss your ideas without building up a massive transatlantic phone bill.

The 'Sensoria' video won the Los Angeles Times video award. Is that right?

Richard: Yeah, it's also in the Museum of Modern Art so there must be something to it.

Do you think that 'Sensoria' has been your most successful record to date?

Richard: No. 'Nag Nag Nag'. (laughs) I don't really know. I mean 'Sensoria' never got an American release, if it had that could probably have done a lot more. I mean it's still feasible that it might be re-released at some time.

Some of your most successful records have been those that have been re-mixed. Do you think that says something about the way that you record?

Richard: Yeah, I think the most successful records we've ever done in terms of sales have been done with producers – whether it is true artistically I don't know.

Does that not beg the question of whether a fully recorded and produced record is not the best step forward?

Richard: Well, we've really already done that. When I say that we've had people come in and re-mix the stuff, we've worked with people like Adrian Sherwood and John Robie – but the idea has always been there, not finished but semi-completed. If we actually set something up from zero, it would be quite interesting to see where it ended up – it might end up with complete chaos and violence. (laughs). But on the other hand it might be something that is really good.

Certainly the added touches to the single of 'Sensoria' seemed to liven it up from the original LP track.

Richard: It was two tracks edited together on multi-track, literally just cut together – which I suppose was a bit ahead of its time again, so much as that is how people tend to make records these days – a lot of dance music now consists of different tracks just glued together – cemented with a few different beats.

Do you think that EMI signed you on the strength of 'Sensoria'?

Richard: That and 'I Want You' – I think they saw a lot of pop potential in there. We're not as big a gamble as people would actually think. Companies like EMI sign up a lot of groups, spend about 5 times as much money on them as they have on us, and they sell about 2,000 records. But when they signed us, the whole thing was presented by Amrik in terms that business affairs people could understand. 'This is the amount of records the group sells... etc. They're not just a group, they do audio-visual stuff as well".

How do Amrik and Stevo compare as managers?

Richard: I'd decline to comment on that one actually. At least not in print anyway. They have such different musical tastes you just can't begin to compare them. They're two different kettles of fish altogether.

But a manager of some kind is essential?

Richard: Yeah, I think if you're dealing with major labels and operating on that kind of level, I think they expect there to be a manager there. I think it freaks them out if they have to deal direct with the group.

I heard Dave Gahan from Depeche Mode recently saying on the radio that they do a lot of the day to day running of the group, setting up tours etc.

Richard: I'd be very sceptical about that. I'm sure they have people who organise it for them. I mean, we used to set up tours, I used to do a hell of a lot of that type of work – ringing people up and haggling over the price and the riders. I quite enjoyed it actually but there comes a time when you think, "Fuck it, I don't want to be doing this all the time – this isn't my job, I want to concentrate on recording". I think you have to be able to delegate things to other people – you can't clone yourself – at least not yet. (laughs)

STEPHEN MALLINDER

What have been your main changes in attitude in the three years since we last spoke?

Mal: I think since then I have become slightly less serious about it. It's really difficult because you don't go into the studio and think, "Oh, my attitude's changed"... (pause) I don't suppose it has changed that much apart from a slightly more frivolous approach with which I want to do it now. Having stopped working for a few months and having the chance to look at other people, both on major labels and independent ones – because I see both sides – it' s amazing how serious they have got about it all, either musically serious or artistically serious. I don't think anyone really started off like that – in the punk days it was never that serious. I think I've started to take it a bit more tongue-in-cheek. I still take what I do seriously – but not the end result.

In terms of recording, we've done two albums since then. One was *The Covenant* where we went back to basics and did it all in our own studio in Sheffield – and then there is the first EMI album, *Code*.

You mention going back to basics, presumably referring to the fact that 'The Crackdown' was recorded in a studio in London. Do you think that you took a step backwards in recording subsequent material in your own studio and as a result of that the material has suffered?

Mal: Yeah, I think so. For me personally we didn't make the best of the position we were in. I think there was a danger, looking back, that Cabaret Voltaire had very much become a sacred cow – which is where Richard and I differed – and I got fed up with becoming the sacred cow that we must respect and had to represent something. Whereas really it didn't, because what people thought it meant in 1978/9 had gradually been eroded away – rather than it being a case of saying, "Oh, it doesn't mean that anymore, it's changed to this". The music had gradually changed, it had become more mainstream – which was intentional. But at the same time there was this horrible, "It has to represent something" – which is true to a certain degree but I don't know why we should have been so respectful of it anyway.

In the first stages we were tongue-in-cheek, we were dadaist in our attitude towards it, so regarding this name, this anonymous entity that was Cabaret Voltaire, with ultimate respect was ironic. I think we held it in too much esteem, so when we were going back to doing recordings in our own studio, and when we were writing with Adrian Sherwood, we were holding ourselves back a little. Whereas we were in the position where people were saying, "Well, you've achieved everything else, why don't you do this, why don't you do that?" – because people knew what we stood for, it wouldn't make any difference what music we made, because we'd established those things in the first place so there is no need necessarily to hold true to them.

It sounds to me as if you are saying that you should have launched yourselves more into becoming a 'pop' band.

Mal: Yeah, I think that's true. It's partly true about the music, but I think it's more true in terms of the way that we presented ourselves. I think that was the downfall with the last EMI album – which was a lot more listenable even though it has got the elements that we held true to – but people still saw us as two distant people, one standing behind the other.

Were you selling yourselves in the wrong way?

Mal: Yeah, I think so really. The records would have warranted being sold in a different way. I think now my attitude is that it's more appealing, more interesting and more valid, to make tough records but actually present yourself in a ridiculous way – than actually do safe records and present it in a very tough way. The music is the important thing and not the personality behind it. The pop medium treats personalities as a joke anyway, so you might as well take the piss out of yourself because they're going to take the piss out of you anyway. So, I think over the last two years we shouldn't have presented ourselves as seriously – as I've already said that is where Richard and I differ, because Richard does have this self-respect, which is fair enough, but there is also a danger of becoming caricature of yourself.

Do you think you moving to London had anything to do with your change in attitude?

Mal: I didn't move to London to get away from being regarded as part of that Northern industrial funk sort of thing – but it was purely by chance – partly because of my then girlfriend Karen – and partly because I wanted to get away from Sheffield because I felt it was more valid – and it has been. Although Richard would probably think that I deserted Sheffield. In a lot of respects I've managed to achieve a lot more for the group being in London because it has meant that I'm a lot more available – I can do interviews, I can do things on spec that I couldn't have done otherwise. So, it has been helpful although I didn't come for those reasons, I came for personal reasons.

London has had a very good effect on me in the fact that when you move to London you realise that you are a very small fish in a big pond, whereas in Sheffield I was a big fish in a very small pond, and you tend to get a rather perverted view of your own worth, esteem or position. I realised, when even up to a year ago and I used to go in to places like The Leadmill (a club in Sheffield) people would recognise you – but really that means fuck all. So, moving down to London did actually deflate my ego, but for me it had a beneficial effect because it put it more in perspective.

Would it be right to surmise that some of the major differences of opinion of late have been over promotion and playing live?

Mal: That is where Richard and I differed because we wanted to do it on different terms. Richard wanted to do it on his terms, which is doing very selective dates – which is fine and was OK ten years ago. But particularly abroad, if you want to do something you have to play a number of dates. It's fine if you're the Pet Shop Boys, then you can get by without actually doing gigs – but the point is they do the equivalent of gigs as they're out of the country all the time doing promotion. Their actual image and the way they present themselves lends itself to TV, video and to all the interviews and all that. For us we have to go about it in a roundabout way because people view us in a certain way – so therefore if you're going to play live then you've got to do it quite intensively.

Also, there's the finances of it. The last time we played America we did a selective number of dates – took it easy – and we actually lost money on it. So, I respect that Richard doesn't regard promotion as his area – that's fine to a point but because he was part of the group it meant that there were certain things that were demanded of him. For instance, about three months ago, we were supposed to go to Greece to do two TV appearances and Richard said that he couldn't be bothered to go – which is not very healthy when there's only two of you in the group.

Many of the records in the charts at the moment use similar features to yours, found voices over a funk backing track. Why do you think you have been unable to corner any of that commercial success?

Mal: Because I think we used those features in a different way – we opened the door for a lot of people to be able to use those things. But those people are using it in a more accessible but somewhat more gimmicky way. I think that's why the public are far more open to the 'Bomb the Bass' record or the 'Pump up the Volume' record it's just done in a more palatable way – that's all. I think we used it in a more upfront, challenging way – and they use it in a more musical, restrained way.

Do you think you are incapable of making commercial music?

Mal: I don't think that either of us have that make up – that doesn't mean that we couldn't do it – it's just that from what I know now I realise there's a certain craft or subtlety involved. That's why I've found using producers useful because they can actually use those elements to better ends and a better effect – whilst we use them in maybe a cruder way. We have the bass line, rhythm track, string line, but there is an actual skill and a craft in putting that together and we haven't actually achieved that in the past – there's been hints and suggestions of it – but there's always been the fact that if there had been that extra input, that extra nurturing of those elements then I think it would work. I don't think it has been totally absent – there have been catchy things in our stuff but I think maybe it's always needed an outside view of it – that's all.

Might the missing element just be that of sitting down and writing a song, like say New Order do, rather than a piece of music?

Mal: I think New Order are much more musical in their approach. Also, there's an inter-communication because they are a group. With two people, the system has very much been Richard working on the music, me doing the vocals – and when they gel they gel, and when they don't it's tough shit. I think a lot of it is the inter-relation between myself and Richard, which needed that outside thing because you know what Richard's like, he's very single-minded about the way that he wants to work, but it has probably always needed an extra person if it was supposed to have that extra added 'poppier' aspect to it.

Do you think you have been hampered by sticking to some of the statements you have traditionally made, such as, "We're not musicians". Some people might view that with a certain amount of cynicism.

Mal: Yes, it's a classic line, it just means that you're not a trained musician. It' s bullshit to say that in doing this for ten years we haven't learnt a certain degree of musicality. And also, you know what's in tune, what's out of tune, you know when you're coming in on the wrong beat – therefore the point is that it' s almost admitting the rules are there and tying yourself to them, but not using them to their proper effect – which we were starting to do on the last album. But, yes it' s held us back – that goes back to the notion of this 'sacred cow' aspect of the group, which is the fear of doing it, whereas we should just tucking let loose and do it.

You have also had some financial problems recently, were you just naive in letting that side of it get out of hand?

Mal: I think it is a two way thing. Yes, I think we were very naive and we trusted the wrong people in terms of our accounts – not management but accountants. I think it was purely that we were lulled into a false sense of security. We were naive – and also man can not live by advances alone, you can't do it – so it was bound to catch up on us.

Do you think the fact that a lot of the people involved with the group are doing other things has been to the detriment of the group?

Mal: It would be nice to say that we have a manager that handles us all the time – 100%. But we don't actually do enough work to warrant that – no one could live on just working for us. If we were touring a lot it would be different.

Your videos have been quite widely critically acclaimed, but again not shown to a great degree. Is that still a basic underlying uncommerciality?

Mal: I think it' s our name – full stop. I think the name actually puts a block on certain things – radio play, video play. I don't think the content of the videos themselves actually stops them from being shown, just as the records don't stop themselves from being played. But I think because of the way we presented ourselves there is a very stand off attitude towards them. I think videos in general have actually spiralled inwards to a degree where the effect of a video now is very diminished. I don't think we could ever make another 'Sensoria' and I don't think anyone ever could – I thought that was a ground-breaking video. I don't think anyone could do it again and that's because everybody makes videos now and it has become less valid. I don't think the form itself is actually valid.

Godley and Creme have tried to take it out of its current genre and make it into an artform in itself.

Mal: I personally don't think it'll work. I admire them for doing it and I admire Godley and Creme immensely, I like their attitude, I think it's great. But the whole notion of video now as an artform has just disappeared and I don't know whether it has gone too far toward a commercial thing for people to pull back from it. I think the odd person will try and make an arty video – Sting or whoever – and that is probably as arty as you can probably get on mainstream TV. I'd like to think it would happen, but people have tried it so much and it doesn't work, because people expect certain things from video -people don't want art.

Is that a reflection on the eighties?

Mal: I think it's a reflection on the music business – I think it's a reflection on the records. I just mean in this climate I don't think it will change. I think the climate has got to change before anyone can make greater inroads into using video as an artform.

There seems to be a more restrictive attitude in this country – partly as a response to AIDS – do you think that hampers people expressing themselves visually in videos?

Mal: I think if you're big enough you can still express yourself any way you want. Nobody stopped George Michael smoking cigarettes in his last video – you're not supposed to, but he did. Nobody stopped him showing scantily clad women in the video – they stopped us, but that is because it is us, and not because of the scantily clad women.

Your biggest progress recently has been an increase in your popularity in America. Why do you think that is?

Mal: Because we didn't have records out there before, I think that's all it is. We'd been over to America and played two or three times, we'd had good press, the videos had been shown and we'd had good press for them, and I think people were aware of the name but had not been able to get the records – now they're able to get the records so our popularity has gone up. It's not been a massive increase but at least the records have been available. You could say that it was because of the danceability of the records to a degree – but America is still very M.O.R. and A.O.R., it's not changed that much. But really it is down to changing from being a cult group where people couldn't get the records outside of LA and New York, to a situation where people can get the records a little bit more. There is an increase in awareness in the States that we've been able to capitalise on from having a release over there.

Perhaps you can start afresh over there and not be tied to that 'long mac' po-faced image?

Mal: I think that's true anywhere outside of England where they don't take that much notice of the *NME* and that sort of thing.

But also it's the only place where you've played live in the last two years. Is that because America appeals to you?

Mal: America still appeals to me, I still like America a lot. I still don't know whether I could live there but it does appeal to me. It's the basis of this popular culture that we're in now – so you might as well go and see it at its source. I mean, it revolts me, but it also attracts me at the same time?

What sort of music do you like listening to now?

Mal: Well, it's a bit of a cliche but it's still a lot of dance music – a lot of the 'house' stuff, the 'acid house' stuff, the 'go-go' stuff, all that fascinates me.

Do you think that white people can successfully recreate that?

Mal: I think they can, because music is music, I don't think that colour matters anymore. A lot of that is image anyway, and the way that it's presented. On most black records there's white people working behind the scenes, so I don't think it makes that much difference. It's a bit awkward to answer because it actually brings out the latent snobbery in people – because if they listen to a record and they find out white people have made it and it's a very soulful or funky record, the tendency is not to like it. That's why you or I would probably not dream of buying a Simply Red record but we would buy a Bobby Womack record. It just brings out snobbery in people really, and I'm just as much a victim of that as anyone else. And that's because we all like to personally own music – and there's nothing wrong with that – people like to get the latest thing, it's just like collecting Dinky cars really. People always want new things, and it's the same with black music, people want it from its source. But that's coming from me talking in England where you can get Chicago records easier than you can in Chicago. (laughs)

How long do you think you can carry on with what you are doing at the moment without having any major success?

Mal: I wouldn't want to carry on much longer because I have become ambitious – I was always ambitious, but the longer you go on the more it aggravates you and the more you want to actually achieve a certain degree. It's not just financial success, or an ego thing, but you do want to achieve it – see some sort of physical reward for it, that sort of profile. So, therefore I don't really want to bring out records that I don't believe in 100% or that I don't think would be 100% successful anymore – because using things as an art statement is crap now and I think it was very much a mystery thing that we lived in for four years – everybody did. I still believe in my own credibility and I'm still an elitist in a lot of ways – I still think I'm better than anyone else. But having said that I want to make records that I'm proud of and that I think will be successful.

So, you still see that ambition taking the form of making records?

Mal: There's this horrible attitude when you get to a certain stage of making music, of wanting to be whisked off to the hinterlands of making soundtrack music – which is fine, it's a valid point but I wouldn't want to do that and nothing else. Because I wouldn't want to be that sort of person locked away doing soundtrack music. I mean it's wonderful if you're Enio Morricone or John Barry – the music they make is incredibly valid but that's a different sort of thing. I don't really want to see myself for the rest of my life making music for artforms. I would like to do it but I would also like to counterbalance it. That's the reason why I started making music in the first place and the reason why we stopped making music in a loft and why we started going out and playing and making records. There's a danger in this sort of fear of putting yourself public hiding behind soundtrack music – things like that.

So you have always felt the most commercially minded of the group – even going way back to those days in the loft.

Mal: Well, obviously that stands out. I suppose it does go without saying. Chris did it for a certain reason, he left for a certain reason to go off and do other things. Richard doesn't want to be involved in the promotion side whereas I, whether I like it or not, see it as a valid part of it. It's like anything else – you have to take the shit with the good side of it. The good side of it is being able to go into studios and do the records you want, but you've got to actually take the crap side of it if you want to get somewhere. Which involves acting like a complete plonker in Milan. It's funny – it's sick.

The Milan incident refers to you dressing up as Father Christmas?

Mal: Fuck, who told you about that – did I tell you that? (laughs)

A bit of an own goal there, I think. Do you think the independent band ethic is a thing of the past?

Mal: I don't think it was ever particularly valid as an ethic, I think it has always paralleled the major labels. But that's the unique thing about the set up in England which I've been part of and been very proud of, because it was actually very valid at the time. But England is unique in that it does have a totally independent set-up that works alongside the majors and it's success-ful. But if they are successful it's because they play the games that everybody plays. They don't do it without making videos, they don't do it without get-ting records on the radio. Apart from some dance records, where there are back ways into the charts which records like 'Pump Up the Volume' have proved.

Do you not get a feeling with some of those records, 'Pump Up the Volume' in particular, that you have been caught up and overtaken?

Mal: I think we were always caught up and overtaken anyway. Because with the things that we have done in the past there have been people working on the same ideas that we were a part of – not that we weren't innovative but we weren't that original. I've never seen ourselves as carrying the flag for something and now all of a sudden everybody's run past us. I don't think it makes any difference – I mean people were saying that to us four years ago, "Aren't you pissed off because so-and-so has got into the charts, because you were doing that two years ago", people have always been saying that about us. That's nobody's fault but our own, because if you want to capitalise on it you can do – it depends if you want to, really.

Certainly it is true that of all the groups that started around the same time as you, most of them have either had some chart success or split up.

Mal: Yeah, it's true. But they probably knew what they wanted a little bit more, we never knew particularly what we wanted – or at least maybe the realisation of it was that Richard and I want different things. I don't know.

One reviewer picked up on this when reviewing the first edition of this book by saying something on the lines of, "200 pages of interviews with two people who haven't a clue what they are doing".

Mal: It's true. But there again I fucking challenge anyone who does know exactly what they do. That's why I've become a lot more cynical and tongue-in-cheek about what I do – now I see people and they're so fucking serious about what they do. I see this real musicianship thing from people that if they'd have carried on like that in the punk days they would have been beaten up for it – so I don't see why I should fall into that trap.

Isn't that true of most people though – that they end up doing what they started off attacking?

Mal: Yeah, well I'm doing what I started off attacking. But the difference is that I don't see that I should have to defend what I do as so fucking phenomenally important. You're as good as your next record – and a record is just an idea that goes on to tape and it's nothing more than that – it's nothing that's going to fucking change the world. If you've got belief in an idea then you follow it through in whatever way you can – and if it takes something to do it – then you fucking do it.

That's a more mercenary approach than I've heard from you before. It's a bit of a new attitude?

Mal: I know it is. But there again I didn't want to stay the same. I'm sure when you interviewed me three years ago my attitude was different from when 'Nag, Nag, Nag' came out. Nobody should be so set in their ways. I'm not a fundamentalist – or like these die hard Marxists – you have to adapt your ideals in what you do. Yeah, I know I've changed – but the world's changed as well. (laughs)

Without sounding cruel, it does sound a bit like the footballer at the end of his career who has suddenly decided he wants to score goals.

Mal: Yeah, probably. No not really, because as you say I was always the more commercially minded of us.

You were always a goal hanger!

Mal: Yeah I was always a bit of a Gary Lineker. It's true. A lot of it is because that role was hoist upon me because I was the singer. I was aware that I was in the position of being able to sell the records. When you've spent the last six months promoting a record like I have done for the last two singles and the last album it would be pretty pathetic if I didn't believe in my ability to promote records.

Will there be many more Cabaret Voltaire records?

Mal: And if there are, who will be on them. (laughs)

Neither of you. Chris Watson?

Mal: Actually, neither of us own the name – EMI own the name Cabaret Voltaire.

So perhaps someone else could tour as you?

Mal: Oh, yeah. But seriously, that is a bone of contention at the moment – I don't really want to tour but I'm getting pressured to do dates. Richard doesn't really want to do dates – and if he does it is only four of five at a time. With things as they are at the moment, I don't really want to tour – just because of personal reasons really.

I understand that one of the possibilities at the moment is selling the studio? Although that decision to do so would presumably affect Richard more than you?

Mal: The thing is with Richard is that it is his lifeline because if you take the studio away – not being nasty – but he doesn't have a reason to carry on. The reason he's in Sheffield is because of the studio. Whereas I've been in the position for quite some time where I've had to book studio time if I want to record solo material. Which is a bit silly when we have our own studio – but the thing is Richard's grown up with it so much that it has become his studio and I can't just say I'm coming in to record and I'll be there for two weeks. I would feel odd doing it. But may be it would be good for Richard for us not to have the studio – it would always have been good for the group over the last two years if we hadn't had our own studio because it would've put us in the position of having to do it another way.

What about your interests outside of music?

Mal: What do I do when it gets dark. (laughs)

Yeah, how do you spend these long winter evenings?

Mal: I have the same interests I always had – which is reading, going to see films. I haven't got a video, so I don't watch videos anymore – which is a bit ironic when I'm the director of two video companies and I haven't got a video machine.

What sort of books have you enjoyed recently?

Mal: Nothing incredibly unusual really. I've gone back to reading a lot of Dashiell Hammett and Patricia Highsmith books – things like that. I'm reading *An Interview with a Vampire* by Ann Rice at the moment, that's really good. Actually it's a bit like this – only it's set in current day San Francisco and there's this kid doing a fanzine interview with a vampire that's 200 years old.

It's very like this actually – I'm the kid and you're the vampire. (laughs)

Mal: Alright (laughs). As for films (pause). *Robocop* was wicked. *Withnail and I* was good.

Would you say that your interests have become more mainstream as well, getting away from the initial influences like Burroughs?

Mal: Burroughs' books have become more mainstream. (laughs) No, I still look for things – I'm still interested in that sort of thing. But as you get older you're bound to ...God, I've gone middle class and middle aged – shit. (laughs) But what's on offer these days is more mainstream. I mean if you go to an art film I can give you 10 to 1 that it's at least 10 years old. Unless it's Derek Jarman and he does mostly videos now.

What about your video company, Doublevision? Is that dead or dormant?

Mal: I would say pretty dead, actually. It's not fair for me or Richard to say whether it's dead or whatever, because we became less part of it, we let Paul take over – and now Paul has got other interests, so we can't really say whether Doublevision is alive or not. It had to take a back seat for us because we were on Virgin and EMI. Also, if Doublevision is dead, all the other video labels that were around at the same time are dead as well because there isn't that sort of thing coming through. It goes back to what I was saying about the art films. A lot of it is you've got to tailor to people's needs. It's alright going, "It's great, I bring out art videos", but if people don't want them then that's bullshit really.

Is there any particular video that you've seen that sticks out for you?

Mal: I don't know, I haven't got a video machine. (laughs)

Back to that old chestnut. When do you want the donation?

Mal: Yeah, I could have a whip round, eh? (laughs) No, seriously video requires a certain amount of discipline that people don't want to give it. And that's fair enough because people don't have time to sit down and watch them – and particularly now they've put *Night Network* on rather than MTV so people would far rather sit down and watch that.

Some of the chapters in the previous edition covered your opinions on religion and politics etc. Would you say that your opinions in those areas have changed much?

Mal: No, I don't think my views about those sorts of things have changed. What we've been discussing has been about my personal, local environment, my ambitions and what I see the music as. But on a broader scale I don't think my views on something like politics have changed – apart from becoming a fascist. (laughs) A fascist catholic. (laughs)

But I couldn't really state any particular area or issue where my attitude has changed. I'm still left wing by inclination but not by dogma. I'm still a fucked up catholic same as I was last time. (laughs)

But a vegetarian fucked up catholic.

Mal: Yeah, I suppose that's the only major change. And I still can't work out why I gave up meat, actually. I was with Robin from the Cocteau Twins and we were sat there and for some reason he had a craving for eating a bucket full of Kentucky Fried Chicken – and he doesn't eat meat either. And I can't work out why I don't eat meat now.

Some people say that it makes them feel healthier.

Mal: Oh God, not when you drink as much as I do! I mean it was never food that made me feel unhealthy. (laughs)

So would still say that you had a pretty hedonistic life-style?

Mal: Oh yeah, I haven't changed in that. The only thing that's changed with me now, is that if I have a really late night or I don't go to bed it takes me a day to get over it – a bit longer to recover.

That's alright I'm safe – as you're older than me.

Mal: But I still do it – that's the point. I still love it. I went to see the Butthole Surfers on Friday night and then I went with the Jesus and Mary Chain to a free drinks party and got incredibly drunk.

What are the Jesus and Mary Chain like?

Mal: Oh, they're brilliant. I only really know Jim but he's great. He's a really nice bloke.

Obviously living in London you get more of a chance to meet a lot of other groups.

Mal: Yeah, it's quite funny because the people that I do meet, they're all from outside London and there's this sort of odd camaraderie between all these people who don't come from London and all go out and get drunk.

Presumably when those sort of people get together the last thing they talk about is music.

Mal: Everybody talks about going out, where they live, drinking. You'd be surprised at the people who are a lot more career-minded than I am. Gibby from the Butthole Surfers is a lot sharper than I am – financially – he knows exactly what he's doing. That bloke will make a lot more money than I ever will. And he comes from a lot weirder group than I do. To be honest, meeting people from groups comes a lot less from being in London, 'cos I've been in London for four years, it's come from since I've been a bachelor, or by myself should I say – since Karen and I split up. I suppose that's all it is really – I don't have a girlfriend so I go out more.

Is being unattached a situation you prefer?

Mal: I quite enjoy it actually, I quite enjoy my freedom. Oh God, I hope Karen doesn't read that, she'll kill me! (laughs) Actually Karen and I get on alright – now. (laughs)

Do you think that London night life is up to much?

Mal: I don't know. I don't go out that much. If I do it's just to meet up with friends for a drink. But I don't go out every night – I know people who do.

Unfortunately, Pete Wylie is a friend of mine, so I don't have a social life I just monitor Wylie's. (laughs)

You've not become paranoid about being a semi-famous person.

Mal: I don't even think about it. I don't think I'm famous at all so it doesn't worry me in the slightest. That's what does worry me – I want to be. (laughs) As I said before I think London's a good ego flattener. Just Like New York – anywhere like that.

What about travel – are there places you'd still like to visit?

Mal: The one place I'd really like to go to that I haven't been is Australia. That's just a fascination in the same way Tokyo and Japan was a few years ago. It is a bit like saying, "been there – done that one – go somewhere else now". (laughs) But the number of places I've been to without working is very, very small – and when I have been it has been on package tours.

But you did take your tours quite easily. It was hardly a gig a night stuff.

Mal: Well, yeah that's become the bone of contention between Richard and I really. Because if I'm going to travel and work I'd rather do it intensively and say that's it finished and then take two weeks off and do what I want to do, rather than try and fit it in over a spread out period. You can never really forget you're working and you're always getting hassled by people.

Although a lot of touring inevitably means a lot of flying. As a fellow hater of flying myself, I can understand Richard not wanting to tour too much.

Mal: The point is I don't knock Richard for not wanting to tour, or not wanting to fly, I don't knock him for not wanting to do those things. But I don't think it should affect myself and what I want to do. That's all it is, really – because I would never want to force him into doing anything. I think quite frankly that doing a tour that was any more than about ten dates would kill Richard – because he's very highly strung in that sense – I can shut off a bit more.

So, tell me about this Father Christmas incident in Milan?

Mal: No, the tape stops now. (laughs) These things are a laugh really, they're not embarrassing at all. Let's face it you'd do it at your own party, or you'd do it at someone else's house for a laugh so what's the difference. In fact if I could do in public what I do at somebody else's house and it would sell more records, then I'd fucking do it. I don't care.

We've come around to this way of thinking as well just recently about books.

Mal: I think you've got to be quite frank, nobody particularly wants to read about groups nowadays because most of them are quite boring.

I think that was one of the interesting things about the last book we published, 'Tape Delay', seeing who had something interesting to say and who didn't.

Mal: I think with the areas that book covered it's fair enough, people do want to read about it. But with groups that are more successful, people don't want to read about their pension schemes and things like that.

People would prefer to listen to the records. Mind you, you are probably the exception – people might prefer reading about you than having to listen to your records. (laughs)

Mal: Yeah, I was talking to Amrik earlier in the day and he asked me what I was doing tonight. I told him I was doing an interview with you and he said what for. I told him that you were doing a second edition of the book – I said, "I think they've twigged that we might be splitting up and they're going to cash in on it". Amrik said, "That's great, it's a really good idea – I would do the same thing."

Is there anything you would like to say finally as a coda to the Cabaret Voltaire story?

Mal: Not really, just that it has been good fun so far (pause) – but that's rock 'n' roll! (laughs)

appendix 3

Bibliography
Wreckers of Civilisation: The Story of Coum Transmissions and Throbbing Gristle by Simon Ford (Black Dog)
Industrial Culture Handbook by Vale (RE-Search)
Tape Delay: Confessions from the Eighties Underground by Charles Neal (SAF)

Websitses
Info and Cabaret Voltaire/Richard Kirk discography: www.brainwashed.com/cv/
Early Cabaret Voltaire/TG records can be bought from: www.mute.co.uk/store.htm
Check out: www.blindyouth.co.uk for information about the early Human League.

Recommended Listening: By no means an exhaustive list, but merely a flavour of the best.

Cabaret Voltaire
The Voice of America (available of CD through Mute)
2x45 (available of CD through Mute)
Living Legends – (Mute "Best Of" containing the best early singles and EPs)
Yashar (12" mix - Factory Benelux)
The Crackdown (Virgin)
Sensoria (12" single mix - Virgin)
The Conversation (Apollo-R&S)

Richard H. Kirk
Disposable Half-Truths (available on CD through Mute)
Test One/ Test Two/ Test Three (with DJ Parrott as Sweet Exorcist - Warp))
Virtual State (Warp)

Stephen Mallinder
Pow Wow Plus (available on CD through Mute)

Throbbing Gristle
Second Annual Report (available of CD through Mute)
Twenty Jazz Funk Greats (available of CD through Mute)
Heathen Earth (available of CD through Mute)
Greatest Hits: Entertainment Through Pain (available on CD through Mute)

Clock DVA
White Souls in Black Suits (Originally released by Industrial, currently unavailable on CD)
Thirst (Originally released by Fetish, currently unavailable on CD)

Other related Sheffield releases:
Neutron Records EP: *1980 The First Fifteen Minutes*:
(features Vice Versa, Clock DVA, I'm So Hollow, the Stunt Kites)
Reproduction by the Human League (Virgin)

Lexicon of Love by ABC
Penthouse and Pavement by Heaven 17
Nagasaki's Children (EP) by The Must Be Russians 4 track EP
Secret's Out by The Box (originally released by Go! Discs, currently unavailable on CD)
Murmur by Hula (originally released by Red Rhino, currently unavailable on CD)
Emotion/Sound/Motion by I'm So Hollow (originally released by Illuminated, currently unavailable on CD)
One Afternoon in a Hot Air Balloon by Artery (originally released by Red Flame, currently unavailable on CD)
Out of the Flesh by Chakk (original 12" released by Doublevision,)

Other related records:
Nothing Here but the Recordings by William Burroughs (Originally released on Industrial)
23 Skidoo/Subliminal by Eric Random (Les Disques Du Crepescule – single)
The Gospel Comes to New Guinea by 23 Skidoo (produced at Western Works)
Bang! An Open Letter by The Hafler Trio (originally released on Doublevision, currently available on CD through Mute)
Force the Hand of Chance by Psychic TV
Heartbeat by Chris & Cosey
Scatology by Coil

Available Now from SAF Publishing

Tape Delay: Confessions from the Eighties Underground
by Charles Neal

ISBN: 0 946719 02 0, Paperback. 256 pages (illustrated)
Price UK £15.00 US$ 20.00

"Tape Delay investigates those rare underground performers who've stuck their forefingers up the butt of commercial (in)sensibility to pursue their own visions. On that level alone it should be welcomed... A virtual Who's Who of people who've done the most in the past decade [the eighties] to drag music out of commercial confinement." NME

Contributors to Tape Delay include:

Marc Almond - Dave Ball - Cabaret Voltaire - Nick Cave - Chris & Cosey - Coil - Einsturzende Neubauten - The Fall - Diamanda Galas - Genesis P. Orridge - Michael Gira - The Hafler Trio - Matt Johnson (The The) - Laibach - Lydia Lunch - New Order - Psychic TV - Boyd Rice - Henry Rollins - Clint Ruin - Sonic Youth - Stevo - Mark Stewart - Swans - Test Dept. - David Tibet (Current 93) and more...

Coming Soon from SAF Publishing

England's Hidden Reverse:
Coil-Current 93-Nurse With Wound
A Secret History Of The Esoteric Underground

ISBN: 0 946719 40 3

Birthed in the fall-out from legendary "Industrial" units Throbbing Gristle and Psychic TV, David Tibet's Current 93, John Balance and Peter Christopherson's Coil and Steven Stapleton's Nurse With Wound represent the real English underground in all its sexual, cultural and artistic variety. An individually numbered limited edition, lavishly illustrated with photographs and original artworks, complete with previously unreleased CD, this volume will become a collector's item. David Keenan's work has been published in *The Wire, Mojo, NME, Melody Maker* and *Uncut* amongst others.

Check www.safpublishing.com for details.

SAF, Helter Skelter and Firefly Books

Mail Order

All SAF, Helter Skelter and Firefly titles are available by mail order from the world-famous Helter Skelter bookshop.

Telephone: +44 (0)20 7836 1151
or Fax: +44 (0)20 7240 9880

Office hours: Mon-Fri 10:00am - 7:00pm,
Sat: 10:00am - 6:00pm, Sun: closed.

**Helter Skelter Bookshop, 4 Denmark Street, London,
WC2H 8LL, United Kingdom.**

If you are in London come and visit us and browse the titles in person.

Order Online

For the latest on SAF, Helter Skelter and Firefly titles, or to order books online, check the SAF or Helter Skelter websites.

You can also browse the full range of rock, pop, jazz and experimental music books we have available, as well as keeping up with our latest releases and special offers.

You can also contact us via email, and request a catalogue.

info@safpublishing.com

www.safpublishing.com

saf publishing